SELFISH REASONS TO HAVE MORE KIDS

SELFISH REASONS TO HAVE MORE KIDS

why being a great parent is less work
and more fun than you think

■   ■   ■   ■   ■

Bryan Caplan

BASIC
BOOKS

A Member of the Perseus Books Group
New York

Books published by Basic Books are available at
special discounts for bulk purchases in the United States by
corporations, institutions, and other organizations. For more information,
please contact the Special Markets Department at the Perseus Books Group,
2300 Chestnut Street, Suite 200, Philadelphia, PA 19103, or call (800)
810-4145, ext. 5000, or e-mail special.markets@perseusbooks.com.

Book design by Linda Mark
Set in 10.5 New Aster

Library of Congress Cataloging-in-Publication Data
Caplan, Bryan.
Selfish reasons to have more kids: Why being a great parent is
less work and more fun than you think / Bryan Caplan.
p. cm.
Includes bibliographical references and index.
ISBN 978-0-465-01867-3 (hardcover : alk. paper)
ISBN 978-0-465-02341-7 (e-book)
1. Parenting. 2. Parenthood. 3. Children. I. Title.
HQ755.8.C37 2011
306.874—dc22
2010040085

10 9 8 7 6 5 4 3 2

*To my parents, who gave me life—
and my children, who give me joy*

Contents

ACKNOWLEDGMENTS

MANY AUTHORS SAY THEY COULDN'T HAVE WRITTEN THEIR BOOKS without their families' inspiration and support. In my case, it's literally true. I was familiar with most of the facts in this book years before I became a dad. But my children inspired me to ponder what the facts *mean*. They transformed my cool curiosity into an enthusiastic philosophy of parenting. And while my wife thinks I go too far, she has always been happy to hear me out and work side by side to make our family something special. I love you all.

My other great debt is to blogging. I'm a professor by trade, but the blogosphere is my intellectual home. To me, academic writing feels too narrow and timid. Blogs are the New World of the mind—the land where science meets common sense, and logic meets life. For years, I largely kept my parenting thoughts to myself because I lacked a forum to develop them. Then I became a blogger for Econ-Log. My second post was called "The Selfish Reason to Have More Kids"—and before long, parenting was my favorite topic. I owe the most to Marginal Revolution's Tyler Cowen and Alex Tabarrok, who gave me my start as a guest blogger; Cafe Hayek's Don Boudreaux and Russ Roberts, who paved the way for me to become an EconLog regular; my co-bloggers Arnold Kling and David Henderson; Liberty Fund for hosting us; and our many thoughtful readers. I also thank the Mercatus Center and George Mason University's economics department for every kind of support.

The Internet has made it child's play to get feedback from all over the world. Omar Al-Ubaydli, Jim Bennett, David Bernstein, Peter Boettke, Sara Bumgarner, Corina Caplan, David Cesarini, Tyler Cowen, Bill Dickens, Brian Doherty, David Friedman, Patri Friedman, Joshua Gans, Daniel Gilbert, Zachary Gochenour, David Gordon, Ananda Gupta, Robin Hanson, Tim Harford, Judith Harris, Teresa Hartford, Lara Heimert, Lisa Hill-Corley, Steve Horwitz, Garett Jones, Tim Kane, Steve Landsburg, Daniel Lurker, Greg Mankiw, Jane Perry, Robert Plomin, Marta Podemska, David Romer, Charles Rowley, Amy Schneider, Jim Schneider, Lenore Skenazy, Ilya Somin, Ed Stringham, Tim Sullivan, Peter Twieg, Michele Wynn, Matt Zwolinski, and anonymous reviewers all responded to drafts. It would have been hard to improve without them. I'm extra grateful to Alex Tabarrok and Tim Harford for organizational insight, Robert Plomin for expert reassurance, Bill Dickens and Judith Harris for expert criticism, David Gordon for sage proofreading, and Matt Zwolinski for the subtitle.

No matter how far the Internet develops, however, it will never replace lunch. When a new idea strikes me, I yearn to defend it face-to-face over a meal. Luckily, I have many heroic colleagues who habitually indulge me, especially Robin Hanson, Garett Jones, John Nye, and of course Tyler and Alex.

Still, my deepest intellectual debts are to thinkers I see less often, if at all. Sheldon Richman piqued my interest in population issues almost twenty years ago when he ran the Cato Institute's summer interns program. Judith Harris's *The Nurture Assumption* awoke me from my dogmatic slumbers on the nature-nurture question—and convinced me that the issue was anything but academic. Bill Dickens was the first economist I knew who took human genetics seriously—and always knew what he was talking about. Lenore Skenazy's *Free-Range Kids* demonstrated how wise and beautifully written a parenting book could be. My greatest thanks, though, go to the late Julian Simon, who opened my eyes to the blessings of population. Out of all the people I'll never meet, I miss him the most.

INTRODUCTION

> This above all: To thine own self be true.
>
> —*Hamlet*

DURING MY LIFETIME, THE AMERICAN FAMILY HAS DRASTICALLY downsized. Women in their forties are about twice as likely to have one child—or none—as they were thirty years ago. Big families have all but disappeared. In 1976, 20 percent of women in their early forties had five or more kids; by 2006, less than 4 percent did.

If you ask people to explain why we don't have as many kids as we used to, the answers are all over the place. "People can't afford big families anymore," "Women have real careers now," "We don't need kids to help out with farm work," "Women want to live like men," "Americans have lost faith in God." In Athens, the Greeks blame air pollution.

If you make the question personal, however, the answers are very much alike. When asked, "Why don't *you* have as many kids as we used to?" both men and women respond with groans. As best I can tell, the English translation of these groans is "Kids are a lot of work," or maybe "Imagine all the dirty diapers and sleepless nights," or perhaps "Are you trying to kill me?"

To be brutally honest, we're reluctant to have more children because we think that the pain outweighs the gain. When people compare the grief that another child would give them to the joy that the child would bring, they conclude that it's just not worth it. As Bill Cosby put it, "The reason we have five children is because we do not want six."

You could easily call this a very selfish outlook. How can you focus exclusively on whether another child would make *you* happier? What about the child? Unless your baby is truly unlucky, he will almost certainly be happy to be alive. Aren't you? This is your child we're talking about. If you have to make yourself a little less happy in order to give a son or daughter the gift of life, shouldn't you?

The question is serious, but I'm going to dodge it. While I accept the natalist view that more births should be encouraged because they make the world a better place, asking others to sacrifice their happiness for the good of the world seems futile. Preaching against selfishness is usually about as productive as nagging a brick wall. When people weigh the costs and benefits of having another child, I'm not going to call them sinners for using a scale.

The claim of this book, rather, is that current and prospective parents have accidentally tipped their scales against fertility. We may feel sure that the pursuit of happiness and kids (or at least more kids) are incompatible, but it is in the average person's enlightened self-interest to have more kids. That's right—people are not having enough children for their own good. Prospective parents need to take another look before they decide not to leap. Current parents need to take another look before they decide not to leap again.

My theory is not one-size-fits-all. The claim is not that everyone should have *lots* of kids, but that the average person should have *more* kids. More than what? More than they were otherwise planning to have. If you live in a tiny urban apartment and love fancy foreign vacations, this might mean one kid instead of zero. If you live in a suburban McMansion and love theme parks, this might mean five kids instead of three. I'm here to provide information, not run your life.

There are many selfish reasons to have more kids, but there are four big reasons to put on the table right away:

■ First, *parents can sharply improve their lives without hurting their kids*. Nature, not nurture, explains most family resemblance, so parents can safely cut themselves a lot of additional slack.

- Second, *parents are much more worried than they ought to be*. Despite the horror stories in the media, kids are much safer today than they were in the "Idyllic Fifties."
- Third, *many of the benefits of children come later in life*. Kids have high start-up costs, but wise parents weigh their initial sleep deprivation against a lifetime of rewards—including future grandchildren.
- Last, *self-interest and altruism point in the same direction*. Parents who have another child make the world a better place, so you can walk the path of enlightened selfishness with a clear conscience.

PARENTS CAN SHARPLY IMPROVE THEIR LIVES WITHOUT HURTING THEIR KIDS

> A second child always undermines parents' belief in their power to mold their children, but child-rearing books hush this up because their market is first-time parents.
>
> —Steve Sailer, "The Nature of Nurture"

When we consider whether one more child is worth it to us, our calculations usually include a lot of needless parental unhappiness. Every generation of parents probably sees itself as exceptionally dedicated, but careful measurement confirms that parental effort is at an all-time high. Stay-at-home moms used to just tell their kids to go outside and play. Now, moms *and* dads tag along with their kids as supervisors, or servants. When we think about the effect of a child on our lives, then, we automatically picture the spartan schedule of Today's Typical Parents. We *have* to give up our hobbies and nights out, we *have* to make our lives revolve around our kids' activities, and we *have* to handle all the extra cooking, cleaning, and babysitting ourselves.

When kids justify foolish behavior with the excuse that all the other kids are doing it, parents try to show them the error of their ways. Few of us notice that by swallowing the high-effort standards of our peers, we are making the same mistake. Today's Typical Parents give up their independence and free time for the sake of their kids, but you still have a choice. If all the other parents were jumping off the Brooklyn Bridge, would you?

My alternative is not child neglect. I spend more time with my kids than most parents. When my sons were infants, I always manned the night shift. I play with my baby every day. My older boys and I share many common interests—especially games and comic books. But most parents don't share my enthusiasm for childish pursuits, and that's fine. Diverse parenting styles deserve our respect. Some parents fill their kids' days with crafts and extra homework. That may be a good approach for them, but it is not the *only* good approach. More relaxed parenting styles are also on the menu—like letting your kids watch *The Simpsons* while you steal a daily hour of "me time."

Aren't parents risking their children's future when they let Homer and Marge share the work? This self-reproach haunts many parents when they're so tired they can barely keep their eyes open, but it's overblown. Even if there were a clear trade-off between parents' present happiness and their children's future, there is no reason for parents to *maximize* their effort. Parents count, too, and there's nothing wrong with a happy medium.

In any case, the obligation to put your children's future above your personal happiness has a lot less bite than you'd think. Adoption and twin research provides strong evidence that parents barely affect their children's prospects. If parents gave themselves a big break—or redoubled their efforts—kids would turn out about the same.

Before you dismiss this claim as crazy, imagine you adopt a baby girl and raise her to adulthood. Who do you think she will resemble more by the time she graduates from high school: Her biological parents, or you? I don't just mean physical resemblance; I'm also talking about smarts, personality, achievements, values, and so on. Can you honestly say you'd be shocked if your adopted daughter had a lot more in common with the strangers who conceived her than she did with you?

You don't have to merely imagine this scenario. It's been done— repeatedly. A small army of researchers has compared adoptees to their relatives—biological and adopted. They find that when adopted children are young, they resemble both the adopted relatives they see every day and the biological relatives they've never met. However, as adopted children grow up, the story has a shocking twist: *Resemblance to biological relatives remains, but resemblance to adopted relatives mostly fades away.* Studies that compare identical to fraternal twins reach the same conclusion.

The lesson: It's easy to change a child but hard to keep him from changing back. Instead of thinking of children as lumps of clay for parents to mold, we should think of them as plastic that flexes in response to pressure—and pops back to its original shape once the pressure is released.

We'll explore adoption and twin research in great detail later in the book. For now, I'll just say that it actually fits my experience as a father. When I put my kids in the "naughty corner," they apologize for their offenses, and their behavior improves. But it doesn't stay better for long. A few hours, days, or weeks later, my sons are up to their old tricks—and back in the corner they go. Which makes me wonder: If I can't change what my sons are going to do next month, how can I hope to change what they're going to do when they're adults?

Whatever your experiences, suppose for the sake of argument that adoption and twin research is sound. Then in purely selfish terms, parenting is a much better deal than it looks on the surface. If massive parental investment is the only way to turn a child into a normal adult, groaning at the thought of a new addition to the family is natural. If your child is virtually destined to become a normal adult, however, you should rethink that groan—especially if you're happy with the way you and your spouse turned out. Odds are, your kids will painlessly inherit your brains, success, charm, and modesty.

The implication: Parents can give themselves a guilt-free break. Children cost far less than most parents pay, because parents *overcharge themselves.* You can have an independent life and still be an admirable parent. Before you decide against another child, then, you owe it to yourself to reconsider. If your sacrifice is only a fraction of what you originally thought, the kid might be a good deal after all.

PARENTS ARE MUCH MORE WORRIED
THAN THEY OUGHT TO BE

You might respond that the real point of parenting isn't to change what kids do when they're adults but to ensure that they reach adulthood in one piece. One of the hardest parts of parenthood is worrying that something terrible will happen to your child. The news is full of stories about parents who failed to shield their children from the dangers of the world—enough to make anyone sick.

Fortunately, news is one thing and real life is another. On the news, the world is going to hell in a handbasket. Even (especially?) innocent children aren't safe. In real life, however, things are looking way up. Children under five years old are almost five times as safe today as they were in the Idyllic Fifties. Children age five to fourteen are almost four times as safe. During the Fifties, American society was great at presenting the image of secure childhood. Modern American society actually delivers this dream. To make the appearance match the reality, most people merely have to turn off their TVs and look out their windows.

If kids were in as much danger as most parents imagine, reluctance to have another child—or any children at all—would be understandable. We'd face a choice between kids and peace of mind; every extra child would be another tragedy waiting to happen. Fortunately, we live in happier times. Our main challenge isn't keeping our kids safe, but appreciating how safe they really are. Far-fetched fears aside, today is a great time to have a child—great for the child, and great for the parents who protect him.

MANY OF THE BENEFITS OF CHILDREN COME LATER IN LIFE

When people weigh the pros and cons of another child, they often suffer from myopia. Literally, myopia is another word for nearsightedness; if you clearly see only what's right in front of your nose, you're myopic. When I talk about myopia, I'm not talking about bad eyesight. I'm talking about bad foresight: focusing too much on the short-run costs of kids and forgetting the big picture.

The short-run costs of kids are clear. When young, they're a lot of work. If you wait until you're thirty to start a family, biology only gives you a brief window of time to finish. So when parents weigh whether to add a child, they're already up to their ears in toil. If they base their decision purely on how tired they feel when they're still young enough to have more kids, parents of two children (or even one!) will likely refuse.

Unfortunately, when a couple of toddlers are running around, you lose sight of the big picture. Namely: Your kids will grow up. Your workload will lighten. By the time you have teens, you'll wish your kids had more time for *you*. Once they move out, even three of them won't seem like enough. You'll want more phone calls and more visits—and some grandchildren while you're still young enough to enjoy them.

My point is that your "best number of children" changes over time. When you're a parent of youngsters, two feels like plenty. You may quietly declare, "I'm too selfish to have any more." But who's going to benefit down the line if you go beyond your comfort point and have another child or two? You. Four kids are a handful when you're thirty. When you're sixty, the story reverses. By that stage, each of your four children—and whatever grandchildren they give you—will probably be a joy.

If you're not just selfish, but good at being selfish, you will take these long-run benefits into account when you decide how many kids to have. This doesn't mean that you should make yourself miserable when you're young in order to have a perfect retirement. It means that you should factor a lifetime of consequences into your decisions, then strike a happy medium.

When you shop for food, you buy enough to last until your next trip to the store. You don't leave the store empty-handed because you ate a big lunch. Similarly, when you decide how many kids to have, you should have enough to last you during your forties, sixties, and eighties. You shouldn't stop having kids merely because your two-year-old won't let you sleep. Basing your long-run decisions on your short-run crankiness doesn't make sense.

SELF-INTEREST AND ALTRUISM POINT IN THE SAME DIRECTION

Sometimes it's wrong to encourage people to pursue their self-interest. If I had ironclad evidence that crime pays, I definitely wouldn't write a book called *Selfish Reasons to Steal More Money*. Stealing's good for thieves, but it's bad for everyone else. Does fertility work the same way?

No. Despite popular fears about overpopulation, more people make the world a better place. Our population and our standard of living have risen side by side for centuries, and it's no coincidence. New ideas, from iPhones to genetically modified crops, are the main reason we keep getting richer. The source of new ideas, without a doubt, is people—creative talent to make discoveries, and paying customers to reward their success. More talent plus more customers equals more ideas and more progress.

Larger populations also expand choices. Almost no one wants to live in the middle of nowhere, because there's nothing to do. Instead, people prefer to live near other people. They may not like the crowds, but they choose crowds, stores, restaurants, and jobs over splendid isolation. You might think that a few hundred thousand neighbors would sustain all the choices anyone would want; but then why do millions of New Yorkers pay a premium to live next to millions of other New Yorkers?

Fertility is also vital for our retirement systems. Programs like Social Security and Medicare are pyramid schemes: As long as there are a lot of young workers for every retiree, low taxes can fund high benefits. As populations age, however, the pyramid gets top-heavy and starts to wobble. Back in 1940, America had almost ten workers per retiree; now it's about five; in fifteen years, it will fall to three. Parents who have extra kids aren't just doing future retirees a favor; they're also making the tax burden on future workers a little more bearable.

The effect of fertility on the environment is more mixed, but conditions are better than they seem. We're not running out of food, fuel, or minerals. Despite setbacks and exceptions, resources have been getting cheaper for well over a century. Air and water quality have improved in recent decades, too, despite large population increases. Admittedly, the news isn't all good. Carbon dioxide emissions, for example, are still on the rise. But given all the offsetting benefits of population, restricting our numbers is a draconian cure. Concerned citizens should prefer eco-remedies that ignore population. We're going to see that they aren't hard to find.

WHO THIS BOOK IS FOR

When I tell people that I'm writing a book called *Selfish Reasons to Have More Kids*, the most common response is, "Because they'll take care of you in your old age?" Now is a good time for a disclaimer: That is *not* what I'm saying. Indeed, I doubt that "they'll provide for me when I'm old" has *ever* been a good reason to have kids. Love tends to run downhill; as an old saying ruefully observes, "One parent can care for five children, but five children cannot care for one parent." In any case, there are more cost-effective ways to provide for your old age than starting a family. In a backward farming community, you can use the money you would have spent on your children to buy land, then sell or rent your holdings when you're ready to retire. In the modern world, self-help is simpler yet. Invest in a retirement fund or buy an annuity. No muss, no fuss.

An especially devoted or successful child might become a high-yield investment, but that's a long shot. The only promising way to meet the "What's in it for me?" challenge is to appeal to the *intrinsic* or "consumption" benefits of children. If someone asks, "Why should I buy a high-definition TV?" you don't assure them that their HDTV will provide for them in their old age. You tell them that their HDTV will be fun, neat, or awesome. In the same way, if someone asks "What's in parenthood for me?" you have to highlight kids' cool features: They're ridiculously cute; they're playful; they look like you; they share half your genes; it's all part of the circle of life.

If kids' cool features have absolutely no appeal to you, then you probably *don't* have any selfish reasons to have more kids—or any kids at all. If you don't like what's on TV, a sales pitch about HDTV's great picture and sound quality is a waste of your time. Similarly, if the phrases "my son" and "my daughter" leave you unmoved, none of my arguments will sway you. A customer won't buy a product if he rejects its basic premise.

That's OK. I'm not trying to convince everyone to have kids. I'm trying to convince people who are at least mildly interested in being a parent that they should have *more* kids than they originally planned. That's a big audience. About 80 percent of Americans twenty-five and older have kids. Even among the childless by choice, many decide against kids because the sacrifice appears too great, not because the thought of kids leaves them cold. As long as you are among the vast majority with a seed of desire to be a parent, we have much to discuss.

MAKING THE RIGHT PERSONAL DECISION

Whether to have a child is plainly one of life's most personal decisions. Just because a decision is personal, however, does not mean that whatever decision you make is the right one for you. The decision to have a child is complex. The consequences are easy to misjudge. If you make your ruling with undue haste, you're only cheating yourself.

Selfishly speaking, children have pros and cons. But these days we're good at counting the cons. A book called *Do I Want to Be a Mom?* has a chapter for every reason you've heard *not* to have a child—from "Will I Get Enough Sleep?" to "Will I Like My Child? Will My Child Like Me?" Even strangers eagerly highlight the drawbacks, whether they're chuckling that your life will change or looking at you with pity and asking if you're getting any sleep.

We've got the cons covered. When it comes to the pros, though, we've got a lot to learn. Parenting is stressful, but much of the stress is unnecessary. Parents can have a much better life without disadvantaging or endangering their kids. In any case, you should not let the short-run stress of an extra child dominate your decision. Many of the benefits of children come later in life. If you are *wisely* selfish, you will not allow a few months of sleepwalking to stand between you and your future as a parent and grandparent.

When I argue in favor of fertility, people occasionally ask, "Do you even have kids?" The notion of selfish reasons to have more kids sounds so crazy to them that they wonder if I'm cooking up my ideas in solitary confinement. The truth is that I have three sons: a pair of seven-year-old identical twins, and a new baby. Before I became a father, I was already familiar with the research upon which this book rests. Only after my wife and I had twins, however, did I appreciate its practical significance.

If the research is right, many prospective parents are making a big mistake. They are missing the chance to have another child who, if born, would enrich their lives. That's sad. It's one thing to refrain from having a child who would make your life worse. You can always insist that it's the people who really exist who count, not people who could have existed but don't. But to deny the gift of life to a child who would have made your life better is a tragic missed opportunity.

1

You Count Too: A Commonsense Guide to Happier Parenting

> We've tried nothing and we're all out of ideas!
> —Ned Flanders's beatnik mother on *The Simpsons*

Soon after you announce that you're going to be a parent, the hazing begins. The nice people say, "Your lives are going to change," with a knowing grin. The not-so-nice chuckle about dirty diapers and sleepless nights. Once, when my wife and I were strolling our twin infants, we overheard a passing jogger tell her friend, "Now *there's* a reason to shoot yourself."

Babies are very cute, and people are pretty superficial. Yet many of us hear "baby" and think "misery." It's not just that we believe that kids *happen* to make their parents miserable. We perceive parental misery as inevitable: If you become a parent, you have to kiss your independence and free time good-bye, and resign yourself to eighteen years of hard labor.

Popular perceptions are mostly wrong. Today's Typical Parents push themselves so hard that you'd expect them to be miserable, but they aren't. Some evidence suggests that kids make people *slightly* less satisfied with their lives, but even that depends on how you ask. By and large, parents feel fine. In any case, once you know how laborious modern parenting has become, making parents happier is like finding hay in a haystack.

PARENTS: HOW ARE THEY DOING?

Count Olaf rubbed his hands together as if he had
been holding something revolting instead of an infant.
—Lemony Snicket, *A Series of Unfortunate Events:
The Bad Beginning*

Is parenthood good for you? The simple stubborn answer is, "It must be; otherwise people wouldn't do it." When you're deciding how many kids to have, however, this answer is unhelpful. People make mistakes. Some of their choices bring them unhappiness and regret. If you want to measure how parents are doing, you need to take human error seriously. Three main approaches fit the bill: studies of customer satisfaction, studies of overall happiness, and studies of momentary happiness.

CUSTOMER SATISFACTION

To learn whether a consumer expects to like a purchase, you only need to find out whether he bought it. To learn whether a consumer *really* likes a purchase, however, you need to find out whether he'd make the same decision over again. If so, he's a satisfied customer. If not, he's got buyer's remorse. After you try a restaurant, hire a mechanic, or upgrade your computer, it's hard not to weigh your experience on the scale of customer satisfaction. Before you try a restaurant, hire a mechanic, or upgrade your computer, it's wise to check the customer satisfaction of people like you.

In practice, do parents feel like their kids were a good deal—or end up with buyer's remorse? The book *Do I Want to Be a Mom?* ominously warns that having a child for "unhealthy reasons" "could cause a lifetime of disappointment in yourself and with your child." But in 1976, *Newsday* commissioned the highest-quality survey ever conducted on the subject—and found buyer's remorse was awfully rare. When asked, "If you had it to do over again, would you or would you not have children?" 91 percent of parents said they would have children all over again. Only 7 percent said they wouldn't.

You might object that people merely rationalize whatever decision they made, but the best available survey finds that *nonbuyer's remorse* is common. In 2003, Gallup asked childless adults over the age of forty, "If you had to do it over again, how many children would you have, or would you not have any at all?" Over two-thirds of the people without kids confessed regret.

Bottom line: A supermajority of parents want every kid they've got. That's part of the magic of having kids. Even parents of unplanned children often confess, "I can't imagine my life without them." The magic of not having kids, in contrast, is elusive. The childless can readily imagine being parents, and by the time they're in their forties, most prefer this fantasy to their reality.

Overall Happiness

In terms of customer satisfaction, parenthood does well. Few parents want their money back, and most of the childless wish they bought back when they had their chance. But customer satisfaction isn't everything. There's also *happiness*—how people feel about their lives. Who's happier: people with kids, or people without?

If you know a few sunny parents, it's tempting to conclude that kids are the path to happiness. If your neighbor has a short fuse and a houseful of hellions, it's hard to believe flowery talk about the joys of family life. To move beyond our own little worlds, we need statistics. Strange as it sounds, high-quality surveys have spent decades asking all sorts of people, "How happy are you?"

On the surface, people with kids are indeed happier than those without. On closer look, however, parenthood is slightly depressing. People with kids are more likely to be older, married, and churchgoing. All three traits—age, marriage, church attendance—predict greater happiness. Once you adjust for these patterns, happiness falls as the number of children rises. The unhappy effect of kids is robust: You can crunch the numbers for months, and your computer will stubbornly continue to tell you that happiness and number of offspring move in opposite directions.

Before you join the "children make us miserable" chorus, however, it's worth staring at the numbers more closely. The negative effect of kids on happiness is robust but *small*. In the General Social Survey, a massive, decades-long study of Americans, every child makes you about 1 percentage point less likely to call yourself "very happy." The difference is real, but you need a statistical microscope to detect it. Married people, in contrast, are *18* percentage points more likely to be very happy. If you're married with children, you're far more likely to be happy than if you're single and childless. Taken too literally, the statistics imply that married couples require over a dozen kids to feel worse than childless singles.

Also striking: The main hit to parental happiness comes from child number one. Otherwise identical people who have one child instead of none are 5.6 percentage points less likely to be very happy. But once you've got a child, enlarging your family is practically painless. Whenever parents install another child seat in the family car, their chance of being very happy falls by a barely perceptible .6 percentage points. Intuitively, people sharply rearrange their lives with the arrival of their first child. They lose privacy and stop going out Saturday nights. When more children come along, however, parents' lifestyle stays about the same.

In the movie *Saved!* a pregnant teenager named Mary learns that cancer and pregnancy have common symptoms—and suddenly feels hopeful. "Please be cancer, please be cancer!" she frantically pleads. When happiness researchers talk about kids, they often sound like Mary. In *Gross National Happiness*, Arthur Brooks, now president of the American Enterprise Institute, jokes, "There are many things in a parent's life that bring great joy. For example, spending time away from their children." When you look at the numbers, the picture's much brighter. If you compare two otherwise identical people, but only one has kids, smart money says that the childless one will be only a tad happier.

MOMENTARY HAPPINESS

Can you trust what people say about their overall happiness? On such an abstract question, answers might depend more on how we're supposed to feel than how we really feel. To get around this problem, some happiness researchers change gears: Instead of asking subjects how they feel overall, they ask them how they spent their day, and how each of their activities made them feel. How does parenting measure up?

The most famous work along these lines, Nobel laureate Daniel Kahneman and coauthors' study of working moms, appeared in *Science* in 2004. According to secondhand reports, Kahneman and company discovered that taking care of kids is virtually the low point of the day. A piece in *Time* announced that "an act of parenting makes most people about as happy as an act of housework." The *Economist* added:

> When researchers ask parents what they enjoy, it turns out that they prefer almost anything to looking after their children. Eating, shopping, exercising, cooking, praying and watching television were all rated more pleasurable than watching the brats . . .

Popular summaries of the original paper turn out to be awfully misleading. Here is how moms actually rated their enjoyment of their days' activities on a scale from 0 ("not at all") to 6 ("very much").

Activity	Average Enjoyment (0–6)
Intimate relations	5.10
Socializing	4.59
Relaxing	4.42
Pray/worship/meditate	4.35
Eating	4.34
Exercising	4.31
Watching TV	4.19
Shopping	3.95
Preparing food	3.93
On the phone	3.92
Napping	3.87
Taking care of my children	*3.86*
Computer/e-mail/Internet	3.81
Housework	3.73
Working	3.62
Commuting	3.45

As far as happiness researchers go, Arthur Brooks is proparenthood. Yet even he looks at these very numbers and concludes that women "enjoy almost *everything* more than they enjoy taking care of their kids." But child care comes in twelfth out of sixteen activities, and easily beats the most time-consuming activity of the day—working. And there is virtually a six-way tie between shopping, preparing food, talking on the phone, napping, taking care of children, and computer use. Last, notice that the top seven activities—from sex ("intimate relations") to watching TV—are all forms of recreation. As far as worklike activities go, enjoyment of child care is slightly above average.

If the Kahneman study has a big social message, it's not that kids are a disaster for happiness. It's that women enjoy taking care of their children more than working outside the home. The only thing women like less than being at their jobs is getting to and from their jobs. Child care isn't a picnic, but it beats a paying job.

In *Stumbling on Happiness*, psychologist Daniel Gilbert contrasts our dreams about children with the harsh reality of parenting. Our dreams:

> When people think about their offspring—either imagining future offspring or thinking about current ones—they tend to conjure up images of cooing babies smiling from their bassinets, adorable toddlers running higgledy-piggledy across the lawn, handsome boys and gorgeous girls playing trumpets and tubas in the school marching band, successful college students going on to have beautiful weddings, satisfying careers, and flawless grandchildren whose affections can be purchased with candy.

The harsh reality:

> Although parenting has many rewarding moments, the vast majority of its moments involve dull and selfless service to people who will take decades to become even begrudgingly grateful for what we are doing.

After you sift through the evidence, Gilbert's harsh reality looks more like a recurring nightmare. The not-so-harsh reality is that parents are far better off than nonparents by the standard of customer satisfaction, and only slightly worse off by the standard of personal happiness. Married couples with big families are much happier than childless singles. Child care is a form of work, but it's nice work if you can get it.

TOIL AND TROUBLE: A WEEK IN THE LIFE OF TODAY'S TYPICAL PARENT

> A British nanny must be a gen'ral! / The future empire lies within her hands / And so the person that we need to mold the breed, / Is a nanny who can give commands!
>
> —*Mary Poppins*

When he was a boy, my dad rode his bike all over downtown Los Angeles. My friends and I had more supervision, but our moms still got us out of their hair by ordering us to play outside until dinner. My mom kindly let me read in my room, but the philosophy was the same: Entertaining myself was my job, not hers. Today, I almost never see kids playing outside without a watchful parent—and several have told me they wouldn't have it any other way. Parents spend their weekends bringing their children to activities I never heard of when I was a kid: Tae Kwon Do classes, Pokemon tournaments, Mandarin immersion.

These are just anecdotes. But they fit the systematic research on the question "What do people do all day?" Sociologists have measured how Americans spend their minutes for over four decades. Their favorite tool is the time diary. You contact a random sample of Americans and ask them to walk you through their previous day. "When did you wake up?" "What did you do then?" "What happened next?" Questions continue until the respondent tells you when he went to bed. Methodically reliving your day makes it hard to stray far from the truth.

According to time diaries, modern parents spend an incredible amount of time taking care of their kids. As expected, dads do a lot more than they used to. Since 1965, when the average dad did only three hours of child care per week, we've more than doubled our efforts. Given how little dads used to do, though, doubling wasn't hard. What's amazing is the change in the typical mother's workload: *Today's mom spends more time taking care of children than she did in the heyday of the stay-at-home mom.*

Back in 1965, when the typical mom was a housewife, she spent ten hours a week specifically focusing on her children's needs. By 2000, this number had risen to thirteen hours a week. This happened despite the fact that today's moms are much more likely to work outside the home, despite the fact that moms have fewer kids, and despite the fact that dads are a lot more helpful. Everything suggests that modern moms would put in fewer hours than ever—except the facts.

One pattern hasn't changed: Stay-at-home moms spend more time with their kids than working moms. However, both kinds of moms try harder than they used to. Stay-at-home moms went from about eleven hours per week in 1975 to seventeen hours per week in 2000. Working moms went from six hours per week in 1975 to eleven hours per week in 2000. Modern working moms spend as much time caring for their kids as stay-at-home moms did thirty years ago.

These weekly totals sound low because they define "child care" narrowly. Reading a book on the couch while my sons fight Playmobil wars wouldn't count—even if I occasionally urged them to play nice. When parents get full credit for multitasking, measured child care shoots up about 50 percent. But however you measure, the main patterns remain. The average dad has roughly doubled his effort. The average mom spends more time taking care of her kids than she did when the average mom was a housewife.

When people learn about these patterns, they're usually relieved. But why? If the statistics are right, it's clear why raising kids feels like a chore. By the standards of the Sixties, modern dads do enough child care to pass for moms—and modern moms do enough child care to compete for Mother of the Year. Kid time has crowded out couple time: Parents in 2000 spent about 25 percent fewer hours with each other than they did in 1975. To use an expression I often heard during my childhood, parents are working their fingers to the bone. Considering how much time we spend caring for our kids, the real surprise is that parents' happiness deficit isn't a lot bigger.

HOW TO BE A HAPPIER PARENT: A PRIMER

It is better to light a candle than to curse the darkness.
—Chinese proverb

If I'm merely cementing your preexisting reservations about children, hold on. Modern parenting has turned kids into a heavy burden. But it's not kids that changed; it's us! We frequently meet demands that our elders would have rejected out of hand ("I'm not your chauffeur"). We even invent demands on our children's behalf ("M-o-m, I don't *want* to take karate"). Why can't parents learn to say no, or at least learn to take no for an answer?

If you want to make parents happier, it's tempting to simply turn back the clock to the more relaxed standards of the Sixties or Seventies. But the smarter approach is to look at parents' lives with a modern eye and target the parts that are least useful and least pleasant. Of course, "Stop doing stuff with big costs and small benefits" is good advice whether or not you're a parent. It's on par with "Buy low, sell high." But comparing costs and benefits is especially helpful for parents, because so many avoid it out of the mistaken sense that only bad parents would do it. As a result, there is plenty of low-hanging fruit to pick.

When my twins were infants, our baby monitor was a godsend. If the kids were crying for food or a change, we wanted to know **ASAP**. Without the monitor, we would have endlessly visited their room to double-check their status. The monitor let us relax, secure in the knowledge that we'd know as soon as our babies needed us.

As our boys got older, the tears tapered off. By the time they were two, my wife and I would tuck them in, then head downstairs to watch TV. The baby monitor was still broadcasting. But instead of cries, we heard laughs. The twins were joking when they were supposed to be sleeping. We'd start *24* and hope for the laughter to die down. Ten minutes later, I'd pause the show, lumber upstairs, and quiet the troublemakers. My first warning rarely took. The aggravating cycle often took an hour.

Then one great night, my wife and I found a way out: We turned off the monitor. Our evenings immediately improved. After tuck-in, we could relax—and the boys still felt fine in the morning. The experience taught us a valuable lesson: We, not our kids, were causing our own aggravation. Our sons never asked us to spy on them. The monitor was a good idea at first; our mistake was to listen long after it stopped making sense.

Turning off the baby monitor did not revolutionize our lives. Yet small changes add up, and they're not hard to find. Review your most unpleasant chores: How many could you safely scale back? Review your least useful chores: How many could you safely forget? Don't look for "solutions" for your problems; you'll rarely find them. Look instead for sensible adjustments to brighten your days. Before you do something for your child, try asking yourself three questions.

1. Do I enjoy it?
2. Does my child enjoy it?
3. Are there any long-run benefits?

I don't pretend to have adjustments that work for everyone. But four great places to start looking are sleep, activities, discipline, and supervision.

SLEEP

Sleep deprivation is new parents' leading complaint. Part of the problem is unavoidable biology—newborns need small, frequent feedings. But infants' needs explain only a sliver of what parents endure. Kids often refuse to sleep through the night for years, long enough to turn their parents into zombies.

A sliver of kids stubbornly refuses to sleep. Normally, though, the root cause of sleeplessness is overparenting. What do people do when their child cries instead of sleeping? If their baby isn't hungry, thirsty, or in need of a fresh diaper, they try attention. The child gets picked up, rocked, and serenaded. He calms down until his parents put him back to bed—then cries louder than ever. What do you expect if he can avoid sleep *and* get attention merely by carrying on? As Joshua Gans writes in *Parentonomics*:

> Sleep is a negotiation. We want sleep, while the baby wants attention. There is an inherent conflict here. The screams of a baby are like an

offer: "I'll stop screaming if you give me some attention." And it is not a vague offer. Give the baby attention and the crying stops. After only a few goes, a little baby can train its parents nicely.

You could argue that nighttime coddling is bad for kids because they'll be tired the next day. Perhaps, but they enjoy the appeasement and can catch up on their sleep any time they please. The clear losers are the parents—and who's to say that the child's reign of terror won't go on night after night?

If parents *only* cared about themselves, the obvious solution to sleeplessness would be to shut the child's bedroom door and let the troublemaker cry himself out. Sleep researchers call this "systematic ignoring." It works, but it's harsh. "Parents count too" doesn't mean "Kids don't count at all." Fortunately, there are intermediate options. The Ferber method—let the child cry for a few minutes, comfort him, repeat—is the most famous, and it works wonders, too. When our twins were about a month old, my wife and I invented our own version. By the time they were three months old, both slept through the night.

I want to believe that our approach was better for us *and* them, but I'm not convinced. During cry time, the twins were two unhappy campers. Still, we're raising their baby brother the same way. While a coddling regime might mean an extra daily hour of fun for our son, it also means an extra dozen daily hours of sluggishness for us.

Getting your kids to sleep through the night is crucial for livable parenting. If you want better than livable, you'll mandate regular naps until your kids are old enough to quietly entertain themselves for an hour. I don't know how bad it is for toddlers not to nap. Many seem fine either way. What I do know is that if they don't, it is bad for parents. Nap time gives parents of young children quiet time to catch up on their work, relax, or take a nap of their own.

Granted, mandatory naps can't go on forever. Parents should be looking for sensible adjustments, not solutions. Still, parents who take their own interests into account will retain a daily nap for a year or two more than their child needs. We kept the twins on a daily napping schedule until they were almost six. By that point, they were mature enough to switch from nap time to quiet time.

Instead of a two-hour nap, they have to keep down the noise for the same duration. For the twins, quiet time is a big improvement. For us, it's a distinction without a difference.

ACTIVITIES

To the naive, activities are a great way for parents to get a break. Why not let their soccer coach mind them for a while? But in reality, kids' activities are a time pit for parents. Kids usually need a ride, so the parent has to take them where they're going, wait around, then take them home. If mom didn't need a break before, she'll need one by the time the car pulls back into the garage.

Chauffeuring kids to activities has always been a little stressful for parents. For Today's Typical Parent, it's more exhausting than ever, because kids have so many structured activities. These excesses would be bad enough if parents' sacrifices actually made their children happy. But parents often reluctantly admit that their kids don't even enjoy their activities. This is no surprise. How would you like it if an authority figure enrolled you in a weekly piano lesson?

A crucial step to happier parenting is to abandon "recreation" enjoyed by neither parent nor child. As Lenore Skenazy advises in *Free-Range Kids*, "Find one thing you've pushed your kids to do that they don't really like and aren't good at, and let them drop it. Be prepared for cheers." Step two is to cut more activities, starting with the ones that parents dislike the most and kids like the least. You don't have to drive your toddler to story time on a rainy day. He can just skip a class.

When parents hear this advice, they soon wonder, "What are my kids supposed to do with all their extra free time?" Notice: Moms and dads don't ask how they'll spend *their* extra free time. On that front, they're full of ideas. When they imagine their kids with idle hands, however, the devil's playground swiftly comes to mind.

Kids have plenty of wholesome stay-at-home options. Many simply want more time to play with their toys. Now that my twins are in school, they feel like they're losing touch with their Playmobiles. "The problem with kindergarten," they soon announced, "is that it takes away all your time." Other kids would get some fresh air in the backyard; you don't need a team to exercise. Still, parents worry that kids will spend most of their newfound free time on television, video games, and other plug-in babysitters.

Their suspicions are almost certainly correct. If you give mature adults extra free time, many relax in front of the TV or computer. It would be amazing if childish children didn't do the same. But what's wrong with that? Electronic babysitters are a vital component of cultural literacy. I hope my kids grow up to know both *The Simpsons* and Shakespeare. In any case, electronic babysitters are undeniably a lot of fun for kids, and—as a cheap, dependable substitute for a human babysitter—a blessing for parents, too. So why the hostility? It's as if parents think that anything that feels good for every member of the family must be bad.

I'm not advising people to put their kids in front of the television and forget about them. My wife and I don't let ours watch more than an hour or two a day, because we don't want them to miss out on the other joys of childhood. I'm merely suggesting pragmatic adjustments in the way that families spend their time. If parents feel exhausted by their kids' busy schedule, they should trim a few hours of activities from their week—even if their kids spend most of their extra hours on TV and video games. The parents will be happier, and the kids will probably be happier, too.

The case for fewer family activities is especially strong when you've got teenagers. Parents and teens habitually complain about each other. Teens say parents are mean and controlling, parents say teens are hostile and ungrateful. These mutual recriminations suggest that parents and teenagers spend too much time together. When your teenager feels like a prisoner, and treats you like a jailer, less is more.

Family vacations are another nightmare for millions of parents. Why pay thousands of dollars for the worst week of your year? Children may appreciate their parents' sacrifices of cash and sanity, but don't count on it. The typical kid is not a fan of long car rides and museums. Most pathetic of all is when aggravated parents let down their masks and scream—giving their kids truly ugly "memories that last a lifetime."

Fewer days and shorter distances would improve most family vacations, but my personal favorite is the parents-only getaway. If kids prevent their parents from enjoying a trip and won't appreciate it themselves, including them is a bad idea. Getaways are mainly an option for families with helpful grandparents, but many parents stubbornly turn down their elders' repeated offers to watch the kids for a few days. They successfully raised you to adulthood. What are you so worried about?

If you insist on family bonding, try a "staycation." Instead of driving for hours and cramming the whole family into a tent or hotel room, stay home together. Every day, you enjoy your regional attractions—then relax in your own home while your kids relax in their own rooms. Staycations are ideal for residents in major tourist areas; I grew up in Los Angeles but never saw Hollywood's Walk of Fame until I was in my thirties. Given the hazards of the family vacation, however, a staycation is worth a try even in the middle of nowhere.

DISCIPLINE

Parents have always made excuses for discipline: "This is for your own good." "This is going to hurt me more than it hurts you." These excuses may sound phony, but Today's Typical Parents actually buy their own propaganda. Benefit to the child is almost the *only* socially acceptable justification for discipline. As a result, parents use a lot less discipline than they would if they counted their own interests.

I can't forget the day I saw a father allow his five-year-old daughter to punch and kick him. She struck hard and often. I felt like I was watching a villain in a bad kung fu movie called *Fists and Feet of Fury*. The dad outweighed his daughter by over a hundred pounds, but all he did to defend himself was say, "Now, now. There, there."

You could blame the dad for retarding his daughter's social skills, but that's arguable. Her social skills were very impressive for a five-year-old. She didn't try to punch or kick anyone else at the party. She knew that different people have different rules—and only her parents would endure her abuse. What's not arguable is that the father was hurting *himself* with bad parenting. He had the bruises to prove it.

Parents who want a happier life need to rethink the justification for discipline. The welfare of the child is one legitimate goal. If your toddler runs into the street, zero tolerance really is for his own good. But the child's welfare is only the beginning. Another legitimate function of discipline is to keep the child from abusing the people around him—and no one is more susceptible to a child's abuse than his own parents. Your kid knows where you live. You're stuck with him, and he knows it. He also knows that you love him, so you're inclined to forgive him his trespasses. Armed with these advantages, your child can make your life awful—unless you stand up for yourself.

The smart disciplinary adjustment to make is just the wisdom of the ages: Clarity, Consistency, and Consequences. Adopt firm rules, clearly explain the penalties for breaking the rules, and impose promised penalties to the letter. If your child punches or kicks you, you've got to tell your child that it's against the rules and that the punishment for transgression is, say, one day without television. Every time your child breaks the rule, harden your heart and impose the punishment. Clear, consistent punishment isn't foolproof, and some kids are tougher to crack than others, but it beats being a punching bag.

If you're skeptical of the wisdom of the ages, there is solid experimental evidence in its favor. When parents ask psychologists to help control their children's disobedience, tantrums, and aggression, psychologists often respond by training the *parents*. They call it "behavioral parent training," but it's Clarity, Consistency, and Consequences by another name. Researchers have run dozens of experiments to see whether behavioral parent training really works. It does. Suppose you have a list of parents who want help with their problem children. You randomly train some, and leave the rest on a waiting list. Experiments typically find that the average child of the trained parents behaves better than 80 percent of the children of the parents on the wait list. The main weakness of the training is parental backsliding: Once parents tire of Clarity, Consistency, and Consequences, their children go back to their old tricks. Discipline is like dieting: It works when tried.

When you're trying to improve your kid's behavior, other authorities—teachers, grandparents, nannies, and so on—often frustrate you by undermining your rules. What good is it to practice the Three Cs if no one else does? Selfishly speaking: Plenty of good. Kids quickly discover that different people have different rules. If the typical teenager treated his friends the way he treats his parents, he wouldn't have any friends. A central criticism of behavioral parent training is that it "only" improves children's behavior in the home. But an optimist would draw a different lesson: Parental discipline is enough to make children treat their parents decently. If other authorities in your child's life have lower standards, that's largely their problem.

One of the human child's charming traits, by the way, is responsiveness to token punishments. You can scare kids straight by credibly threatening to take away one night's TV or one dinner's dessert. In fact, these wrist slaps often turn out to be overkill. When our twins were infants, I watched *Supernanny* in disbelief. The Supernanny, Jo Frost, punished monstrous children merely by putting them in the naughty corner—and their behavior sharply improved. Once my boys got a little older, I was shocked to discover that the naughty corner works. At least in my family, two minutes of mild humiliation was enough to deter nine out of ten toddler tantrums.

When I praise discipline, then, don't imagine that I'm Captain von Trapp from *The Sound of Music*. I never spank my kids. I don't even raise my voice to them. If I did, their behavior would probably be better still. But as I've said, "Parents count, too" doesn't mean "Kids don't count at all." If I can sharply improve my quality of life by mildly punishing my kids, I'll do so without apology. If cruelty is the price of slightly better behavior, I'm not buying.

SUPERVISION

When you google "Worst Mom in America," journalist Lenore Skenazy is the first hit. Her offense: Letting her nine-year-old son ride the New York City subway by himself. The boy had a safe trip, enjoyed a taste of independence, and made it home in about an hour. Yet when Skenazy bragged about his odyssey on television, viewers were horrified—and she soon won her infamous title. Needless to say, Skenazy wears it as a joke. She wants to keep her progeny safe, too. She let her son ride the subway alone because he had years of practice and she knew the safety statistics. The point of her book, *Free-Range Kids*, is that children can handle—and would enjoy—a lot more independence than modern parents allow.

All this suggests another judicious way for parents to give themselves a break. More independent kids equal less parental supervision. If your kids want to stretch their wings, you don't feel like supervising them, and everyone stays safe, go for it. Even if your kids lobby against more independence for themselves, there's nothing wrong with balancing their mild separation anxiety against your desire for a little more space.

There are many thoughtful ways to safely cut back on parental supervision. No one raises "free-range babies," but you don't have to play with them during every waking moment. They often cry for attention because it works. If you have toddlers, gate off a small danger zone, then child-proof the rest of your home until you're comfortable letting them play on their own for an hour.

Once you have school-age kids, chances to safely cut supervision are all around. Let them use public restrooms on their own, stay home alone while you go to the store, or watch the Chipmunks movie in Theater 3 while you enjoy a real movie in Theater 6. Letting your eight-year-old out of your sight may feel dangerous, but as we'll see later on, popular fears of abduction are almost pure fantasy. Driving your third-grader to the store is vastly more dangerous than leaving him home without a bodyguard.

If you're looking for more creative ways to supervise less, Skenazy's *Free-Range Kids* is a gold mine. A few favorites:

> Volunteer to watch the kids who are waiting with your own kid for soccer to start or school to open—whatever. Explain to the other parents that you're offering them a little free time. If they say no, ask them to watch *your* kid.

> Think of one activity you did as a child that you are unwilling to let your own sweetheart do at the same age (baby-sitting, biking to a friend's), and make a list of twenty things that could conceivably go wrong. If there are any worries that strike you as realistic, help your child prepare for them.

> Have your middle schooler start doing a task that *you* would normally do, like taking the dog to the vet or buying the groceries for dinner.

Policing kids' books, shows, movies, and games for "inappropriate content" is also usually a waste of time. Scariness is one thing. If your kid won't be able to sleep after he watches *Paranormal Activity*, don't let him. (But remember: Action is not horror. Violent movies rarely scare kids if the good guys win.) If your children imitate bad behavior they see on TV, denying access is poetic justice. Otherwise, relax. Whatever you do, your kids will see and hear it all long before it's "age appropriate."

IN PRAISE OF THROWING MONEY AT YOUR PROBLEMS

The day after my wife and I got married, we prepared for a cross-country drive from Los Angeles to our new home in Princeton, New Jersey. Though we were eager for the honeymoon to begin, I spent four hours at my in-laws' house struggling to change our Volkswagen's oil. Meanwhile, my wife inventoried the wedding presents, including thousands of dollars in cash and checks. Yet it never crossed my mind to take $20 out of the gift box and drive to Jiffy-Lube. By the time the oil was changed and the car was packed, it was midnight—and I was ready to bang my head against the windshield.

The oil-change incident wasn't merely a failure of common sense. We were moving to Princeton so I could finish my PhD in economics, yet the well-known fact that money can be exchanged for goods and services slipped my mind. My only excuse has to be some kind of post-wedding dementia. But at least I learned a lifelong lesson: Money *can* buy happiness if you spend it the right way.

When you're tired, stressed, or disgusted, outsourcing your worst hours of child care can make your whole day. This may sound like "Let them eat cake," but parents don't need a lot of money to escape a lot of misery. *Most* Americans can afford a few more hours of babysitting a week. Even if the money only purchases a little extra free time on the weekend, the benefits are large, because the last hours of child care are the hardest. And many parents can afford much more. In 2005, over 15 percent of American families earned six-figure incomes. That's roughly 18 million households with the income to hire a lot of help—up to and including a full-time nanny. One day, this could be you, if it isn't already.

One hundred thousand dollars a year might not seem that rich to you, but it's a question of priorities. Families earning six figures have plenty of fat to cut. If you have two kids, a part-time nanny will probably do more for your quality of life than a new car. If you're feeling too short on cash to hire help, there are plenty of ways to cut the cost. A nanny doesn't need fluent English or a driver's license to provide loving care for your children. It's a little less convenient, but costs half as much—and before long, your kids will be fluent translators.

Now that you've got your wallet out, consider a few other ways to turn your money into happiness. The obvious ones: Spend freely on take-out meals, electronic babysitters, and cleaning services; they're a tired, stressed, disgusted parent's best friends. Less obviously, and more controversially: When you want your kids' help, nag them less and reward them more.

When I was a boy, my mom paid me a penny for every ten weeds I pulled. When I complained, she'd object, "You're lucky to get paid at all. You live here, and you should contribute." Just imagine how persuasive her lecture was. Under my mom's slave-wage regime, she had to heavily nag me to lift a finger.

Now that I'm a dad, my mom's penny-wise labor policies still strike me as pound foolish. Why should parents drive themselves crazy squeezing free labor out of their kids? Your boss doesn't have to nag you to do your job. Instead, he makes you an offer—and if you don't like it, you can quit. This seemingly cold system is far more harmonious in practice than "From each according to his ability, to each according to his need."

Don't pay your children for every little thing. But when you want to give your kids a major project or a recurring chore, make it worth their while. Trading favors works well, especially for younger children. "If you eat your dinner without complaining, you get dessert," "You can watch TV after you clean up your toys," and "I'll give you a ride to the mall if you put the dishes away" are all good options. At the same time, there's absolutely nothing wrong with paying cash. You're not trying to raise a communist.

If generous terms fall on deaf ears, you're probably giving your kids too much for free. Handing out goodies to your kids "just because" is fun, but you shouldn't expect a child with a $40 weekly allowance to be hungry for work. Instead of redoubling your nagging, turn a portion of your welfare into workfare.

Using money to make parenting easier isn't just doable; it's done. High-income parents actually seem to "buy" themselves less regret and more happiness. In the *Newsday* survey, only 4 percent of the richest parents regretted having children—compared to 13 percent of the poorest. In the General Social Survey, richer parents have a much smaller happiness deficit. In the poorer half, otherwise identical people with one child instead of zero are 6.6 percentage points less likely to be very happy. In the richer half, parents' happiness deficit is only 3.6 percentage points.

You might look at these results and conclude, "Don't have kids until you are financially secure." Not bad advice, assuming fertility problems are far in the future. However, I'm making a totally different point: Rich parents successfully use money to make parenting easier—and the rest of us can profit by their example.

PROTECTING YOUR KIDS FROM SECONDHAND STRESS

"If mamma ain't happy, ain't nobody happy." On the surface, the saying reminds us to be nice to mom, but there's a deeper meaning: Beware of sacrifices for the good of the family. If you don't feel like taking your kids on a ski trip, your bad mood could easily ruin the outing. On balance, your kids might be happier if you said no. They'll feel disappointed, but at least they won't be traumatized when you scream at them for changing the radio station. By the same logic, your child might be happier if you saw more movies alone on your way home from work. While you'd spend a little less time with your family, you'd have a better attitude during your time together.

Many parents worry about the dangers of secondhand smoke. But few consider the dangers of secondhand stress. If you make yourself miserable to do a special favor for your child, he might enjoy it. But if he senses your negative feelings, he might come to share them.

Secondhand stress is one of kids' leading grievances. In the Ask the Children survey, researcher Ellen Galinsky interviewed over 1,000 kids in grades three to twelve and asked parents to guess how kids would respond. One key question: "If you were granted one wish to change the way that your mother's/father's work affects your life, what would that wish be?" Kids' answers were striking. They rarely wished for extra face time with their parents. They were much more likely to wish their parents would be less tired and stressed. The parents were completely out of touch. Virtually none guessed that kids would use their one wish to give their parents a better attitude.

Galinsky also asked kids to grade their parents' performance on a dozen dimensions. Overall, parents did pretty well. Moms had an overall GPA of 3.14, versus 2.98 for dads. A majority of moms *and* dads got As for "appreciating me for who I am," "making me feel important and loved," and "being able to attend important events in my life." Anger management was parents' Achilles' heel. More than 40 percent of kids gave their moms and dads a C, D, or F for "controlling his/her temper when I do something that makes him/her angry"—the very worst marks on their report card.

When I preach that "Parents count, too," there's a lot of push back. I feel like I'm on *The Simpsons* and Helen Lovejoy's shouting, "Won't somebody please think of the children?" However, if you not only think of the children but *listen* to them, you'll end up following a lot of my advice. Kids may not realize that they can make themselves unhappy by demanding too much from their parents. Parents, however, should be mature enough to protect their kids from secondhand stress. When you can't help your child with a sincere smile, it's often kinder to gently refuse.

FROM HAPPIER PARENTS TO BIGGER FAMILIES

Parental unhappiness is not a complete myth. The average parent is slightly less happy than the average nonparent. My reaction is not to deny the facts but to ask, "Why settle for average?" Parents put an enormous amount of time and money into their children, and in terms of happiness, they *almost* break even. If you're trying hard and almost succeeding, the natural response is not to give up but to rethink your strategy. With a little insight and creativity, parents can sharply improve their experience.

A dad once joked to me, "The first kid takes 99 percent of your free time; the second kid takes the remaining 1 percent." The one-liner seems to affirm the inevitability of parental sacrifice but actually does the opposite. How can the second child be so much less work than the first? Because parents *reallocate* their time away from the firstborn to care for the baby. The implication: The elder child never really "required" 99 percent of their time in the first place. The parents could have given themselves a break all along, because much of their toil was superfluous.

If all my book does is make you a happier parent, I'll be satisfied. Still, I want to push my luck—to convince you to be the happier parent of a larger family. The argument is simple: Once you adjust the kind of parent you plan to be, you should also reconsider the number of kids you want to have. When you weigh whether to have one more, you shouldn't base your decision on the lifestyle of Today's Typical Parent. You should base it on the lifestyle you've chosen for yourself. When you live by the philosophy that "Parents count, too," you buy your kids at a hefty effort discount. Why not stock up?

Now it's time to grapple with the strongest objection to my self-styled "commonsense guide to happier parenting": In the future, your children will pay the price for your lackadaisical attitude. We all know how important parenting is, right? Energetic parenting supposedly turns children into healthy, smart, successful, virtuous, and possibly even happy adults. When young adults fall short of this ideal, we round up the usual suspects—bad, lazy, or absent parents who failed to do their job.

From this perspective, a take-it-easy approach only *seems* better for parents. Letting your kids watch Saturday-morning cartoons while you sleep in feels pleasant at the time. When eighteen years of shortcuts turn your son into an unemployed dropout who spends his days playing video games in your basement, though, a single question will torment you: "What have I done?"

I will not respond to this objection by trotting out a bunch of studies claiming that hands-off parenting leads to independence or that video games build brain cells. I don't claim to know the *real* way to mold your children into adults you can be proud of. My response is more modest, yet more radical: The best available evidence shows that large differences in upbringing have little effect on how kids turn out. While healthy, smart, happy, successful, virtuous parents tend to have matching offspring, the reason is largely nature, not nurture.

When I say "the best available evidence," I'm not talking about a handful of studies that are slightly less bogus than the competition. The best available evidence on the nature-nurture question is excellent. Twin and adoption studies aren't quite as good as controlled laboratory experiments, but many are close. Thousands of research papers have applied these methods to hundreds of controversial questions. They reach an amazing consensus about what counts for kids.

2
■ ■ ■

THE CASE AGAINST GUILT: A PARENT'S GUIDE TO BEHAVIORAL GENETICS

> When I was just a little girl / I asked my mother, "What will I be?" / "Will I be pretty?" / "Will I be rich?" / Here's what she said to me: / Que sera, sera / Whatever will be, will be; / The future's not ours to see. / Que sera, sera.
>
> —Doris Day, *The Man Who Knew Too Much*

KIDS BORN TODAY REQUIRE FOOD AND SHELTER, JUST AS THEY DID a hundred thousand years ago. Meeting these basic needs is far easier than it once was—we buy at the store rather than hunt in the wild. As we've gotten better at providing food and shelter, however, we've also upped our standards of good parenting. Modern parents feel obligated to make many extra credit investments in their children's future. Their "free time" revolves around their children: preparing them, shuttling them around, and watching them from the bleachers.

Why do parents kill themselves, instead of taking my easy way out? Unlike a lot of expert recommendations, it is hard to deny that my approach would work as advertised. At least in the short run, parents would clearly be happier if they gave themselves a break. Moms' and dads' central objection is that if they cut corners, they risk their children's future. Indeed, they often shudder when they hear my advice. Their heads fill with images of lazy parents fiddling while their oversized packs of barbaric children burn down Rome.

We're going to see that these fears are mostly, if you'll pardon the expression, old wives' tales. You can do a lot less without risking your children's future, because children are far more resilient than we realize. Once upon a time, nature versus nurture was a matter of opinion, but now there are hard answers: Nature wins, especially in the long run. If your child had grown up in a very different family— or if you had been a very different parent—he probably would have turned out about the same.

This may sound discouraging. No parent wants to hear that his sacrifices have been in vain. I insist, however, that the glass is more than half full. Do you think your kids will turn out all right? You probably should; most eventually do. Well, if I'm telling you the truth about nature and nurture, you don't need to make great decisions to get kids you can be proud of. You don't have to live up to the exhausting standards of the Supermom and Superdad next door. Instead, you can raise your kids in the way that feels comfortable for you, and stop worrying. They'll still turn out fine.

HOW TO TELL NATURE FROM NURTURE

Patri Friedman is one of the most exciting characters I've ever met. He's the grandson of Nobel Prize–winning economist Milton Friedman, known for his staunchly libertarian views, and the son of economist David Friedman, who makes father Milton look like a socialist. At Patri's 2005 wedding, a year before Milton passed away, guests saw three generations of Friedmans side by side. All were short and hyper. All were brilliant, creative, and loved a good debate. None were religious. All were libertarians. All were obsessed with economics. Admittedly, only Milton and David became economics professors. But after working for Google's prediction markets project, Patri decided to bring his sires' libertarian economics to life by founding the Seasteading Institute, a think tank that explores the feasibility of floating city-states on the high seas.

What should we think about the Friedmans' eerie family resemblances? We tend to see their physical similarity as hereditary.

The first time you set your eyes on Patri, you'll hail the power of the Friedman genes. Elfin Jew begat elfin Jew begat another elfin Jew. In contrast, we tend to see their psychological and behavioral similarity as proof of the power of parenting. The first time you argue with Patri, you'll probably imagine that he spent decades learning the family business over the dinner table. Patri is brilliant and hyper, economistic and libertarian, because he was raised that way, right?

If you share these musings with Patri, however, he'll disagree. His parents divorced when he was a baby, and his dad lived in another state. How then did he come to his distinctive outlook? Patri tells me he's been this way as long as he can remember. He entered the family business long before he knew it *was* the family business.

Perhaps Patri understates his family's influence. Once he was eight or so, he started spending summers with his dad. Perhaps people who knew about his Nobelist grandfather treated Patri in subtly different yet life-altering ways. Still, Patri's story raises a red flag: We might draw the line between nature and nurture in the wrong place. What makes us so sure that we're good at telling the two apart?

The naive reaction to these doubts is to carefully study lots of families. Alas, you can't get anywhere on the nature-nurture issue merely by looking at typical families, because the typical family seamlessly blends biology and upbringing. We normally share half of our siblings' genes, plus a childhood in the same home. As long as these two treatments are woven together, we'll never figure out what's going on. Intelligent bystanders' reaction is usually to split the difference and decree, "*Both* nature and nurture are important," or else declare the question insoluble.

Fortunately, active researchers in this area aren't so quick to admit defeat. After they concede that nature and nurture seamlessly go together in the typical family, they retort that *not all families are typical*. The secret to unraveling the nature-nurture mystery is to study special kinds of families where there is a clear seam—or even a complete separation—between biology and parenting. From this standpoint, two kinds of families are special: Families that adopt, and families with twins.

We can clearly learn a lot by looking at families that adopt. When a couple raises the child of a perfect stranger from birth, any family resemblance is probably due to nurture. If you've never even *met* your birth parents but resemble them anyway, the reason is probably nature.

What about families with twins? At first glance, they have the same problem as "regular" families—they seamlessly blend biology and upbringing, making it impossible to tell the two apart. But there are two kinds of twins: identical and fraternal. Identical twins share all of their genes. They usually look so similar that strangers have trouble telling who's who. When people ask me how to tell my identical twin sons apart, I point out that one has a barely visible birthmark on his chin. Fraternal twins share only half of their genes—no more than ordinary siblings. So if identical twins resemble each other more than fraternal twins, the reason is probably nature.

Not good enough for you? We can go to the next level by looking at twins who were separated and raised by different families. If identical twins raised apart are more similar than fraternal twins raised apart, the reason almost has to be nature. If twins raised together are more similar than twins raised apart, the reason almost has to be nurture.

A few decades ago, twin and adoption methods were little more than neat ideas. Since then, hundreds of researchers have taken these neat ideas and run with them. The result is a new discipline— behavioral genetics—and an imposing stack of studies that use twin and adoption methods to settle the nature-nurture debate, trait by trait.

What do these studies reveal? Most expect the middle-of-the-road answer that both nature and nurture are important. Indeed, most have trouble believing anything else. But believe it or not, twin and adoption studies do *not* support the middle-of-the-road answer. Identical twins are *much* more similar than fraternal twins—even when separated at birth—and their similarity often increases as they age. When adopted children are young, they moderately resemble their adopted family. By the time adoptees reach adulthood, however, this resemblance largely fades away. Taken together, there's a striking lesson: *Nature matters a lot more than nurture, especially in the long run.*

NATURE VERSUS NURTURE: CLARIFYING THE QUESTION

Twin and adoption studies are powerful microscopes on the human condition. Before we start looking through the microscope, however, let's take the device apart and see how it works.

EXPLAINING VARIATION

It is easy to devise examples where nurture matters tremendously. If you raise a child in a closet and make sure he never hears a word, he won't learn how to speak. It is equally easy to devise examples where nature is all powerful. If a child gets two copies of the gene for Tay-Sachs disease, he'll almost surely die by the age of five. How can nature or nurture "matter more" if either can make all the difference in the world?

Researchers handle this issue by focusing on what's important in practice, instead of mere hypotheticals. They don't ask, "What *could* make people different from each other?" They ask, "What *does* make people different from each other?" They don't ask, "How would this child have turned out if he were raised by wolves?" They ask, "How would this child have turned out if he were raised by one of the other families we interviewed?" If an adoption study concludes that nurture doesn't matter for height, this means that existing parenting differences do not affect kids' height. If a twin study, similarly, reports that upbringing doesn't affect income after age thirty, this doesn't mean that your dad *can't* hire you for double your market value, merely that such nepotism is vanishingly rare in the real world.

Nurture has two distinct ways *not* to matter. One is simple; the other is subtle. The simple way is when height is completely out of parents' control. If nothing in the parental toolkit affects height, we won't find a nurture effect. The subtle way is when all parents affect height to the same degree. If every parent takes actions that raise her children's height by four inches, *differences* in parenting won't explain why some kids are taller than others. The same distinction applies if you say that nurture doesn't matter much. It could mean that parents only have small effects; it could mean that parents have *similar* effects.

Notice: If your goal is to understand differences that we actually observe, it's important to specify where we actually look. Most twin and adoption studies focus on people raised in advanced Western countries in modern times. So if a study finds that nurture doesn't matter for height, this tells us that mixing up two babies at an American or a Swedish hospital will leave their adult stature unchanged. If a mix-up sent a Haitian baby to food-rich America, and an American baby to hungry Haiti, the effect on height could be massive.

From a social scientist's point of view, this is an important distinction. You can't look at families in the United States or Sweden, conclude that almost all are good enough to allow children to flourish, then infer the same about families in Haiti. From a *parent's* point of view, however, this distinction is rarely relevant. If you're reading this book, you probably live in the First World—or at least enjoy a First World standard of living. When you decide what kind of parent to be, you aren't wondering whether you should emigrate to Haiti to raise your children in dire poverty. Instead, you're weighing the pros and cons of the parenting styles used by people like you. If you discover that these styles are equally good for kids, you have the information you need.

NURTURE AND ENVIRONMENT ARE NOT THE SAME

No two people have exactly the same environment. Two children who live under one roof have different teachers and friends. They watch different TV programs and eat different foods. One has the top bunk, the other has the bottom bunk. One gets a spanking, the other gets a bedtime story. Most, but not all, eventually leave their childhood home. How then can researchers say that two kids were nurtured in the same way?

The answer is that researchers equate "nurtured in the same way" with "were raised by the same people." If parents' income, education, marital status, parenting philosophy, religion, school district, or favorite color affects their children, it counts as nurture. What doesn't count as nurture? Any feature of children's environment that varies despite the fact that they were raised by the same people. Researchers call such features "unique environment" or "nonshared environment," but you could just as well say "none of the above." Anything from peers, germs, and television to parental favoritism, dumb luck, and free will could qualify as unique environment.

Unique environment is a provably powerful force. My first two children share all their genes. They've lived with my wife and me since their birth. Yet they're different. One twin is more argumentative, the other eager to please; one focuses on following the rules, the other on making friends. If we took the nature-nurture debate literally, the individuality of my sons—or any identical twins raised together—would be impossible. The solution to this paradox: Instead of picturing a two-way race between nature and nurture, picture a three-way race between nature (also known as heredity and genes), nurture (also known as upbringing, family, parents, and shared family environment), and unique environment (also known as nonshared environment and none of the above). If you're studying height, for example, there are three questions to ask. First: How much height variation is due to genetic differences? Second: How much is due to differences in family environment? Third: How much is due to everything else? The fact that genes don't explain everything does not imply that family environment explains the rest.

NATURE AND NURTURE:
DIRECT VERSUS INDIRECT EFFECTS

Twin and adoption studies are great ways to distinguish nature from nurture. However, they rarely help us distinguish different kinds of nature, or different kinds of nurture. Instead, they bundle *all* direct and indirect effects together. If researchers report that genes affect income, for example, the reason might be that genes matter for intelligence, and intelligence matters for income. It could just as easily mean that genes matter for looks, and looks matter for income. There doesn't need to be an "income gene." Similarly, when researchers report that nurture matters for religion, the reason might be that parents instill religious values; yet it could just as easily mean that parents control religious education, which in turn instills religious values.

Since researchers bundle together direct and indirect effects, their results are a lot stronger than they look. Suppose an adoption study finds that nurture doesn't influence smoking. A parent could *not* reasonably object, "Right, but since peers influence smoking, and parents influence peers, I still matter." The flaw in this argument is that a normal adoption study includes *any* and *all* indirect effects. If the "parents influence peers, peers influence smoking" channel worked, then an adoption study would report that parents matter. The same goes for neighborhoods. If parents choose their neighborhood, and neighborhoods affect kids' drinking or college attendance, then a twin study would conclude that nurture matters for drinking and college. So remember: Researchers' failure to detect an effect doesn't just undermine simple stories of parental influence; it throws cold water on whatever stories you might propose.

MEASURING NATURE AND NURTURE EFFECTS

It's easy to understand what it means for nature or nurture to have *zero* effect. What does it mean, though, for nature or nurture effects to be "small" or "large"? The clearest measures come from a thought experiment I call "Switched at Birth":

> Imagine you have an identical twin, but there's a mix-up at the hospital: A nurse accidentally switches your twin with another family's baby. You and the strangers' baby grow up with your biological parents. Your twin grows up with the strangers. Decades later, the hospital discovers its mistake and arranges a meeting between you, your identical twin, and your accidentally adopted sibling.

To measure the effect of nature, just answer this question:

> Suppose you're higher on some trait—height, intelligence, income, conservatism, you name it—than 80 percent of your peers. How high on this trait should you expect your TWIN from Switched at Birth to be?

To measure the effect of nurture, just answer this question:

> Suppose you're higher on some trait—height, intelligence, income, conservatism, you name it—than 80 percent of your peers. How high on this trait should you expect your ADOPTED SIBLING from Switched at Birth to be?

Most twin and adoption studies report enough information to measure both effects; if you're curious about the math, see the appendix at the end of this chapter on "Where the Nature-Nurture Effect Sizes Come From." Intuitively, if nature didn't matter at all, you would expect your separated twin to be average—in the 50th percentile. If nature were destiny, you would expect your separated twin to match you in the 80th percentile; you'd both be higher in the trait than four out of five peers. Similarly, if nurture didn't matter at all, you would expect your adopted sibling to be average; if nurture were destiny, you would expect your adopted sibling to be in the 80th percentile, just like you.

I'm going to use Switched at Birth's measures of nature and nurture over and over. Once we get to specific twin and adoption studies, I'll usually tell you their precise predictions about your separated twin or adopted sibling. As shorthand, if your counterpart in the thought experiment is in the 51st through 55th percentiles, I'll call that a "small" effect. If he's in the 56th through 65th percentiles, I'll call that a "moderate" effect. Anything more I'll call "large."

THE PARENTAL WISH LIST: CAN PARENTS MAKE THEIR DREAMS COME TRUE?

> The children must be molded, shaped and taught /
> That life's a looming battle to be faced and fought!
>
> —*Mary Poppins*

Parents are supposed to love their children unconditionally, but that doesn't stop them from having an extensive wish list for the next generation. Some parents map out their kids' future in great detail: You will go to Harvard, become a cardiologist, marry a nice Jewish girl, and live in the house across the street. You're probably much more accepting, but you'd still *prefer* your kids to become healthy, smart, happy, successful, virtuous adults who share your values and appreciate what you've done for them. And if things don't pan out, even the most accepting parents wonder, "Where did I go wrong?"

The underlying assumption is that parents have the power to grant their own wishes. Do they? How much influence do parents really have over their children's traits? To answer these questions, I now climb upon the shoulders of giants—the hundreds of researchers, past and present, who have used twin and adoption methods to unlock the secrets of nature and nurture. Researchers have carefully studied every entry on the typical parent's wish list. It's time to confront their evidence, wish by wish.

Wish #1: Health

My mom is a longtime antismoking crusader. When I was growing up in Los Angeles, she always requested the nonsmoking section—even if she knew quite well that the restaurant didn't have one. My mother was so opposed to smoking that she offered her kids a cash prize—payable on our twenty-first birthdays—if we stayed away from tobacco. I never smoked, and my mom paid up. Yet to be honest, the prize was overkill: Smoking disgusted me from an early age. While my mom *tried* to shape my behavior, and got the result she wanted, that hardly shows that her bribe worked.

The same goes for a long list of health habits that parents struggle to instill. Parents pressure their kids to eat right, get fresh air and exercise, brush their teeth, and stay away from tobacco and drugs. Part of parents' motivation is to protect their kids' *current* health, but the typical kid is too full of life to expect much immediate payoff. The main rationale for health-related nagging is to instill healthy habits that last a lifetime. My parents put strict limits on sweets, even though I was a skinny kid with perfect teeth. However harmless and tasty candy might seem, they weren't going to let me develop bad eating habits that would hurt me when I grew up.

If you take parents' rhetoric literally, there are strong implications. For example, if health nagging really works, then parents should affect how long their children live. If you influence your child's decision to smoke, and smoking affects life span, it follows that your child's life span is partly under your control.

If parents want to convince themselves that their efforts pay off, it won't be hard: Long life runs in families. But there are two explanations for family resemblance in health, just as there are two explanations for family resemblance in anything: upbringing is one, heredity is the other. When medical researchers use twin studies to weigh the importance of these competing explanations, nurture turns out to be far less important than parents think.

Parents don't affect life expectancy. Major twin studies find no influence of family environment on life span. One looked at almost 3,000 pairs of Danish twins born between 1870 and 1900. By the time the study was conducted in 1994, virtually all of the twins were dead, so researchers could easily compare the longevity of identical versus fraternal twins. They found moderate genetic effects: If you lived longer than 80 percent of the population, you could expect your separated identical twin to live longer than 58 percent of us. Yet the Danish twin study found "no evidence for an impact of shared (family) environment." Growing up in the same home, being nagged by the same people about the same things, does not make your life expectancy more alike.

Another study looked at the mortality of about 9,000 Swedish twins born between 1886 and 1925. Since the Swedish sample was younger, some of the subjects were still alive; the goal of the study was to study twins' *probability* of surviving to a given age. The Swedish twins study found strong genetic effects, especially for males—and zero effect of upbringing.

Parents have little or no effect on overall health. There's more to health than staying alive. Do parents make their children's years healthier even if they don't make them longer? Probably not. Researchers have examined twins' objective health (what particular health problems they've had) and subjective health (how healthy they say they feel). A study of over 3,000 elderly Danish twins found moderate effects of heredity on hospitalizations and self-reported health, but no effects of family environment. Another team of researchers looked at about 2,500 Swedish twins and found moderate genetic effects on self-rated health, but small or nonexistent nurture effects. A smaller study of older female Finnish twins found moderate effects of upbringing on self-rated health, but no effect of upbringing on health ratings based on doctors' examinations.

The most notable exception comes from the Swedish Adoption/ Twin Study of Aging. Researchers studied over 700 twin pairs, about half raised apart. For respondents seventy and older, they found a moderate-to-large nurture effect on objective health. If you were in the 80th percentile of objective health, you could expect your adopted sibling to be in the 65th percentile. For all younger groups, however, the nurture effect was zero.

Parents don't affect height, weight, or teeth. We all want our kids to grow up to be tall and fit, with sparkling white teeth. Most of us try to make these wishes come true. We push healthy foods, limit sweets, encourage exercise, and smell our kids' breath to make sure they use toothpaste. Parents probably recognize that genes play a role, but we clearly think we make a difference. Otherwise, what's the point of telling your kids how big and strong they'll be if they eat their vegetables?

In reality, genes strongly influence both height and weight, while upbringing influences neither. In the Swedish Adoption/Twin Study of Aging, twins raised together were about as similar in height and weight as twins raised apart, and identical twins were about twice as similar as fraternal twins—both strong signs that nature matters and nurture doesn't. Suppose you're six inches taller than average, and twenty pounds overweight. Expect your separated identical twin to be five inches taller than average, and fifteen pounds overweight— and your adopted sibling to be perfectly average.

A major survey article on the genetics of obesity confirms the power of nature and the impotence of nurture. Parents may not even affect the weight of young children, though one study finds a small family effect for girls in their tweens. If it seems hard to believe that parents are this powerless, remember the old saying that you can lead a horse to water, but you can't make him drink. It's a big pain to make a picky eater clean his plate—or keep *South Park*'s Eric Cartman on a low-carb diet. And if parents refuse their kids the food they crave, they'll find it somewhere else.

What about teeth? Surely parents' commitment to brushing, flossing, and regular checkups has to matter. A major study of adult Swedish twins looked at gingivitis, periodontal disease, and complete tooth loss. All three conditions showed moderate genetic influence. Family environment, in contrast, mattered only for the rare problem of losing all your teeth.

Parents might *have a small effect on smoking, drinking, and drug problems.* I understand why my mom paid me not to smoke. I don't want my kids to smoke, either. I don't care whether drugs are legal or not; I don't want my kids to use them. When relatives give my seven-year-olds a little beer, it irks me. Still, the question remains: "How much can I as a parent do about it?" When I bite my tongue and let my kids take a sip of alcohol, do I risk their future?

The answers from twin and adoption research aren't completely one-sided. Some conclude that nature fully explains why smoking, drinking, and drug use run in families. A study of over 3,000 male twins from the Vietnam Era Twin Registry found almost no family influence on nicotine and alcohol dependence; another study of the same group of twins found that nurture mattered for regular use of marijuana, but not amphetamines, cocaine, or sedatives. A study of Australian twins found that family environment made almost no difference for alcoholism. Researchers using the Virginia 30,000 sample—a massive study of Virginian twins and their families— concluded that being raised by smokers makes you a little *less* likely to share their vice. Maybe cigarettes are a lame way to rebel against parents who smoke.

But other researchers find that nurture plays a role as well. One team studied the tobacco, alcohol, and drug use of about 1,000 seventeen- and eighteen-year-olds from the Minnesota Twin Family Study. They found moderate family effects for boys, and large family effects for girls. A couple of other studies conclude that parents don't affect drinking, but siblings do. One looked at about 1,000 adoptees and their families, and found that adoptees drank like their adopted siblings but not like their adopted parents. Another study of over 1,000 Koreans adopted by American families found that children raised by mothers who never drank alcohol were almost 20 percentage points more likely to never drink themselves.

What's a parent to think? You should put more stock in the larger studies that find small or nonexistent nurture effects. If you have paternalism to spare, though, you might as well try to keep your kids off tobacco, alcohol, and drugs. You probably won't change your child, but there's an outside chance that you'll make a big difference.

WISH #2: INTELLIGENCE

New parents get excited by the faintest signs of their babies' intelligence: "She could crawl, use a spoon, and say no before she was one." By the time they're toddlers, we're furtively comparing our kids' brain power to their playmates'—and struggling to give our off-spring an edge with books, educational videos, museum trips, and tutors. If our child does poorly in school, we comfort ourselves with the thought that "he just needs to apply himself." We care so much about our kids' intelligence that we try to increase it prenatally. One misreported study about "the Mozart effect" led moms to play the classics for babies and fetuses alike.

However, a large scientific literature finds that parents have little or no long-run effect on their children's intelligence. Separated twin studies, regular twin studies, and adoption studies all point in the same direction.

The Minnesota Study of Twins Reared Apart reunited almost 100 separated identical twins and triplets and gave them two standard IQ tests. It found large effects of genes on adult intelligence. If you did better than 80 percent of the population on both tests, you should expect your separated identical twin to do better than 72 percent on one test, and 74 percent on the other. In contrast, when researchers compared the reared-apart twins to a control group of reared-together twins, the effect of nurture was barely detectable. If you did better than 80 percent of the population on both tests, you should expect your adopted sibling from Switched at Birth to do better than 56 percent on one test, and just 50 percent on the other.

The Swedish Adoption/Twin Study of Aging studied the intelligence of about 150 pairs of middle-age and elderly twins. Some of these twins were identical, some fraternal; about half were raised apart, half together. Researchers individually administered a four-hour test of spatial and verbal intelligence, memory, and processing speed to each twin. They found an even larger effect of genes on intelligence than the Minnesota study and confirmed the irrelevance of upbringing for adult intelligence: "Growing up in the same family does not contribute to similarity in cognitive abilities later in life."

Another team of researchers tested about 1,600 reared-together adult twins from the Dutch Twin Registry. Identical twins got extremely similar scores on a standard IQ test, and the similarity between fraternal twins was about half as strong—implying a big effect of genes, and no effect of upbringing. In the Switched at Birth experiment, if you were smarter than 80 percent of the population, you should expect your separated twin to be smarter than 76 percent but your adopted sibling to be perfectly average.

In 1975, the Colorado Adoption Project began studying 245 adopted babies, their birth mothers, and their adoptive parents. It also set up a control group of 245 comparable babies being raised by their biological parents. By the age of twelve, adoptees raised in high-IQ homes were no smarter than those raised in average homes. The researchers double-checked this result four years later and found the same thing. The Texas Adoption Project, which spent decades studying over 300 adoptees and the families that adopted them, also found no effect of upbringing on the IQs of late adolescents.

From a parent's point of view, these are strong results. Today's Typical Parents strive to mentally stimulate their children and struggle to protect their brains from being turned to mush by television and video games. Yet by adulthood, the fruit of parents' labor is practically invisible. Children who grew up in enriched homes are no smarter than they would have been if they'd grown up in average homes.

WISH #3: HAPPINESS

Good parents want to make their children happy. In the short run, they often succeed. If I want to put big grins on my sons' faces, I buy them ice cream. Works every time. But most parents are more ambitious. They believe that if they raise their children in the right way, they'll grow up to be happy adults. Maybe the recipe is unconditional love; maybe it's daily sermons about gratitude and "how much harder life was when I was a kid." Parents differ on the best approach but agree that parenting makes a big difference for the happiness of the next generation.

Parents grossly overestimate their influence. The Minnesota Twin Registry gave personality tests to over 1,300 pairs of adult twins raised together. Fraternal twins' happiness resemblance was barely perceptible: If you're happier than 80 percent of people, your fraternal twin will typically be happier than 53 percent. If all of this were due to nurture, it wouldn't be much. On closer look, though, the credit belongs to nature, not nurture. Identical twins were far more similar in their happiness than fraternal twins, leaving no room for nurture effects.

One of the main problems with happiness tests is that the subject might be having a bad day or a bad year. To deal with this concern, the Minnesota Twin Study waited about a decade, then retested. As expected, the research team found that happiness is fairly stable over time; humans have a "happiness set point" to which they gravitate. The researchers were amazed, however, to discover that people are as similar to their identical twin a decade ago as they are to *themselves* a decade ago. The implication: "Nearly 100 percent of the variation in the happiness set point seems to be due to individual differences in genetic makeup."

The most striking evidence on nature, nurture, and happiness comes from the Minnesota Study of Twins Reared Apart. Twins raised apart were *more* alike in happiness than twins raised together. If you're happier than four out of five people, expect your separated identical twin to be happier than 67 percent of us. If the identical Pollyanna twins were separated at birth, both sets of parents would probably claim responsibility for their daughters' happiness—and they'd both be wrong.

The same goes for self-esteem. The single most impressive study interviewed almost 8,000 twins from the Virginia Twin Registry and found zero effect of parenting on self-esteem for both men and women. Parents try to build their kids up, but science backs the slogan that "self-esteem comes from within."

Finally, what about *un*happiness? We're quicker to blame our parents for our misery than thank them for our joy, but further research using the Minnesota Twin Registry concluded that nurture is equally irrelevant for both. The twins' personality test measured many different ways to feel bad: nervous, upset, guilty, mistreated, betrayed, angry, vindictive, and so on. Upbringing didn't matter. By the time you're an adult, your parents' past mistakes are not the reason for your present unhappiness.

Parents like to think they're giving their children the love and support they need to become happy adults. Unhappy adults like to blame their problems on their parents' lack of love and support. According to the best evidence, however, both groups are wrong. Nature isn't the sole author of our happiness, but nurture barely gets a word in.

If you just can't believe this, I know where you're coming from. It's easy to recall times when your mom or dad made you angry or sad. But if you'd grown up with a very different family, you'd still have a Rolodex of stories about how your parents hurt your feelings. In what sense, then, are your parents the reason for the way you feel today? You might as well just blame "life."

WISH #4: SUCCESS

> "Do you know, mother, I shall have our children educated just like Lucy. Bring them up among honest country folks for freshness, send them to Italy for subtlety, and then—not till then—let them come to London. I don't believe in these London educations—" He broke off, remembering that he had had one himself . . .
>
> —E. M. Forster, *A Room with a View*

Strangers often advise you to follow your dreams, but parents are more likely to tell you to get your head out of the clouds. Doing what you love is all well and good, but don't you want to make something out of your life, to get ahead? Parents might add that in the long run, you'll be happier if you take their advice. Being a successful lawyer is more fun than being a failed actor.

I'm not taking sides here. My point is merely that parents want their children to be successful—and that doesn't just mean "follow your bliss." Instead, success roughly equals high income and a fancy degree. These are the kind of accomplishments parents can brag about to their friends—as in "my son, the doctor."

Many parents obsess over their children's success. They don't just help them a little with their homework. They plan out their lives, beginning with elite preschools—and use any chance they get to give their kids a leg up. Successful parents have successful kids. The reason, most parents assume, is that the winners had more help from mom and dad.

Twin and adoption studies say almost the opposite. Successful parents may give their kids a small edge, but heredity is much more important. Kids literally inherit educational and financial success from their parents. The most influential gift that parents give their children is not money, connections, or help with their homework, but the right stuff.

Parents have little effect on how much school their kids get. Parents feel an intense obligation to be involved with their kids' education. Does their involvement yield fruit? Most twin and adoption studies respond, "slightly"; a few say, "yes, for earlier generations"; the rest give a flat-out "no."

In 1955, Harry Holt, an Oregon businessman, and his wife, Bertha, adopted eight Korean orphans. Soon they set up a charity to help other Americans adopt disadvantaged Koreans. The adopting families were unusually diverse. To be eligible, couples had to be married for at least three years, twenty-five to forty-five years old, with no more than four children, and a minimum income just 25 percent above the poverty line. In 2004–2005, economist Bruce Sacerdote tracked down over 1,600 of the Korean adoptees and their adopting families to see how they turned out.

Nurture influenced the Koreans' educational success. More educated moms and fewer siblings both helped—but only slightly. If the mother had an extra year of education, the child finished five extra weeks of education, and was 2 percentage points more likely to graduate from college. For every extra sibling, the adoptee finished six fewer weeks of education, and was 3 percentage points less likely to graduate from college.

The Korean adoption study is most remarkable, though, for what it *failed* to find. Rich parents routinely try to give their kids an edge by moving to good school districts, hiring tutors, and paying tuition for fancy schools. Yet neither family income nor neighborhood income increased adoptees' academic success. If you ever thought it unfair for rich parents to buy their children's way through school, be at peace; apparently they don't get what they pay for.

Another major study of over 2,000 Swedish adoptees plus their adoptive and birth parents got almost the same results. The main difference: In Sweden, dads matter more, moms matter less. If the dad who raised you had one more year of education, you got five more weeks; if he finished college, you were 10 percentage points more likely to do the same. The only clear effect of maternal education, in contrast, was that kids were 10 percentage points more likely to finish college if their adopted moms did the same.

Twin studies also find small effects of nurture on education. The most remarkable examined about 2,000 pairs of American twins who served in World War II, plus their grown children. The results? Genes matter *a lot* for educational success. If you're more educated than four out of five people, you can expect your separated identical twin to be more educated than three out of four. Upbringing makes little difference. Only two nurture effects stand out in the veteran twins study. First, if your father is a professional or manager instead of an unskilled worker, you typically complete one more year of education. Second, every extra sibling depresses your educational achievement by seven weeks.

Researchers who looked at about 2,500 Australian twins confirmed these results. Identical twins' educational success is markedly more similar than fraternal twins'. Nurture does matter, but only slightly. If either parent gets an extra year of education, you get four or five extra weeks. If your family has an extra kid, you complete three fewer weeks.

While twin and adoption studies usually find that your family has a small effect on how far you get in school, exceptions exist. Some twin research reports that upbringing used to be more important and continues to be more important for women. An early study of Norwegian twins found strong family effects for female twins born before 1961, and male twins born before 1940. During the prewar era, if you had one extra year of education, you could expect your adopted sibling to have about six extra months. Researchers using the Minnesota Twin Family Registry and the Finnish Twin Cohort Study similarly found moderate to large nurture effects for Americans and Finns born between 1936 and 1955.

Other twin researchers conclude that children's families have *no* long-run effect on educational success. Their reasoning: Husbands and wives don't pair up randomly; married couples usually have similar levels of education, intelligence, and other genetically influenced traits. (The catch phrase is "assortative mating.") The slightly yucky implication is that most of us are the fruit of mild incest. Since married couples are somewhat genetically similar, siblings share *more* than half their genes. Implication: Fraternal twins are genetically closer to identical twins than we thought, so standard twin methods underestimate nature and overestimate nurture.

When researchers fix this flaw, educational nurture effects go away. One team combined thousands of observations from earlier studies of spouses, parents, their children, siblings, and twins. After adjusting for spouses' educational similarity, it found that family environment has no effect on how far you get in school. A more recent study of Australian twins reports moderate nurture effects on education, *assuming* people marry at random. Once the researchers discard this unrealistic assumption, nurture effects vanish for both men and women, even for those born in the first half of the twentieth century.

Parents have no effect on grades. All of the twin and adoption studies we've seen so far focus on years of education and college graduation. When parents help with homework, though, maybe their goal is to help their kids learn more or get better grades. Do they succeed? While this question has received less attention, the signs point to no. An early study of about 500 Australian twins reported little or no effect of upbringing on college-bound students' knowledge of arts, science, English, geography, math, or biology. A research team investigating the attitudes of almost 700 Canadian twins discovered that family had no effect on high school seniors' GPA.

The most impressive evidence, however, comes from the U.S.-based National Longitudinal Study of Adolescent Health, a nationally representative survey of seventh- through twelfth-graders living in the same household. The subjects were a mix of identical twins, fraternal twins, siblings, half siblings, cousins, and nonrelatives—about 1,700 kids in all. Genes had a strong effect on grades. If you're in the 80th percentile of your class, expect the identical twin you've never met to be in the 71st. Parental effects, in contrast, were literally invisible. The GPAs of unrelated kids raised together were no more similar than strangers'.

The lesson: If you've ever felt angry about parents who do their kids' homework for them, you can stop. In the long run, these parents aren't inflating their kids' grades. As far as we can tell, they're either wasting their time or reliving their youth.

Parents have little or no effect on how much money their kids make when they grow up. Most parents feel secondhand greed; or to be polite, they want their kids to be financially successful. True, more parents nag their kids to do well in school than to make a lot of money. Yet a lot of educational nagging is income nagging in disguise. Think about how parents react when their children choose a major. You want your kid to study medicine or law—not French poetry or sociology.

Parents who want their kids to get ahead encourage education, but that's only part of a bigger strategy. You're also supposed to teach your child the value of a dollar, an honest day's work, teamwork, initiative, and ambition. No matter what your income is, you've got something to stress about. If you don't have money, you stress about the advantages you can't give your children. How will they get ahead without the right connections? If you do have money, you stress about giving your kids *too many* advantages. If you spoil them, won't it kill their drive and self-reliance?

All this fretting is much ado about nothing. Yes, wealth and poverty run in families. According to twin and adoption studies, however, the main reason is not upbringing, but heredity. Nurture has even less effect on income than on education.

In Sacerdote's Korean adoption study, biological children from richer families grew up to have much higher incomes, but adoptees raised in the same families did not. The results are strong to the point of shocking. The income of the family you grew up with has literally no effect on your financial success. Korean adoptees raised by the *poorest* families have the same average income as adoptees raised by the *richest* families. While adoptees' moms have a small effect on their education, that extra education fails to pay off in the job market. Growing up in a rich neighborhood is equally impotent. Small families boost kids' incomes, but the effect is tiny: Every sibling depresses your adult income by about 4 percent. The Swedish adoption study mentioned earlier finds small effects on income rather than no effects at all. Being raised by a dad with 10 percent higher earnings causes you to earn 1 percent more when you grow up.

Twin studies also find small to zero effects of nurture on financial success. Identical twins' incomes are much more similar than fraternal twins'. A recent working paper looks at over 5,000 men from the Swedish Twin Registry born between 1926 and 1958. Identical twins turn out to be almost exactly twice as similar in labor incomes as fraternal twins—precisely what you would expect if family resemblance were purely hereditary. A study of over 2,000 Australian twins finds the same thing.

Contrary evidence? In the U.S. Twinsburg Study, which looks at about 400 American male twins, nurture matters a bit more and nature matters a bit less. If you earn more than 80 percent of your peers, your adopted sibling can expect to earn more than 55 percent. A study of American full and half siblings using the National Longitudinal Survey of Youth (NLSY) implies an even more modest effect— the adopted sibling is expected to have a higher income than 53 percent of the population.

You want your kids to succeed. But how much do you really help them? According to twin and adoption studies, not much. If your family is legally qualified to adopt, your parenting is good enough to allow your child to realize his potential. Whether he takes advantage of these opportunities is largely up to him.

WISH #5: CHARACTER

> OK, so maybe I *am* lazy, but it's not really my fault. I've been lazy ever since I was a little kid, and if someone had caught it early on, maybe I wouldn't be the way I am now.
>
> —Jeff Kinney, *Diary of a Wimpy Kid: Dog Days*

"A Boy Named Sue" is one of Johnny Cash's most famous songs— and certainly his funniest. In it, a deadbeat dad adds insult to injury. Before he abandons his son, he names him "Sue."

The name gives Sue a lifetime of grief, and he vows revenge. Years later, he finally bumps into his dad in a Gatlinburg bar. Father and son have a battle royal, then reach for their guns. The younger man's a little quicker. Before Sue can commit patricide, however, his father reveals his true motive. He didn't name him Sue out of cruelty. He did it to build his son's character—and it worked:

> And he said, "Son, this world is rough, / And if a man's gonna make it, he's gotta be tough, / And I knew I wouldn't be there to help ya along. / So I give ya that name and I said good-bye / I knew you'd have to get tough or die / And it's the name that helped to make you strong."

Sue's almost convinced. He spares his dad's life, and calls him "Pa." But he's not convinced enough to put his own son through the same ordeal: "And if I ever have a son, I think I'm gonna name him . . . Bill or George, any damn thing but 'Sue.'"

Most parents aren't as ruthless as Sue's father, but his motive should be familiar. We want our children to grow up to be men and women of substance—of character. Like Sue's dad, we want our children to be strong and determined, but that's only the beginning. We also want our kids to be hardworking, diligent, honest, polite, cooperative, and kind—and we certainly don't want them to become common criminals. If we have to occasionally hurt their feelings to raise them right, so be it.

When you tell parents that they overestimate their influence, they often retreat to the bunker of character: "Maybe I can't affect his IQ or his income, but I *can* control whether he grows up to be a decent person." For health, intelligence, happiness, or success, most parents eventually learn some modesty. For character, they're practically parental determinists: If you raise your children right, they *will* grow up to be good people—and if they turn out bad, the reason *must* be that you raised them wrong. Is there any truth to this? Is character a genuine exception to the rule that nurture doesn't matter much?

Parents have little or no effect on conscientiousness or agreeableness. To answer, we need plausible ways to measure character. Luckily for us, personality psychologists have been studying human personality for decades, so plausible measures of character already exist. According to most psychologists, personality traits fall under five big umbrellas: openness, conscientiousness, extroversion, agreeableness, and neuroticism. If you make a list of the traits that almost all parents want to instill—hardworking, diligent, honest, polite, cooperative, kind, and so on—they fall under just two of the psychologists' umbrellas: conscientiousness and agreeableness. One good way to test for parental influence on character is to use twin and adoption methods to figure out where conscientiousness and agreeableness come from.

Personality psychologists have been there and done that. Some find small effects of family environment on character; the rest find none at all. Good kids do tend to come from good families. Yet contrary to what almost everyone thinks, the overarching reason is heredity, not upbringing. Sue had strength and determination because he inherited them from his strong-willed father, not because his girly name "made him strong."

Hillary Clinton outraged many people by insisting, "It takes a village to raise a child." Her offense was not to deny the importance of parents but to hint that good parenting is not enough. The results from twin and adoption studies are more outrageous. You may be tempted to dismiss them out of hand. But before you do, how about a tour of the evidence?

One of the earliest studies of nature, nurture, and character used the Swedish Adoption/Twin Study of Aging. Researchers gave personality tests to 500 reared-apart twins and 600 reared-together twins and found small to moderate nurture effects. Suppose you're higher on conscientiousness and agreeableness than 80 percent of the population. According to the Swedish twin study, you should expect your adopted sibling to be more conscientious than 54 percent of the population, and more agreeable than 57 percent. A survey article published in *Science* a year later reported similar nurture effects for conscientiousness but smaller effects for agreeableness.

More recent twin research finds even smaller effects of parenting on character. One team looked at almost 2,000 German twins. While most personality research simply asks people to describe themselves, the German twin study got three perspectives on each subject: a self-report, plus two independent reports by friends or other close acquaintances. When researchers combined all this information, they found unusually large effects of nature on conscientiousness and agreeableness, and no effect of nurture. Studies of 1,600 American twins and 600 Canadian twins also found that upbringing did not affect character.

If you're skeptical about self-reporting, you might prefer the Swedish approach. Sweden has universal military service. After high school graduation, a professional psychologist reviews each recruit's dossier and interviews him to rate the young man's "emotional stability, persistence, his ability to function in a group and his ability to take initiatives." Researchers often call these traits "non-cognitive skill," but they sound a lot like character. Since Sweden keeps excellent twin records, we can use psychologists' ratings to understand where character comes from. As usual, genes play a serious role: Identical twins are much more alike in character than fraternal twins. Upbringing, in contrast, only has a small effect. If you had more character than 80 percent of Swedish recruits, you should expect your adopted sibling to have more than 54 percent.

In 2005, leading psychologist John Loehlin took a comprehensive look at family studies of personality. Character does run in families: If your parents were higher in conscientiousness and agreeableness than 80 percent of the population, you're typically more conscientious than 53 percent of us, and more agreeable than 54 percent. However, the resemblance is about equally strong when you compare adoptees to their biological parents, and virtually nonexistent when you compare adoptees to the parents who raised them. Heredity wins again.

Parents have little or no effect on criminal behavior. Faced with all this evidence, parents might protest, "I'm not trying to turn my kid into a saint; I'm just trying to raise a law-abiding member of society." As Bart Simpson told Judge Constance Harm:

> Your Honor, it's not easy being my parents. I'm always screwing up in school and getting in trouble with the law. But if I grow up to be a halfway decent person, I know it will be because of my mom and dad.

Bart's not alone. Most of us think that good parenting can keep kids from turning into common criminals. But how much effect on criminality do parents really have? As usual, there are twin and adoption studies to enlighten us.

In 1984, *Science* published a study of almost 15,000 Danish adoptees age fifteen or older, their adoptive parents, and their birth parents. Thanks to Denmark's careful record keeping, the researchers knew whether *any* of the people in their study had criminal convictions. Since few female adoptees had legal problems, the study focused on males—with striking results. As long as the adoptee's *biological* parents were law abiding, their adoptive parents made little difference: 13.5 percent of adoptees with law-abiding biological *and* adoptive parents got convicted of something, versus 14.7 percent with law-abiding biological parents and criminal adoptive parents. If the adoptee's biological parents were criminal, however, upbringing mattered: 20 percent of adoptees with law-breaking biological and law-abiding adoptive parents got convicted, versus 24.5 percent with law-breaking biological *and* adoptive parents. Criminal environments do bring out criminal tendencies. Still, as long as the biological parents were law abiding, family environment made little difference.

In 2002, a study of antisocial behavior in almost 7,000 Virginian twins born since 1918 found a small nurture effect for adult males and no nurture effect for adult females. The same year, a major review of fifty-one twin and adoption studies reported small nurture effects for antisocial attitudes and behavior. For outright criminality, however, heredity was the sole cause of family resemblance.

The lesson: Even if your standards are low, instilling character is hard. Genes are the main reason criminal behavior runs in families. Contrary to popular opinion, good upbringing is not enough to steer a child away from a life of crime. If that depresses you, there are two sources of comfort. First, as long as you and your spouse are law abiding, it's good news, because *non*criminality is hereditary, too. Second, most children of criminals *don't* become criminals; in the Danish adoption study, over three-fourths of the boys born of and raised by people with criminal convictions weren't convicted themselves. You don't have to be hopeful about parenting to be hopeful about your children's future.

WISH #6: VALUES

> Babies, chum: tiny, dimpled, fleshy mirrors of our us-ness, that we parents hurl into the future, like leathery footballs of hope. And you've got to get a good spiral on that baby, or evil will make an interception.
>
> —The Tick

Character isn't controversial; almost all parents want their kids to be hardworking, honest, kind, and so on. Yet few parents stop there. Most of us also try to impart controversial *values*. We teach our children to see the world as we do—even if others say our lessons are wrong or wicked. When your side does it, it's "education"; when other sides do it, it's "brainwashing."

Religion is the most obvious example. Whatever your religious view—Christian, Jewish, Muslim, Zoroastrian, or atheist—I bet you want your kids to believe as you do. In fact, I bet you want your kids to accept not just your religion, but your interpretation of it. If you're a liberal Jew, you don't want your child to join an ultra-Orthodox synagogue.

In politics, there's a little more room for independent thought, but less than we care to admit. If you're a moderate Democrat, you want your kids to be moderate Democrats, too. You don't want Marxist sons who denounce your bourgeois compromises, or Republican daughters who tell you what Ann Coulter said. When controversy erupts, parents want their children on their side.

Religion and politics are only the beginning. Some parents teach traditional values; others call for open-mindedness and tolerance. Some tell their children to have faith; others praise the power of critical thinking. Some parents preach mercy; others demand an eye for an eye. Indeed, some parents raise their children to be fruitful and multiply; others tell them that we need to limit our numbers, lest we destroy the planet.

You know where I stand on the last issue, but I'm not bringing up controversies to take a side. My task isn't to distinguish good education from evil brainwashing. I am simply observing that parents of all stripes want their kids to share their values and believe they can cause this to happen. Then I ask my standard question: "Is this widespread belief *true*?" When parents try to educate/brainwash their kids, do their lessons stick?

As usual, the fact that we often share our parents' values does not prove that upbringing matters. The similarity could be hereditary. If genes affect health, intelligence, happiness, success, and character, why not values? To measure parents' influence, we must once again defer to twin and adoption studies. They find that contrary to the Jesuit motto "Give me a child until he is seven and I will give you the man," the effect of upbringing on values is superficial. If you want your children's lip service, parenting can probably get it for you. But if you want to win your children's hearts and minds, twin and adoption studies show the power of parenting to be greatly overrated.

Parents have a big effect on religious labels, but little on religious attitudes and behavior. Parents strongly affect which religion their children say they belong to. A major study of over 7,000 adult Australian twins finds that identical and fraternal twins are highly *and equally* likely to share a religion—precisely what you would expect if nurture mattered a lot and nature didn't matter at all. Another study of almost 2,000 women from the Virginia Twin Registry reaches a similar conclusion: Family has a big effect on religious denomination, while genes have at most a small effect.

If the key to salvation is merely pronouncing the words "I belong to religion X," these are nurture effects of infinite importance. If you're raised by a family of believers, you'll probably be saved; if you're not, you'll probably be damned. Whatever your religion, though, I bet you hold to higher standards. As the book of James asks, "What good is it, my brothers, if a man claims to have faith but has no deeds? . . . Faith by itself, if it is not accompanied by action, is dead."

Almost all religions have detailed lists of doctrinal and behavioral do's and don'ts that separate the faithful from the hypocrites. Catholics are supposed to attend mass on Sundays and holidays, fast on Ash Wednesday and Good Friday, delay sex until marriage, oppose abortion, believe in transubstantiation, and confess their sins at least once per year. When we call a person religious, we usually mean that he takes his religion's do's and don'ts seriously.

Twin and adoption research reveals surprisingly little parental influence on how truly religious children grow up to be. One early study of almost 2,000 adult Minnesota twins reared together and apart found little or no effect of parenting on religiosity. Researchers measured the twins' interest in both religious activities (such as attending services, volunteering, and religious study) and religious occupations (such as being a minister, priest, rabbi, missionary, or religious writer). Identical twins were much more similar on both measures than fraternal twins. Nurture effects were small for religious activities and zero for religious occupations. A recent follow-up found similar results.

Another team of researchers looked at the religiosity of over 11,000 adult twins from Virginia. Parents have almost no effect on adult church attendance. Suppose your adopted parents attend church more than 80 percent of adults. When you grow up, we should expect you to attend church more often than 51 percent of us. The researchers also measured the Virginia twins' affinity for the "Religious Right." They found a very small nurture effect for men, and none for women. Another major study of American and Australian church attendance looked at over 5,000 families with twins in each country. Parents in both countries have zero effect on the church attendance of their adult sons, and at most a tiny effect on the church attendance of their adult daughters.

A different team of researchers created a test to measure "the centrality of religion in the individual's life." The test covers the frequency of church attendance, prayer, scripture reading, religious discussion, religious moralizing, and religious holiday observance; membership in religious groups; having friends with similar beliefs; and the importance of religious faith in daily life. When over 500 male Minnesota twins in their early thirties took the test, upbringing had only a modest effect. If you're more religious than 80 percent of people, expect your adopted sibling to be more religious than 56 percent. When about 600 female Minnesota twins took the same test (once when they were twenty, then again when they were twenty-five), though, the nurture effect was larger. The source of the discrepancy was apparently age, not gender: The effect of upbringing was large for twenty-year-old women, weaker for twenty-five-year-old women, and weakest of all for thirty-something men.

Parents have a big effect on political labels, but little on political attitudes and behavior. Modern American politics looks a lot like religion: People split into "right-thinking" camps and demonize rivals as stupid and/or evil. The splits usually run along family lines: Democratic parents tend to have Democratic children, Republican parents tend to have Republican children. Religion probably remains touchier than politics; your parents are more likely to disown you for rejecting their church than rejecting their party. Still, parents want their kids to share their political values and try to pass them on.

Twin studies confirm that politics is a lot like religion. Parents have a large effect on your political *label*. In the Virginia 30,000 study, both identical and fraternal twins were highly and almost equally likely to belong to the same political party, implying large effects of nurture and weak effects of nature. Party identification works the same way in Australia: Fraternal twins are highly similar, and identical twins are only slightly more alike.

In politics as in religion, however, the biggest nurture effects are also the most superficial. The Virginia 30,000 study found that parents have little effect on the *strength* of your partisan commitment —whether you always vote for the same party or straddle the fence. A national survey of young American adult twins found that parents have little influence over whether people bother to vote or participate in other political activities. If you're more politically active than 80 percent of people, expect your adopted sibling to be more active than 56 percent. The same goes for overall political philosophy and positions on specific issues. Parents may slightly affect how conservative you are, or your views on immigration, abortion, socialism, or crime. But not much.

Parents have little effect on traditionalism and modernism. "Old-fashioned" parents raise children to be practical, respect authority, and value tradition. "New-age" parents raise children to be creative, question authority, and value diversity. Of course, even bohemians overstate their openness; the parent who says "Question authority" usually means "Question *their* authority," not "Question *my* authority." Whether you're old-school or progressive, you have a mental picture of how your kids ought to turn out, and try to make it happen.

When people compare traditional to modern parenting, they usually argue that one is better. I'm asking a separate question: Do parents' efforts to instill a "traditional" or "modern" outlook succeed? To get an answer, we need to measure people's traditionalism. Once again, personality psychologists are here to help.

Personality psychologists have spent decades studying the trait they call "openness." Open is the opposite of old-fashioned. People high in openness see themselves as creative, interesting, tolerant, curious, and artistic; people low in openness see themselves as practical, normal, upright, respectful, and down-to-earth. When people are less open than us, they seem square; when they're more open than us, they seem weird. The long-running cartoon *King of the Hill* is a fine depiction of the conflict: Hank Hill is a practical, old-fashioned Texas propane salesman who endures habitual embarrassment at the hands of his artistic, unconventional son, Bobby. In the classic episode "Rodeo Days," Hank encourages his son to ride in the local rodeo, but Bobby decides—to his father's horror—to be a rodeo clown instead.

Like other personality traits, openness is largely unresponsive to upbringing. Diverse twin studies find little or no effect of nurture on openness, including studies of over 1,000 Swedes raised apart and together, almost 2,000 Germans, about 1,600 American high school juniors, and 500 Canadians. The average adoption study finds a small but reliable effect of parenting on openness. Suppose two parents have a mixed family with both biological and adopted children. If the parents are more open than 80 percent of the population, we should expect their biological children to be more open than 56 percent of their peers, versus 52 percent for adoptees.

Family values. You probably think your love life is a private matter. But even if your parents officially believe in minding their own business, they probably involved themselves every step of the way. When children are young, parents frantically try to control the flow of sexual information. Some practice blanket censorship, some tell lies about storks, others make sure their kids hear it from them first. Once they've got teenagers, almost all parents want their kids to go slow. But some virtually lock them up, while others hand out condoms. By the time they're in their twenties, parents are pressuring their kids to marry—and vetting the candidates. Soon after the wedding, parents start asking about grandchildren. If you contemplate divorce, your parents will probably eagerly share their opinion on that, too.

Parents clearly *try* to control their children's love lives, but how much influence do they really have? Counterexamples are easy to spot: Boys raised in puritanical homes sneak Internet porn; girls with purity rings get pregnant out of wedlock. Yet despite these counterexamples, our sexual, marital, and reproductive behavior tends to resemble our parents'—or at least the behavior of our parents when they were our age. The question is not whether people resemble their parents, but why. How much is due to upbringing, and how much to heredity?

Parents have moderate influence over when their daughters start having sex, but little over their sons. There are two major Australian twin studies of sexual initiation. The first included over 3,000 women born between 1922 and 1965. A follow-up roughly doubled the sample size by adding older and younger female twins. Both studies found moderate to large nurture effects. If you waited longer than 80 percent of girls, the first study found that you could expect your adopted sister to wait longer than 58 percent of girls; the second study, longer than 65 percent. Another research team used the National Longitudinal Survey of Youth to study the sexual initiation of about 2,000 American twins, siblings, half siblings, and cousins. For women, upbringing had as much effect in the United States as it did in Australia.

In contrast, parental influence on sons' sexual initiation is weak. The first of the Australian twin studies included about 1,800 males. While it found a moderate nurture effect for the older men (born 1922–1952), it found zero parental influence for the younger men (born 1952–1965). The NLSY study similarly found only a small nurture effect for American men born between 1958 and 1965. If you waited longer than 80 percent of boys, the NLSY study estimated that your adopted brother would wait longer than 53 percent.

Parents have little or no effect on teen pregnancy. The fact that parents affect their daughters' sex lives more than their sons' is not surprising. Girls' parents are more likely to take extreme measures due to fear of teen pregnancy. Their precautions largely fail. While the Australian study of almost 7,000 female twins found that parents had a moderate effect on the pregnancy of teens born between 1964 and 1971, parents had zero effect on the pregnancy of teens born between 1893 and 1964. A study of about 2,000 female Swedish twins born in the Fifties also found zero effect of upbringing on teen pregnancy.

Parents have little or no effect on adult sexual behavior. Few parents want their children to be forty-year-old virgins. Less than a third of Americans believe that premarital sex is always wrong. Still, this doesn't mean that anything goes. Parents try to instill values about proper sexual behavior and hope these values last a lifetime.

They hope in vain. Two major twin studies find little effect of upbringing on adult sexuality. The first surveyed nearly 5,000 Australian twins about their "sociosexuality," better known as promiscuity. The survey had questions about sexual attitudes (such as "Sex without love is okay" and "The thought of an illicit sex affair excites me") as well as sexual behavior (such as "With how many partners of the opposite sex have you had sexual intercourse within the past year?" and "With how many partners of the opposite sex have you had sexual intercourse on one and only one occasion?"). Family environment had almost no effect on sociosexuality; if you were in the 80th percentile, you could expect your adopted sibling to stand in the 51st. A second study of 1,600 female twins in the United Kingdom focused on number of sexual partners and infidelity. It found a small effect of family environment on the total number of sex partners, a moderate effect on attitudes about infidelity—and zero effect on the actual *practice* of infidelity.

Parents may have a small effect on sexual orientation. Psychologists used to label homosexuality a mental illness caused by overprotective mothers and distant fathers. Now we tend to see sexual orientation as a preference inherent in our genes. When you look at the evidence, however, neither story quite works. Genes definitely play a strong role—every major twin study finds that identical twins are more alike in their sexual orientation than fraternal twins. Yet genes are far from the whole story—if you're gay, your identical twin is usually still straight. Upbringing might make a difference, too. In surveys, adopted brothers of gay men and adopted sisters of gay women are about *six times* as likely to be gay as the general population. This would normally be a smoking gun, but sexual orientation remains a touchy issue. The adoption results might merely show that gays with gay adopted siblings were six times as likely to mail in their surveys. A large Swedish twin study with an exceptionally high response rate—nearly 60 percent—confirms a small nurture effect for women's orientation, but none for men's.

Parents have little or no effect on marriage, marital satisfaction, or divorce. In Tolstoy's novels, parents decide who their children should marry, and when. In *War and Peace*, set during the early 1800s, parents arrange and forbid marriages without apology. In *Anna Karenina*, set sixty years later, parents preach respect for their children's choices but still practice the old ways:

> The princess realized that in the process of getting to know each other, her daughter might fall in love, and fall in love with someone who did not care to marry her or who was quite unfit to be her husband. And, however much it was instilled into the princess that in our times young people ought to arrange their lives for themselves, she was unable to believe it, just as she would have been unable to believe that, at any time whatever, the most suitable playthings for children five years old ought to be loaded pistols.

Modern parents like to think they're light years from nineteenth-century Russia. Still, we have views about who and when our children should marry, and few of us keep these views to ourselves. Even if we held our tongues, children might learn by example. Growing up in a broken home has to make kids less likely to have a happy marriage later on, right?

Twin research says otherwise. A study of over 4,000 Minnesota twins, most in their thirties and forties, found zero effect of parenting on marital status. A long-running study of almost 6,000 men from the World War II Twin Registry found moderate nurture effects for *early* marriage, but none for marital status at thirty, forty, or fifty. Upbringing also has little or no effect on marital satisfaction. A research team asked 1,000 female Swedish twins and their spouses about the quality of their marriages. The women's parents had no effect on the marital satisfaction of their daughters, but they did have a small effect on the marital satisfaction of their sons-in-law. You might infer that some parents raise unusually good wives, but the simpler story is that some parents are unusually good in-laws.

What about divorce? An early study using the Minnesota Twin Registry found large effects of genes and no effect of family environment. Individuals with a divorced identical twin are almost six times as likely to be divorced; for individuals with a divorced fraternal twin, the risk of divorce less than doubles. A later study expands the sample and reaches the same conclusion: Heredity matters a lot, upbringing doesn't matter at all. One of the main reasons why divorce is heritable, the authors learned, is that marital stability depends upon personality and values, which in turn depend upon genes.

Parents have little or no effect on childbearing. I often half jokingly tell my three sons that they're required to have three kids each, but twin studies say I'm wasting my breath. While fertility runs in families, the reason nowadays is almost entirely genetic. A major study of Danish twins born in 1870–1910 found moderate nurture effects on family size. Half a century later, though, these nurture effects had disappeared. Upbringing had a tiny influence on when Danes tried to start a family, but none on the total number of children produced by those thirty-five to forty-one years old. A different team of researchers looked at about 2,000 American twins, siblings, half siblings, and cousins born between 1958 and 1965 and found minimal nurture effects on fertility.

WISH #7: APPRECIATION

To me, it's more important to deserve my children's appreciation than to get it. I would raise my children with kindness and respect even if I knew they wouldn't reciprocate. Still, I hope they will. I want them to feel good about me and look back fondly on their childhood.

The odds that my efforts pay off are pretty good. Both twin and adoption studies confirm that parents affect how their children *perceive* and *remember* them. When adoptees in the Colorado Adoption Project were ten to twelve years old, researchers asked both biological and adopted children questions about their families. How loving, communicative, and conflict-prone were they? Siblings gave fairly similar answers whether or not they were biologically related. Suppose you rated your family more positively than 80 percent of kids. Expect your adopted sibling to rate your family more positively than 59 percent of kids.

Two research teams using the Minnesota Twin Registry reached similar conclusions. The first questioned about 1,200 Minnesota twins. How much did they like their parents? How much did their parents like them? How involved were their parents in their lives? How much did they fight with their parents? The twins answered twice—once when they were eleven years old, once when they were fourteen. At both ages, parents had moderate influence over how much their children liked them, and small to moderate influence over perceived involvement and conflict. (Parents had less influence, though, over how much kids thought their parents liked *them*.) A later research team doubled the number of twins in the sample to almost 2,500 and interviewed them when they were sixteen to twenty years old. They confirmed that parents continue to have moderate effects on how their young adult children feel about and perceive them.

When they ignore their children's wishes, parents often protest, "You'll thank me later," suggesting a disconnect between how we perceive our childhood and how we remember it. But researchers find that upbringing matters for long-term memories as well as immediate perceptions. An early Swedish study of 1,400 middle-aged and elderly twins asked them how their parents raised and treated them. Most respondents hadn't been children for fifty years—but nurture mattered. Identical twins' portraits of their parents were only moderately more alike than fraternal twins', and twins raised together gave much more similar answers than twins raised apart. The Swedish study discovered moderate nurture effects for seven out of eight measures of parenting style. Suppose you remember your family as more loving and harmonious than eight percent of adults remember theirs. You should expect your adopted sibling to remember more familial love and harmony than 59 percent of adults. Other studies of German, Canadian, and Swedish twins find that parents have comparable or larger effects on how their grown children remember them.

Many parents have found inspiration in the words of Forest Witcraft:

> A hundred years from now it will not matter what my bank account was, the sort of house I lived in, or the kind of car I drove . . . but the world may be different because I was important in the life of a child.

If you halve the number of years, Witcraft has science on his side. Half a century from now, your children will remember how you treated them. If you showed them kindness, they probably won't forget. If you habitually lost your temper, they probably won't forget that, either. Out of all the wishes on the Parental Wish List, "good memories" are one of the few that clearly depend upon how you raise your child. Don't forget it.

BEYOND THE EXTRAORDINARY

"Parents have little long-run effect on their kids." It's an extraordinary claim—and as astronomer Carl Sagan wisely insisted, "Extraordinary claims require extraordinary evidence." But behavioral genetics comfortably passes Sagan's test. Over the last few decades, twin and adoption researchers cast a wide net. They looked at every major trait—and most of the minor traits—that parents seek to cultivate.

They approached each of the main questions from multiple angles: Different subjects, different times, different measures. The researchers come from disparate fields: medicine, psychology, economics, sociology, and more. Despite their intellectual diversity and the ambition of their project, twin and adoption researchers have built an impressively consistent body of knowledge about the causes of family resemblance.

If the only lesson you take away from this book is that scientists have solid but shocking answers to the nature-nurture puzzle, I'll be happy. Behavioral geneticists have done so much great work that it's an honor just to be their messenger. But I don't want to merely deliver their message and go home. Now that we've got solid but shocking answers to the nature-nurture puzzle, it's time to tackle a deeper question: How should these answers change the way we raise our children and live our lives?

APPENDIX TO CHAPTER 2:
WHERE THE NATURE-NURTURE EFFECT SIZES COME FROM

The final products of most twin and adoption studies are their estimates of three variables:

1. the fraction of variance explained by heredity—usually called h^2;
2. the fraction of variance explained by shared family environment—usually called c^2;
3. the fraction of variance explained by non-shared family environment—usually called e^2.

To explain these effect sizes in layman's terms, I take advantage of two mathematical facts implied by standard behavioral genetic models. First, a trait's h^2 equals the expected correlation between identical twins raised apart. Second, a trait's c^2 equals the expected correlation between unrelated individuals raised together.

On the plausible assumption that traits are normally distributed, we can then calculate the expected performance of your separated identical twin or adopted sibling. If you are s standard deviations (SDs) above average on a trait with $h^2=.3$ and $c^2=.1$, we should expect your separated identical twin to be $.3s$ SDs above average, and your adopted sibling to be $.1s$ SDs above average.

On the standard normal distribution, the 80th percentile is approximately .84 SDs above average. If you are in the 80th percentile on a trait, we would therefore expect your separated identical twin to be $.84h^2$ SDs above average and your adopted sibling to be $.84c^2$ SDs above average. Suppose the trait in question is education, and we use Baker et al.'s initial estimates derived from Australian twins: $h^2=.57$ and $c^2=.24$. If you were in the 80th percentile, we would expect your separated identical twin to be .84*.57 SDs=.48 SDs above average and your adopted sibling to be .84*.24 SDs=.20 SDs above average. Using a standard normal table, this translates to the 68th and 58th percentiles, respectively.

When twin and adoption studies explicitly report estimates for h^2 and c^2, I use them. If they report only correlations for identical versus fraternal twins, I estimate h^2 using Falconer's formula: $h^2=2*(r_{MZ}-r_{DZ})$; since $e^2=1-r_{MZ}$, $c^2=2r_{DZ}-r_{MZ}$. When more complex kinship studies distinguish "shared environment" from "vertical transmission," I use the latter as my measure of the effect of nurture. When studies directly report genetically informed regression coefficients, I use them without further ado.

3
...

BEHAVIORAL GENETICS: CAN IT BE TRUE— AND WHAT DOES IT MEAN?

> We worry about what a child will become tomorrow,
> yet we forget that he is someone today.
>
> —Stacia Tauscher

WHEN THEY LEARN ABOUT TWIN AND ADOPTION RESEARCH, SOME parents stonewall, and others despair. Those who stonewall say that behavioral genetics is too counterintuitive to believe. Those who despair say that behavioral genetics is too depressing to embrace. If you're in either camp—or both—I want to change your mind. You don't have to stonewall to protect common sense, and you don't have to deny the facts to avoid despair.

From a distance, the findings of behavioral genetics are indeed counterintuitive. When you look closer at the evidence, however, crucial caveats come into view. Crucial caveats like: Parents' short-run effects are much bigger than their long-run effects. Upbringing has lasting effects on appreciation, and religious and political identity. And: For every kid who yields to parental pressure, there's probably another who rebels against it. Learning about these crucial caveats lets us reconcile science and common sense.

In any case, there's no reason for the science of nature and nurture to drive you to despair. Yes, it deflates some kinds of parenting, like bending kids to your will and riding kids for their own good. But the science also shines a spotlight on exciting opportunities. Exciting opportunities like: Raising kids your own way, guilt free. Treating your kids with kindness and respect, without worrying that you'll make them soft. And: Having more kids—while still having time for yourself. Learning about these exciting opportunities lets us reconcile science and hope.

Behavioral genetics offers parents a deal: Show more modesty, and get more happiness. You can have a better life and a bigger family if you admit that your kids' future is not in your hands. The offer is more than fair. In fact, it's the deal of a lifetime.

"WHO YOU GONNA BELIEVE—ME OR YOUR OWN EYES?" NATURE, NURTURE, AND FADE-OUT

> I gotta say that I'm enjoying adulthood. For a lot of reasons. And, I'll tell you reason number one: As an adult, if I want a cookie, I have a cookie, okay? I have three cookies or four cookies, or eleven cookies if I want. Many times I will intentionally ruin my entire appetite. Just ruin it. And then, I call my mother up right after to tell her that I did it. "Hello, Mom? Yeah, I just ruined my entire appetite."
>
> —Jerry Seinfeld

As a father of identical twins, I readily accept the power of nature but still struggle to deny the power of nurture. Twin and adoption studies of health, intelligence, happiness, success, character, and values seem to contradict firsthand observation. Haven't you repeatedly seen parents change their children's lives? I have. Don't you recall many times when your parents changed *your* life? I do. It's tempting to treat all of this research like a "proof" that 1+1=3: Clearly wrong, but life's too short to figure out why.

If that's what you're thinking, please pause. There is a simple way to sync science and common sense: *The short-run effects of parenting are larger than the long-run effects.* If you think you've changed your kids' behavior, I bet you're right. You could go and change it some more right now. Feel free. The catch is that your efforts won't last. The immediate, visible effects of nurture tend to wear off or "fade out" as children grow up. Think about all the times in your childhood when you got in big trouble and vowed, "I'll be good from now on." How long did your change of heart last? A month? A week? Five minutes? Parents could conceivably compensate for fade-out with extra persistence. But time is against them. No matter how strict or encouraging parents are, their children eventually grow up, and fade-out eventually kicks in.

If you want to discredit twin and adoption research with eyewitness testimony, I have no objection. I only ask to cross-examine you. You've seen parents change their children's lives. You recall times when your parents changed yours. But haven't you also seen how temporary these changes tend to be? Think about how many parents try to inspire a love of books. At the time, they succeed; lots of kids won't sleep without a bedtime story. Ten or twenty years later, however, only a small minority read for pleasure. That's fade-out for you.

If the short-run effects of parenting are as large as I say, why don't twin and adoption studies report them? The answer is that they rarely look for them. Researchers typically focus on long-run effects—whether your parents change the kind of adult you become. That is why they reach the weird conclusion that nurture doesn't matter much. When twin and adoption studies focus on the short run—whether your parents change the kind of *child* you are—they typically support the obvious conclusion that nurture matters. The research is a little sparse, but studies of intelligence, income, crime, and religion all find that upbringing matters less as we grow up.

FADE-OUT AND INTELLIGENCE

Twin and adoption research on young children's intelligence always finds nurture effects. The younger the child, the more parents matter. A team of prominent behavioral geneticists looked at major adoption studies of IQ. They found moderate nurture effects for children, versus none for adults. Suppose an adoptee grows up in a family with a biological child in the 80th percentile of IQ. *During his childhood*, we should expect the adoptee to have a higher IQ than 58 percent of his peers. Nurture effects were largest for the youngest kids under observation, four- to six-year-olds. An average child of this age raised in a high-IQ home will typically test higher than 63 percent of his peers. Not bad—but it doesn't last.

The Colorado Adoption Project provides an especially vivid illustration of fade-out. Nurture effects were already visible when the children were one to two years old and peaked when they were three to four years old. Toddlers adopted by parents in the 80th percentile of IQ scored about 7 percentage points higher than average. By the time the adoptees were age seven, however, two-thirds of this nurture effect was gone. By twelve, nothing was left. As the researchers bluntly concluded, "Adopted children resemble their adoptive parents slightly in early childhood but not at all in middle childhood or adolescence."

FADE-OUT AND INCOME

Swedes have almost no financial privacy; researchers can collect your complete lifetime earnings history from tax records. One study of over 5,000 Swedish twins was therefore able to confirm that the effect of nurture on men's income changes with age. Family has a moderate effect in your early twenties. Suppose you earn more than 80 percent of your peers. You should expect your adopted brother to make more money than 58 percent of his peers when he is twenty to twenty-two years old, and 55 percent when he is twenty-three to twenty-five years old. By the time your adopted brother reaches his late twenties, however, the effect of upbringing on income completely fades out— and remains invisible for the rest of his career. When children first become adults, their parents might find them a good job, or support them so they don't have to work. Within a few years, however, young adults get on their own two feet, and stay there.

FADE-OUT, CRIME, AND OTHER BAD BEHAVIOR

As you may recall, a 2002 study of almost 7,000 Virginian twins found little or no effect of family environment on *adult* antisocial behavior. But if you read the fine print, there are noticeable nurture effects for children younger than fifteen—especially boys. This study is no fluke. A major review of twin and adoption studies of antisocial and criminal behavior finds that nurture matters most for preteens, less for children thirteen to eighteen, and least for adults. Suppose a family has a biological son and an adopted son. The biological child is a bad seed—he starts in the 80th percentile of antisocial behavior, and stays there. When his adopted brother is a child, you should expect his behavior to be worse than 57 percent of his peers. By adolescence, this shrinks to 55 percent. By adulthood, it declines further to 53 percent. The same goes for female promiscuity. Parents influence when their daughters *start* having sex but have little or no effect on their adult sexual behavior.

The moral: Parents are pretty good at putting their children on the right track, but not so good at keeping them there. By adulthood, it's normal for "good kids from bad homes" to get back on track and "bad kids from good homes" to run off the rails.

FADE-OUT AND RELIGION

Twin and adoption studies of religion usually find no more than moderate nurture effects. Especially if you had a religious upbringing, this is hard to believe. To reconcile science and common sense, we simply need to distinguish short- and long-run effects. Most twin and adoption studies of religion look at adults. When researchers focus on *children's* religion, the conflict with common sense goes away. The cleanest study asked over 500 Minnesota twins questions about the "centrality of religion" in their lives during their childhood and today. During childhood, the nurture effect is big. If you're more religious than 80 percent of kids, we should expect your adopted sibling to be more religious than 68 percent. Yet by the time you're thirty-three years old, two-thirds of this effect fades out.

When you're raising a child, you can make him go to church, say his prayers, and shield his impressionable mind from infidels, heretics, and skeptics. When he grows up, however, he will discover the broader world. He will probably continue to pay lip service to his religious upbringing, but the effect on his behavior and beliefs will largely vanish.

Unlike Chico Marx in *Duck Soup*, then, twin and adoption researchers don't have to ask, "Who you gonna believe? Me or your own eyes?" They freely admit that parents matter in the short run. If you think you're giving your kids a head start, you're probably correct. Your mistake is to assume that the head start lasts a lifetime. By the time your child grows up, the impact of your encouragement and nagging will largely fade away.

We often compare children to clay. When they're soft, you can mold them into any shape you like; after they harden, they stay the way you made them. What common sense *and* science tell us, however, is that children are more like flexible plastic. Both respond to pressure. Yet when you remove the pressure, both tend to return to their original shape.

At some point during your childhood, you probably announced, "When I grow up, I'm going to do things my way!" Your parents might have laughed in your face, but you had the last laugh. You're all grown up now, and I bet you do things your own way, as predicted. Your parents might object that when you were seven years old, "your way" included wearing a cape and eating only chocolate. But the obvious response is that your tastes matured because you grew up. When you were seven years old, you probably didn't like the opposite sex much either. What changed your mind—your parents, or your hormones?

When people learn about twin and adoption research, they often object, "If this is true, how come parents haven't figured it out for themselves?" At least part of the answer is that parents' firsthand observation is directly misleading. When they try to mold their kids, the short-run effects are obvious to the naked eye. It is tempting to assume that these short-run effects add up—and explain why children turn into their parents. Without twin and adoption methods, we would never have discovered that the "obvious" effects of parenting are mostly a plausible, powerful illusion.

THE POWER OF PARENTING: CAN REBELLION SAVE THE DAY?

> *The most dangerous party member:* In every party there is one who through his all too credulous avowal of the party's principles incites the others to apostasy.
> —Friedrich Nietzsche, *Human, All Too Human*

Twin and adoption studies usually find that the average effect of family environment is near zero. The simplest interpretation is that parents have little effect. A competing interpretation, however, is that parents have big effects, but their efforts backfire about half the time.

Rebellion is the most plausible mechanism. Almost every item on the Parental Wish List suggests compelling examples. *Health:* Your mom is morbidly obese; you carefully watch your weight so you don't end up like her. *Intelligence:* Your dad watches sports all day long, so you seek refuge in books. *Happiness:* Your mom tells you to cheer up, so you sulk just to spite her. *Success:* Your parents are poor, so you vow with God as your witness never to go hungry again. *Character:* You're habitually late to annoy your rigidly punctual dad. *Values:* You resolve to have at least two kids because you were a lonely only child.

Twin and adoption researchers should take rebellion more seriously. I doubt I'd be such a nerd if my dad and brother weren't sports fans, or as slow to lose my temper if my parents had more often kept their cool. From a practical point of view, however, it doesn't make much difference whether parenting is impotent or just backfires half the time. One story says, "Your efforts won't work." The other says, "Your efforts are equally likely to make things better or worse." Either way, parents can't reasonably *expect* their extra effort to pay off.

GENETIC DETERMINISM VERSUS PARENTAL DETERMINISM

When critics of twin and adoption methods run out of arguments, they turn to name-calling. "Genetic determinism" is their favorite epithet. Fans of twin and adoption research supposedly believe that genes completely control behavior, that heredity is destiny. Clever critics might add that my book is self-refuting: If genetic determinism is true, then our genes fully control our parenting behavior, and the best argument in the world won't change that.

The critics of genetic determinism aren't just wrong; they're not even listening. Twin and adoption studies *never* claim that genes fully explain variation in human behavior. While they often report zero effect of shared family environment, they freely admit that they can't make perfect predictions—even if they observe your identical twin first. Attacks on genetic determinism are a witch hunt. Witches don't exist, and neither do genetic determinists who understand twin and adoption research.

The witch hunt against genetic determinism is particularly odd because it overlooks a truly popular dogma: *parental* determinism. Many imagine that the way your parents raised you is the cause of everything right or wrong in your life. When someone succeeds, they say, "His parents raised him well." When someone fails, they huff, "Just look at the parents." When someone fails despite his parents' efforts, they muse, "If only his parents tried a little harder." No matter what occurs, the root cause has to be parenting. Never mind the brute fact that kids in the same family are often quite different.

At least genetic determinism has a solid kernel of truth: Genes really do have large, lasting effects on almost every item on the Parental Wish List. Parental determinism barely has a kernel: Although parents matter quite a bit in the short run, they leave little lasting impression.

If family environment matters so little, why is human behavior so hard to predict? *Because there's a lot more to "the environment" than the family.* There has to be. Otherwise, identical twins raised together would literally be identical copies. As a father of identical twins, I assure you they're not. One of my sons is a better bicyclist, the other a better swimmer. One prefers reading, the other writing. One worries about tomorrow while the other enjoys today.

So far, researchers have failed to explain why identical twins—not to mention ordinary siblings—are so different. Discrediting popular explanations is easy, but finding credible alternatives is not. Personally, I doubt that scientists will ever account for my sons' differences, because I think their primary source is free will. Despite genes, despite family, despite everything, human beings always have choices—and when we can make different choices, we often do. Some choices are moment-to-moment: To keep working or give up, lie or tell the truth, abandon or defend your views on immigration policy. Other choices are cumulative: You can't change your weight, education, or income by snapping your fingers, but in the long run they depend on diet, study, and effort—all of which you're free to choose.

Most behavioral geneticists will dismiss my armchair philosophy. Several close friends call my stance on free will "my most absurd belief." But embracing behavioral genetics and free will at the same time is at least *consistent*. Remember: Another name for "unique environment" and "nonshared environment" is "none of the above." If free will isn't none of the above, what is?

LINGERING DOUBTS

I don't want to come off as a "true believer" in behavioral genetics. I'm convinced, but not certain. Mediocre research occasionally gets published. When twin and adoption studies recruit one hundred subjects by mail, you shouldn't swallow their results whole. Even excellent studies have flaws; authors often disclose them to beat critics to the punch. And flawless methods don't guarantee clean results. The most eminent behavioral geneticists in the world occasionally shrug and say, "Well, that's what I found. I don't know what it means." I've tried to handle these concerns the best way I know how: weeding out weaker papers, noting major shortcomings of research that made the cut, and acknowledging anomalies.

If the researchers of the next generation toned down some of their teachers' stronger claims, it wouldn't be shocking. We're learning as we go. Behavioral geneticists usually assume, for example, that genetic effects are linear—two copies of a gene have twice the effect of a single copy. If this assumption is wrong, standard models oversell the effect of nature and shortchange the effect of nurture. So far, evidence of nonlinear genetic effects is mixed at best, so I ignore the issue. But better evidence may come along—and if it does, I'll revise my position. Another doubt on the horizon: Cutting-edge studies of the *children* of twins find bigger effects of parenting than traditional twin and adoption studies. If the approach pans out, it won't mean that earlier research was wrong, but nurture will merit a bit more credit.

The most important weakness of behavioral genetics, though, is simply that *research focuses on middle-class families in First World countries*. The results might not generalize. Twin and adoption studies almost never look at people in Third World countries. So you shouldn't conclude that Haitian orphans would turn out the same way if raised in Sweden. Twin and adoption studies also tend to ignore the poor in First World countries. Twins come from all walks of life, but it's usually harder to get twins from lower-class homes to join a study. Adoptees almost never grow up in lower-class homes, even though their biological parents tend to be lower class. Don't assume that poor inner-city kids would turn out the same way if they grew up in a sheltered suburb.

For policymakers, the restricted range in twin and adoption studies is a major blind spot. But middle-class parents in First World countries needn't worry. Families like yours have been studied to death. In your corner of the world, you can safely rely on the postcard version of behavioral genetics: The chief cause of family resemblance is heredity, not upbringing—and while the short-run effects of upbringing are self-evident, they leave little lasting impression.

WHAT THE SCIENCE OF NATURE AND NURTURE MEANS FOR PARENTS

Parents want the best for their children, but parenting has surprisingly little effect on whether or not children get the best. While this discovery might seem too dangerous for human consumption, it's great news for parents and children alike. False hope in the power of nurture leads to wasted effort and wasted opportunities. Parents who understand the facts can help their families and themselves.

LIGHTEN UP

Let's start with the obvious. If parental investments don't pay off, then relaxed parenting is a free lunch: better for parents, and no worse for kids. If you falsely believe that your child's health, intelligence, happiness, success, character, and values heavily hinge on your effort, you will waste sweat and tears. Once you accept the truth, you can drop a lot of painful parenting.

How much pain can parents safely avoid? To answer this question, remember the main limitation of twin and adoption studies: They almost always focus on relatively normal families in relatively rich countries. You can't read an American adoption study and conclude that abject poverty and severe neglect do no lasting damage. But you can conclude that it's okay for parents to move *within the normal American range*. You don't need to fret about whether to sacrifice more for your children than 20, 50, or 80 percent of parents like you. If the typical adoption agency would consider you a suitable parent, you're good enough to let your children to reach their potential. A good rule of thumb: If your parenting style passes the laugh test, your kids will be fine.

When they hear about the evidence from twin and adoption research, parents occasionally respond, "I know I don't matter much, but every little bit helps." But how much pain are they willing to bear for a small gain? For each of the items on the Parental Wish List, there's a big difference between homes with kids in the 50th percentile and homes with kids in the 80th. Suppose you want to turn your child into a churchgoer, even though you're not especially religious. In 2006, the General Social Survey found that the median American went to church "several times a year." But one person in five went every week—or more. Moving from the 50th to the 80th percentile on this one trait therefore takes almost fifty extra services a year. If you don't really enjoy church, that's a lot of effort to make your kids 2 or 3 percentage points more religious.

Or take education. The Korean adoption study found that if a mom has an extra year of education, her adoptee gets five more weeks. To raise her child's educational attainment by a single year, a mom would need more than a decade of extra schooling. That's practically an entire childhood. Even ignoring the massive cost for the mother, it's a lonely life for the child.

I see why parents of *grown* children resist my message. They're proud of their kids and don't want some genetic accountant telling them to write off their investments. What's puzzling is the resistance of people who are still midstream. The exhausted parents of a two-year-old should be thrilled to hear that the next sixteen years of parenting can be less of a chore.

The best explanation is that parents suffer from what psychologists call the illusion of control. Flying is about 100 times safer than driving, but many of us feel safer behind the wheel. When we drive, we're in control. As long as our driving is good enough, we imagine that nothing bad can happen. When we're flying, our safety is out of our hands. If the pilot does a bad job, we die.

This "reasoning" is silly. Imagine you're a passenger on a plane and the pilot hands you the controls. While you'd suddenly have a lot more *control* over your safety, you'd be in mortal danger. Control is vastly overrated.

When parents reflect on the science of nature and nurture, they need to keep this moral in mind. Do not be alarmed when twin and adoption studies conclude that your children's future is outside your control. They're not saying that your children will do *poorly*. They're saying that your children will probably turn out fine, whether or not you're a great parent. If anything, the truth should come as a great relief. If I thought that my sons' future depended primarily on my actions, I'd fret, "We should be reading another book," every time we sat down to watch *The Simpsons*.

Granted, if nature matters as much as I claim, you won't be able to turn your kid into the next Einstein (unless you and your spouse happen to be Einsteins). But if you just want a child you're proud of—a decent human being and a productive citizen—give him the gift of life, feed and water him, don't lock him in a closet, and life will take care of the rest. If this seems impossibly Zen, consider: When teens start to assert their independence, we advise parents to "Step back and trust that you raised your kids right." I'm almost saying the same thing, except that I'm advising you to step back and trust not in your parenting but in your genes.

When I advise parents to lighten up, many object that I ignore peer pressure. Won't other parents severely harass and badmouth the first family to relax? But peer pressure is overblown. Most parents are too exhausted by their own overparenting to pay much attention to yours. Even if you do pop up on other parents' radar, they'll probably keep their opinions to themselves to avoid conflict. In any case, if other parents openly disapprove of you, the consequences are mild. In modern society, we meet most of our needs in the marketplace, not our neighborhoods. Amazon neither knows nor cares how you raise your kids—and your boss probably doesn't either. For practical purposes, parents might as well keep their own counsel.

CHOOSE A SPOUSE WHO RESEMBLES THE KIDS YOU WANT TO HAVE

The most effective way to get the kind of kids you want is to pick a spouse who has the traits you want your kids to have. Genes have a large effect on almost everything on the Parental Wish List. The right spouse is like a genie who grants wishes you are powerless to achieve through your own efforts.

We already do this to some extent. Married couples are fairly similar in health, intelligence, education, income, criminality, and values—all important items on the Parental Wish List. The result, intended or not, is to make children and their parents more compatible. For personality traits, however, spouses are barely alike, suggesting that we aren't so picky about the personalities of the potential mothers and fathers of our children. Behavioral genetics urges us to get pickier. If you want happy or agreeable or conscientious or open-minded kids, avoid dates that lack these traits.

Another implication: The macho, irresponsible "bad boy" is an even worse deal for women than he's reputed to be. Not only will he be emotionally and financially AWOL; the children he fathers will probably give a great deal of grief to any mother who struggles to raise them right.

IF YOU WANT TO DRASTICALLY IMPROVE A CHILD'S LIFE, ADOPT FROM THE THIRD WORLD

The main lesson of behavior genetics is that parenting is about the journey, not the destination. Instead of trying to mold your children into the people you think they ought to be, focus on enjoying your time together. Suppose, however, that you yearn to transform a child's life. Is there any effective way to do it?

Yes: Adopt from the Third World—from lands where poverty, disease, illiteracy, and oppression stifle human flourishing. Twin and adoption research only show that families have little long-run effect *inside* the First World. *Bringing* kids to the First World often saves their lives. Over 13 percent of the children in Malawi—the African nation that initially denied Madonna's petition to adopt a four-year-old orphan—don't survive their first five years. And survival is only the beginning. Life in the First World spares children from hunger, disease, and harsh labor, and opens vast opportunities that most of us take for granted. Merely moving an adult Nigerian to the United States multiplies his wage about fifteen times. Imagine the benefit of giving a Nigerian child an American childhood and an American education.

Adopting disadvantaged children from the First World probably improves their lives in similar, but more modest ways. But if you don't adopt an American baby, somebody else often will. There are even waiting lists for domestic adoption of special needs children. In contrast, the baby you don't adopt from the Third World is likely to stay there.

RAISE YOUR CHILDREN WITH KINDNESS AND RESPECT

I first started thinking seriously about parenting after reading *The Nurture Assumption* by Judith Harris. Like me, she said twin and adoption studies show that parenting is overrated. Yet in my favorite passage, she thoughtfully defended the *power* of parenting:

> People sometimes ask me, "So you mean it doesn't matter how I treat my child?" They never ask, "So you mean it doesn't matter how I treat my husband or wife?" and yet the situation is similar. I don't expect that the way I act toward my husband is going to determine what kind of person he will be ten or twenty years from now. I do expect, however, that it will affect how happy he is to live with me and whether we will still be good friends in ten or twenty years.

As usual, Harris was right. Twin and adoption studies confirm that parents have a noticeable effect on how kids experience and remember their childhood. While this isn't parents' only lasting legacy, it is the most meaningful.

This knowledge should inspire every parent. Raise your children with love, control your temper, and enjoy family time. They'll appreciate it when they're children and fondly remember their happy home when they grow up. When my sons and I read *A Series of Unfortunate Events*, I don't imagine that I'm boosting their adult IQ or reading ability. The point is to enjoy the stories and take away fond memories of our time together.

Even good moms and dads underrate the importance of kindness and respect. When I was young, parents urged children to settle their differences on their own. In practice, this was a green light for older, bigger kids to abuse smaller, younger kids—while adults stood idly by. Today, similarly, many believe that they have to raise their kids to be tough and competitive in a tough, competitive world. From this perspective, too much kindness is dangerous; parents have to strike a delicate balance between making their kids feel loved and preparing them for life. Given the evidence, though, "sentimentally" shielding your kids from petty cruelty makes perfect sense.

Don't get me wrong: I'm a fan of firm discipline. But if I'm going to fall a little in my sons' esteem, I expect something in return. Mild, consistent sanctions are a great way to get better behavior, more sleep, less back talk, and fewer fights. Treating kids harshly "for their own good," in contrast, doesn't pay off.

This doesn't mean that you're to blame if your kids turn into unhappy adults. As we've seen, there is strong evidence that parents have zero long-run effect on their children's overall happiness. Still, if your children remember you as cold, angry, or absent, it's probably because that's the side of yourself you chose to show them.

SHARE YOUR CREED, BUT DON'T EXPECT MIRACLES

Parents' other major legacies are their effects on religious denomination and political party. If you want your children to share your religion or your party, make sure they know where you stand. They will probably follow in your footsteps.

At the same time, realize that your religious and political influence is superficial. You heavily control what your kids will call themselves, not what they'll think or do. If a family of progressive Baptists adopts a kid with a conservative but secular temperament, he'll probably call himself a Baptist and a Democrat when he grows up. Yet don't celebrate too much: He's likely to be a Baptist who doesn't go to church or read the Bible, and a Democrat who opposes national health care and higher taxes.

DON'T WRITE OFF YOUR TEENS

Parents affect juvenile antisocial behavior (for both sexes) and sexual behavior (girls only). If you don't want your teenage son to be a common criminal or your teenage daughter sleeping around, a little extra effort on your part may make a difference. By adulthood, this influence fades out. Still, if your goal is to keep your teen out of trouble, it's doable. You might also try to discourage smoking, drinking, and drug use. The evidence is mixed, but at least some twin and adoption studies find parental influence. If you quit smoking to set a good example for your kids, you might succeed.

HAVE MORE KIDS

If every child's future hinged on massive parental investment, fear of large families would be understandable. If you push yourself, you might be a first-rate tutor, coach, driver, and cheering section for two children. With four kids, there aren't enough hours in the day to wear every hat well. Instead of two children who make you proud, you'll have four disappointments.

Since parental investment is overrated, however, *good kids*—kids you can be proud of—are much cheaper than they seem. As long as you and your spouse turned out all right, your kids probably will, too. And what does enlightened self-interest tell you to do when you find out that something is cheaper than you previously believed? Buy more.

Shouldn't parents worry that if they add another member to the family, the children they already have won't have the support they need to succeed? Not really. Yes, the Korean adoption study provides solid evidence that kids who grow up in bigger families are *slightly* less successful. If you have another baby, expect the children you already have to complete six fewer weeks of education and earn 4 percent less income. Compared to the value of having another brother or sister, however, the downside is tiny. Compared to the value of *being* that brother or sister, the downside isn't worth mentioning.

None of this means that you should try to compete with "Octo-mom" or the Duggars. I only recommend a prudent adjustment in the face of surprising new information. If you used to think that your lifestyle was incompatible with parenthood, maybe one child would work. If you used to believe that one high-maintenance kid was all you could handle, two low-maintenance kids might be better. If you originally planned on two children, how about three or four? Maybe you'll conclude that another kid is a bad deal despite the new low price. Still, for a decision this big, and a price cut this steep, you should seriously ponder a change of plans.

A CLOSING PRAYER

"God, grant me the serenity to accept the things I cannot change, the courage to change the things I can, and the wisdom to know the difference." That's Reinhold Niebuhr's justly famous Serenity Prayer. Unfortunately, as Magneto observes in *X-Men*, God works too slowly. Human beings have spent millennia arguing about what parents can and cannot change. Solid answers would have really helped parents raise their children and plan their families. Yet until recently, mankind was still waiting around for the wisdom to know the difference.

At last, the wait is over. Twin and adoption research has given parents the answers they need. They may not be the answers we wanted to hear. They are, however, the best answers we've got.

To many, the nature-nurture question sounds purely academic. The Serenity Prayer brings it back to everyday life. It's good to know when something is largely outside your control. If I'm beating my head against a brick wall, I want to know. Even if there isn't a better way to break through the wall, at least my head will start to heal.

My sons will grow up to be their own men. Accepting that fact doesn't change it, but it spares me disappointment and aggravation. Not only do I feel better about my life, but I can also take the physical and emotional energy I've conserved and make it count. That might mean taking my kids to the pool. It might mean showing extra patience for a marathon of curious questions about *The Lord of the Rings*. Or it might mean that my wife and I will decide that there is room in our lives to welcome another child.

4
...

WHAT *ABOUT* THE CHILDREN? KIDS TODAY ARE SAFER THAN EVER

> When you open this door, just push on the wood here. Never use the doorknob. I'm always afraid that it will shatter into a million pieces and that one of them will hit my eye.
>
> —Lemony Snicket, *A Series of Unfortunate Events: The Wide Window*

WHEN MY BROTHER AND I WERE TEENAGERS AND WE STAYED OUT late with our friends, my parents had one nonnegotiable demand: If they were in bed, we had to tap them on the shoulder as soon as we got home. Until they knew that their sons were secure, they were too nervous to sleep well. Parents have a lot of worries, but fear for their kids' physical safety has got to be the most traumatic.

If you're trying to make parents feel better, it's counterproductive to remind them that parents have little or no effect on their kids' health. Accepting the inevitability of *minor* risks often makes you feel better. Unless you're Mr. Spock, though, telling yourself "I can't control the horrible things that happen to children these days" will only make you feel worse.

But how would you react if I said that the risks that modern children face *are* minor? You probably wouldn't believe me. I'd have to be blind to miss what happened to this country over the last fifty years. Villainy is all over the news. Still, if you did believe me, you would feel better about being or becoming a parent. What a relief it would be to discover that the nightmarish world we seem to inhabit is only a bad dream.

THE GOOD NEWS ABOUT BAD NEWS

There are many kinds of safety. Some are vague, so let's start with the hardest of hard numbers: mortality statistics. Mortality statistics tell us the fraction of people who died during a year. In the broad scheme of things, how safe are our little ones?

The answers are easy to find and hard to dispute. Every year, the Centers for Disease Control and Prevention publish the authoritative *National Vital Statistics Reports*. Here are the numbers for 2005, the latest available year. They're straight out of the original document, with one small adjustment: Since the report doesn't count overseas deaths, I've added fatalities of U.S. armed forces killed in hostile action.

With the important exception of babies, children are the safest people in the United States. My seven-year-olds may look vulnerable, but they are almost twelve times as safe as I am, and over 100 times as safe as their grandparents. The twins' annual chance of death is 16.3 out of 100,000, which means their chance of staying alive is 99.9837 percent. If my sons could forever remain as safe as they are now, their life expectancy would exceed 6,000 years. Although I wish they were invulnerable, I'm not losing sleep over my own mortality. Wouldn't it be paranoid to sweat bullets about my children's safety when they're far more secure than I am?

Still, weren't kids a lot safer back in the Fifties? Good question. When I'm teaching, I often present a "Standard Story," then explain why the Standard Story is wrong. "The Idyllic Fifties" is one of my favorites. Imagine a comically pompous narrator:

> The year: 1950. The place: The United States of America. There's never been a better time or place to be a kid. Children happily play kick-the-can and stickball on their tree-lined streets. Their parents

Table 4.1: Mortality by Age in 2005

Age	Annual Mortality per 100,000
Under 1 year	692.5
1–4 years	29.4
5–14 years	16.3
15–24 years	82.3
25–34 years	105.4
35–44 years	193.7
45–54 years	432.0
55–64 years	906.9
65–74 years	2137.1
75–84 years	5260.0
85+ years	13,798.6

can relax inside and read the evening newspaper, because they *know* that their children are safe. In 1950, the worst thing an American child has to fear is a skinned knee.

Alas, 1950 is just a distant memory. Now children live in a much darker and more dangerous world. No decent parent would let her kids roam the neighborhood unsupervised. Her precious children could be run down by a careless motorist, snatched by a nefarious stranger, or gunned down by a disturbed peer. True, we're materially richer than we used to be. Yet in the Fifties, parents had something all our money can't buy: peace of mind.

The Idyllic Fifties is a little cartoonish. All my Standard Stories are. But it captures the way we see the evolution of childhood—as a tale of Pleasantville lost.

Fortunately for us, the Idyllic Fifties confuses television and reality. On television, children's lives sharply deteriorated over the

Table 4.2: Annual Youth Mortality per 100,000:
The Fifties versus Today

Age	1950	2005	Safety Gain
Under 1 year	3299	692.5	x4.8
1–4 years	139	29.4	x4.7
5–14 years	60	16.3	x3.7
15–24 years	175.9	82.3	x2.1

last half century. On *Leave It to Beaver*, a kid's worst fate is getting a black eye from a pugnacious girl. On *Law and Order: Special Victims Unit*, child murder and sexual abuse seem as common as jaywalking. If you turn off your television and look at the U.S. mortality numbers for 1950 versus 2005, however, you'll see a different story.

Forget everything you think you know about the golden age of childhood. People are much safer than they used to be—especially kids. In 1950, more than 3 percent of kids didn't live to see their first birthday. That's about one missing child for every classroom in the country. Conditions today aren't merely better. They improved so much that government statisticians changed their denominator from deaths per 1,000 to deaths per *100,000*.

You might think that children under five are safer because they have so little contact with the increasingly frightening outside world. What happens once kids go to school and meet our sick, twisted society? The answer: Even though school-age children were already the safest people in the country back in 1950, we managed to make them almost four times as safe.

If the numbers seem counterintuitive or absurd, riddle me this: Have any of the horrible things you see on TV happened to *you*? To someone you care about? To anyone you personally know? If not, why do you place so much stock in what you see on television, and so little in what you see with your own eyes? Tragedies on *Law and*

Order don't even pretend to be real. Tragedies on CNN are genuine, but they're as misleading as stories about lottery winners. They're news precisely because they are phenomenally unlikely to happen to you. Alas, one of the few things that improved faster than our children's safety is the media's ability to track down the shrinking number of exceptions.

THE FIFTIES VERSUS TODAY: A CLOSER LOOK
AT THE DECLINE OF TRAGEDY

Why did safety improve so much since 1950? To answer this question, we must think some gruesome thoughts. How often do kids die of disease? Accidents? War? Murder? Suicide? The last thing I want to do is freak you out while trying to calm you down. So don't forget our mission: Finding out why childhood is so much *less* tragic than it used to be.

Table 4.3: How Our Kids Got Safer Since 1950

	Under 1 year		1–4 years		5–14 years		15–24 years	
Annual Cause of Death per 100,000	1950	2005	1950	2005	1950	2005	1950	2005
Disease	3179.7	656.1	101.6	16.4	36.6	8.6	62.5	19.6
Accidents	114.9	28.9	36.8	10.7	22.7	6.2	54.8	38.6
War	0	0	0	0	0	0	47.9	0.9
Homicide	4.4	7.5	0.6	2.3	0.5	0.8	6.3	13.2
Suicide	0	0	0	0	0.2	0.7	4.4	10.0
Total	3299	692.5	139	29.4	60	16.3	175.9	82.3

Disease

Stories about sick children rarely make the news, *Leave It to Beaver*, or even *Law and Order: SVU*. Nevertheless, disease has long been youth's leading killer. When the unthinkable happened to a child under one, disease was the cause 96 percent of the time in 1950, and 94 percent of the time in 2005. The pattern gets less lopsided as kids grow up, but disease remains deadlier than all other causes put together for all kids under fifteen years old.

Fortunately, disease isn't what it used to be. The greatest killer of youth has become *much* less deadly—about 80 percent less for younger kids, and about 70 percent less for fifteen- to twenty-four-year-olds. Death from infectious disease has virtually been eradicated. Back in 1950, influenza and pneumonia were responsible for almost 14 percent of the deaths of children age one to four. By 2005, their chance of death from these diseases was about thirty times smaller. Progress on noninfectious ailments hasn't been as rapid, but is still a great gift. Take heart disease. The death rate for children ages five to fourteen fell more than three times.

Suppose that in 1950, a genie let you wish away one cause of death for your children. You would want to pick disease, because it is far and away the greatest threat to their lives. Since 1950, this wish practically came true without a genie's help. And it wasn't just one lucky family that got this wish; we all did. Children and their parents have much to be grateful for.

Accidents

In 1950, accidents were the second greatest killer of youth of all ages. In 2005, accidents remained the number two killer of children under fifteen and had become the number one killer for fifteen- to twenty-four-year-olds. Progress? Absolutely. Accidental death rates sharply declined for every age group. Kids under fifteen are now almost four times as safe as they were in 1950. Even fifteen- to twenty-four-year-olds, who gained the least, are about 1.4 times as safe. Accidents became their leading killer because their death rate for disease fell even faster.

WAR

In 1950, American families were losing their sons to the Korean War. In 2005, American families were losing their sons—and occasionally daughters—to wars in Iraq and Afghanistan. A cynic might say, "The more things change, the more they stay the same." At least from the American point of view, however, he'd be wrong. Since 1950, war has radically changed: It isn't that dangerous anymore. The fatality rate of 1950 was more than *fifty* times as high as the fatality rate of 2005. In 1950, parents really had to worry that the government would force their sons to join the army and send them overseas to die. Now the soldiers are volunteers, and they almost always come home alive.

HOMICIDE AND SUICIDE

The Fifties weren't worse in every way. Our homicide and suicide rates are two to four times as high as they used to be. Before you declare victory for despair, though, remember that homicide and suicide rates continue to be microscopic. They're horrifying, but so rare that you can quadruple the rates for 1950 without having much effect on overall safety. Even fifteen- to twenty-four-year olds—the group most likely to die violently—are still more than twice as safe overall.

A KIND WORD FOR THE FIFTIES

Compared to modern America, 1950 was a death trap. Yet American parents in 1950 were right to feel that they had given their children

Table 4.4: Annual Youth Mortality per 100,000: 1900 versus 1950

Age	1900	1950	Safety Gain
Under 1 year	16,245	3299	x4.9
1–4 years	1984	139	x14.3
5–14 years	386	60	x6.4
15–24 years	586	175.9	x3.3

a better life. By the standards of 1900, 1950 *was* a children's paradise. In 1900, over 16 percent of babies didn't see their first birthday; 1950 was almost five times as safe. In 1900, about 2 percent of kids age one to four didn't make it through the year; 1950 was fourteen times as safe. Tragic deaths for older youths became much less common, too: Safety improved six and a half times for five- to fourteen-year-olds, and more than three times for fifteen- to twenty-four-year-olds. The people of 1950 had a triumph over tragedy to celebrate. But so do we.

VIOLENT CRIME

The devastating loss of a child used to be commonplace. Now it's a freak event. Every actual and potential parent should breathe a sigh of relief that she isn't living in 1950, or—God forbid—1900. Still, there's more to safety than staying alive. What about all the terrible crimes that people commit against children?

Hard numbers again contradict popular perception. Whenever Gallup asks, "Is there more crime in the U.S. than there was a year ago, or less?" a majority of Americans almost always answers, "More." According to crime statistics, however, violent crime has always been rare, especially for children, and recently hit its lowest rate in thirty years. The world is safe—and keeps getting safer. We fear for our children because journalists and screenwriters are scary—and keep getting scarier.

The leading source of American crime statistics, the Bureau of Justice Statistics' National Crime Victimization Survey (NCVS), began in 1973. Its goal is to measure how much crime happens, not just how much crime the police hear about. Instead of relying on police reports, the government interviews a nationally representative sample of about 75,000 households to find out whether they've been victimized. In 2008, it estimated a violent crime rate of 19.3 per 1,000 people over the age of eleven—less than half the 1973 rate. The most common violent crime by far is simple assault (67 percent of violent crimes), followed by aggravated assault (17 percent), robbery (11 percent), and rape/sexual assault (4 percent).

In the NCVS, roughly 4 percent of twelve- to twenty-four-year-olds are the victim of a violent crime during the course of a year. That is about twice the overall rate. Since young people commit most of the violence, it is hardly surprising that they are also its main victims. Fortunately, the more serious crimes are much less common. For twelve- to twenty-four-year-olds, the incidence rate is about one in 144 for aggravated assault, and less than one in 500 for rape/sexual assault.

Since this survey is based on interviews with victims twelve and older, it does not count crimes against young children. But according to police reports, kids under twelve are *much* safer than twelve- to seventeen-year-olds. Their assault rate is about seven times lower, their robbery rate about twelve times lower, and their forcible sex rate about two times lower. The world is far from perfect, but serious crimes against children are rare—and getting rarer.

THE CASE OF KIDNAPPING

When I was a kid, my mom and dad repeatedly warned me never to get into a stranger's car—no matter how much candy he promised. Although they let me bike all over our neighborhood without supervision, my parents were genuinely afraid of what the FBI calls a "stereotypical kidnapping." In a stereotypical kidnapping, the perpetrator is a stranger or slight acquaintance who (1) transports the victim fifty or more miles, (2) detains him overnight, (3) holds him for ransom, (4) intends to keep him permanently, *or* (5) kills him. If my parents were worried about kidnapping thirty years ago—when people were nice—how often does it happen in modern America?

Almost never. For children under twelve years old, the chance of a stereotypical kidnapping is one in a million per year. The best source on child abduction in the United States is the Department of Justice's Second National Incidence Studies of Missing, Abducted, Runaway, and Thrownaway Children. Last conducted during 1999, this survey found a total of 115 stereotypical kidnappings for the year. Older children were more likely to be victims, but even for the highest-risk group—twelve- to fourteen-year-olds—the odds were just four in a million. Your child is about as likely to be the next Lindbergh baby as you are to win world fame for flying from New York to Paris.

Once you know these basic facts, it is clear that Lenore Skenazy, the journalist who let her nine-year-old ride the New York subway alone, is not the "Worst Mom in America." I say she's one of the best. If you merely want to curry favor with other parents, go ahead and base your safety decisions on hearsay. If you really care about your children's safety, however, do what Skenazy did: Look at the numbers. Telling your kid to buckle his seat belt is reasonable. Telling your kid he can't walk to the mailbox alone because he might get abducted is lunacy.

Over 200,000 children were kidnapped in 1999, but the vast majority were nothing like the cases on the news. Kidnappers of pre-teens are almost always relatives who are unhappy with their custody status. While these kidnappings are certainly distressing, they almost never lead to physical injuries. The kidnapper returns the child more than 90 percent of the time. When he doesn't, the rest of the family almost always discovers the child's new location— and can easily pursue legal remedies.

IS SAFETY-CONSCIOUS PARENTING
THE REASON OUR KIDS ARE SAFER?

> Walk through the baby safety department of a store
> with your oldest living relative asking, "Which of
> these things did you need?"
>
> —Lenore Skenazy, *Free-Range Kids*

Modern parents usually say they're safety conscious because the modern world has become so perilous for kids. They're wrong about the peril. Still, is it possible that parental paranoia is the *cause* of the massive increase in our children's safety? Once Today's Typical Parents learn the facts, I assume they'll want the credit.

Despite the weak evidence for nurture effects on children's health, we can't dismiss the possibility out of hand. Drastically reducing a tiny risk has almost no perceptible effect on life expectancy. Imagine a world where any child who survives his first year lives to be 100 years old. If you reduce his risk of premature death from 100 per 100,000 to zero per 100,000, you only increase his life expectancy by about five weeks. That is too small an effect for even higher-quality twin and adoption studies to rule out.

Yet if you recall the main causes of youth mortality, it is hard to give parenting much credit. Parents are primarily hyper about accidents and crime. But the overwhelming reason our kids are safer is that *disease* is so much less deadly. It is unclear how hyper parents could have caused much of this decline. Still, safety-conscious parenting might have played a supporting role. Accident rates declined much less for fifteen- to twenty-four-year-olds than they did for younger children. Perhaps as kids grow up, they take more and more risks that their fretful parents can no longer veto.

Bottom line: While there's no hard proof that safety-conscious parenting works, there is reason to suspect a small benefit. If you have nervous energy to spare, you might as well try a little extra nagging or child proofing. Whatever you do, however, do not mess with Halloween and spoil everyone's fun. Contrary to urban legends about poisoned candy and apples with razor blades, no child has *ever* been killed or seriously injured by Halloween treats.

Whether or not you go the extra mile to protect your child, don't lament that no matter how hard you try, you can't recreate the Fifties. By the standards of the Fifties, almost every modern parent is doing great. If you're especially safety conscious, you're doing better than great. Feel free to pat yourself on the back for making your safe child even safer.

PRUDENCE, NOT PARANOIA

The Baudelaires had not really enjoyed most of their time with her—not because she cooked horrible cold meals, or chose presents for them that they didn't like, or always corrected the children's grammar, but because she was so afraid of everything that she made it impossible to really enjoy anything at all.
—Lemony Snicket, *A Series of Unfortunate Events: The Wide Window*

I have an obsessive personality. It's usually an asset: When I obsess about an idea, I absorb it; when I obsess about a project, I finish it. Sadly, I also occasionally fixate on fruitless topics. I spend hours worrying about unsolvable problems and fantastic scenarios. Sometimes I worry about literally impossible dangers. Negative thoughts stay with me like a song I can't get out of my head.

I know as well as anyone, then, that facts do not instantly bring peace of mind. Still, on the road to peace of mind, learning the facts about children's safety is an important first step. Once you know the facts, you know the kind of problem you face. In an utterly deadly world, worry is a solution: You need to figure out how to protect your kids from danger. In a perfectly safe world, worry is a problem: You need to figure out how to protect yourself from your own anxiety.

The real world is neither utterly deadly nor perfectly safe. Caring parents need to strike a balance between fearing the world and fearing fear itself—to be prudent, rather than paranoid. Unfortunately, Today's Typical Parent strikes an indefensible balance. At minimum, our fear should have mellowed as the safety of our loved ones rose. Since our kids are almost five times as safe as they were in 1950, parents' angst should have mostly melted away. Instead, we've come down with a collective anxiety disorder.

Learning the facts about safety is the first step toward feeling better. What steps come next? Trying to prevent all conceivable dangers is tempting, but futile. Everything's slightly risky—even leaving the house. As Lenore Skenazy wisely observes:

> Once you can picture an eight-year-old . . . being dragged down the street by her Hannah Montana backpack while the bus driver digs Zeppelin on his cranked-up, off-brand iPod, it certainly seems worth warning the kids to undo their backpack belts. And then— whew! That's one worry off the checklist.
>
> The problem is that the checklist just keeps growing. It's like one of those brooms in the story of the sorcerer's apprentice. Chop one in half, and it comes back as two. Two become four.

If parents can't ward off their anxiety by fighting microscopic dangers, what's the alternative? One of psychologists' most effective treatments for anxiety is called *exposure therapy*. People get over their irrational fears by repeatedly facing them. Suppose you accept that leaving your twelve-year-old home alone is as safe as crossing the street, but you're still afraid to do so. After you accept the irrationality of your fear, step two is leaving your child at home while you take a short trip to the store. The catch: You have to do it even if it terrifies you. Once a child-free trip to the store no longer makes your palms sweat, face your next phobia. Baby steps are okay. But the lesson of exposure therapy is that to stop being afraid, you have to start doing things that scare you.

While it's important to face the fears you've got, there's no reason to channel surf for new nightmares. The horrors that parents see on the news and "realistic" crime dramas are insanely rare. If they disturb you, stop watching. If you must watch, watch ironically. Fictional shows are merely gripping lies. Even carefully fact-checked journalism is as misleading as infomercials about "making millions with no money down"; both dwell on weird outliers. The media's job is to point cameras at the most heartbreaking story on earth. In a world with 7 billion human beings, the news will always be horrifying. That's no reason to fear for your children.

If you have kids, or might one day want them, never forget that we're living in a golden age of safety. The false perception that today's world is dangerous for children is a major source of needless parental suffering. Compared to the "idyllic" Fifties, modern children are amazingly secure. Now more than ever, parents should sleep well, knowing that their progeny are safe.

APPENDIX TO CHAPTER 4:
WHERE THE MORTALITY TABLES COME FROM

The raw numbers for mortality from disease, accidents, homicide, and suicide come from *Vital Statistics of the United States 1950, Vol.3: Mortality Data*, Table 57 (for 1950), and *National Vital Statistics Reports* 56 (10), Table 11 (for 2005). Mortality data for 1900 come from Centers for Disease Control/National Center for Health Statistics (CDC/NCHS), National Vital Statistics System, Table HIST290.

My only adjustment to these numbers: The 2005 numbers have separate entries for "legal intervention" (people killed by the police, execution, etc.), "undetermined intent" (violent deaths not ruled homicide or suicide), and "complications of medical and surgical care." I decided to count deaths from legal intervention as homicides, and deaths from undetermined intent and medical complications as accidents.

I had to estimate deaths from war because (1) standard U.S. statistics exclude overseas deaths, (2) military statistics combine deaths from overseas hostile action and other causes, and (3) available military statistics are less detailed than civilian numbers. My raw numbers come from the Office of Medical History's *Battle Casualties and Medical Statistics: U.S. Army Experience in the Korea War*, Table 15, and Richard Kolb, "Korea and Vietnam: Comparing Participants and Casualties," *Veterans of Foreign Wars Magazine* (June–July 2003), pp. 21–23 (for 1950), and the Congressional Research Service Report for Congress's *American War and Military Operations Casualties: Lists and Statistics*, Tables 5, 11, and 15 (for 2005). For 1950, these sources have separate tables for deaths by year, age, and cause of death. For 2005, these sources have separate tables for deaths by year and age.

To estimate war deaths for 1950, I assumed that the age and cause of death breakdowns were constant over the course of the Korean War. During 1950, 14,650 soldiers died in the Korean War, 78.3 percent of the Korean War dead were fifteen to twenty-four years old, and 92.3 percent of deaths in Korea resulted from hostile action. My estimated number of war deaths for those fifteen to twenty-four years old for 1950 was therefore 10,588.

To estimate war deaths for 2005, I assumed that the age breakdown of military fatalities was constant between October 7, 2001 and April 5, 2008—the endpoints of the Congressional Research Service Report. During 2005, 739 soldiers died in hostile action, and 48.8 percent of those killed in Operation Enduring Freedom and Operation Iraqi Freedom were fifteen to twenty-four years old. My estimated 2005 war death count for this age bracket was therefore 361.

To the best of my knowledge, there is no available year or age breakdown for war deaths in 1900, so Table 4.4 does not include war deaths for 1900. This has almost no effect on the results. In 1900, America's only military conflicts were the Boxer Rebellion (1900–

1901) which caused a total of thirty-seven U.S. combat deaths, and the Philippine-American War (1898–1902), which caused a total of 1,020 U.S. combat deaths. If combat deaths were constant over time, and 80 percent of the dead were fifteen to twenty-four years old, there would have been 178 war deaths for those in that age group in 1900, raising their mortality rate from 586 per 100,000 to 586.7 per 100,000.

5
...

ENLIGHTENED FAMILY PLANNING: HOW MANY KIDS DO YOU WANT WHEN YOU'RE SIXTY?

> Nothing I've ever done has given me more joys and rewards than being a father to my children.
>
> —Bill Cosby

IN 1992, GARY BECKER WON THE NOBEL PRIZE IN ECONOMICS FOR one big idea: "Economics is everywhere." He saw economics in discrimination; employers hire people they hate if the wage is right. He saw economics in crime; crooks rob banks because that's where the money is. He saw economics in education; students endure years of boring lectures because they're fascinated by higher pay after graduation. Perhaps most important, Becker saw economics in the family. Human beings plan their families on the basis of enlightened self-interest. Parents look at the world, form roughly accurate beliefs about the costs and benefits of kids, and make babies until they foresee that another would be more trouble than he's worth.

I'm a devotee of Gary Becker. Once when I was visiting the faculty club at the University of Chicago, he unexpectedly sat down for lunch. I barely stopped myself from blurting out, "Oh my God, you're Gary Becker!" Still, my idol doesn't always get things right. One pillar of his family economics is the assumption that the fewer kids you have, the better they'll be. Becker matter-of-factly speaks of the "quality/quantity trade-off." A central lesson of behavioral genetics, as we've seen, is that the trade-off is often illusory. Parents who believe otherwise base their family plans on misinformation. Is this merely one admittedly large oversight on Becker's part, or has the ability of enlightened self-interest to explain the family been oversold?

CAN ENLIGHTENED SELF-INTEREST EXPLAIN THE SHRINKING FAMILY?

> Be nice to your kids, they'll choose your nursing home!
> —Popular bumper sticker

The greatest perceived triumph of the economics of the family is its explanation for the global fertility decline. In the second half of the Fifties, American women had a total fertility rate of almost 4 children. Fifty years later, it was 2.1. We see similar patterns over most of the globe. During the same period, France went from a total fertility rate of 2.7 to 1.9 kids, Germany from 2.3 to 1.3, Japan from 2.2 to 1.3, Mexico from 6.8 to 2.2, and China from 5.5 to 1.8. Becker and the many economists who extended his work are confident that enlightened self-interest explains the worldwide downsizing of the family.

Their position is appealing. When I see a change of this magnitude, I too presume that self-interest is the cause. A few people sterilize themselves to save the planet, but most of us are too selfish to make big sacrifices for what we see—rightly or wrongly—as the common good. Do *you* feel like giving up your car to fight global warming?

Still, a presumption is not an explanation. Why specifically would it be in our self-interest to have fewer kids than before? The answer people often spit out is that big families are no longer affordable, but the opposite is true. Big families are more affordable than ever, because we're more than three times richer than we were in

1950. You can see our mounting riches in our homes. Compared to the tiny dwellings of the Fifties, modern families live in castles, with air conditioning. Why hasn't the size of our families grown in step with the size of our houses?

Becker knows how rich we've grown, so he tells a subtler story about why self-interest implies fewer children. He promisingly begins by focusing on the people who do most of the child care: moms. The women of 2010 give up more to have a child than the women of 1950. Back when women's wages were low, staying home for a few years to raise another kid was a small financial sacrifice. Women earned so little that they didn't have much to lose. Now that working women make good money, staying home for a few years to raise kids can stop mom from earning hundreds of thousands of dollars.

This explanation sounds good, but it's not as smart as it seems. Women lose more income when they take time off, but they also have a lot more income to lose. They could have worked less, earned more, *and* had more kids. Since men's wages rose, too, staying home with the kids is actually more affordable for married moms than ever. If that's too retro, women could have responded to rising wages by working more, having more kids, and using their extra riches to hire extra help.

A variant on the rising-women's-wages story claims that family size shrank because women's bargaining power increased. Since women pay most of the cost of bearing and raising children, it was supposedly in their self-interest to use their newfound leverage to negotiate for fewer kids. But this story falsely assumes that women want smaller families than men do. When the World Values Survey queried men and women around the world about "ideal family size," the sexes saw almost eye-to-eye. In the United States, the average woman wanted .1 children *more* than the average man. Why would women use their new bargaining power to demand changes that they don't desire?

Another selfish explanation for lower birthrates points to birth control: We always wanted sex without children—and now we can finally live the dream. A tempting tale, but it's not as sexy as it looks. Condoms have been widely available since World War II, when the U.S. military started issuing them to soldiers. Families in the Fifties had the technology to keep their families small. Returning veterans and their wives opted for a baby boom instead.

Perhaps the most popular selfish explanation for smaller families, though, claims that people used to have children to support them in their old age. Now that the government provides for retirees, children are obsolete investments. But this story's key assumption is wrong. *Money primarily flows from old to young.* It's long been true and remains true today. Anthropologists who study hunter-gatherer societies have found:

> Children consumed more food than they caught at all ages until age 18. Grandparents continued to work hard to support their grandchildren and produced more than they ate. At almost no time in their adult lives did adults produce less than they consumed.

The same goes for traditional farmers: Investing in your children is less lucrative than stuffing money in your mattress.

In modern societies, little has changed. Parents give more to their children than they can hope to recover. Take the United States in the 1980s. One research team using the Survey of Consumer Finances found that parents gave their kids large cash gifts ($3,000+) much more often than the reverse. Another researcher using the Consumer Expenditure Survey found that—ignoring child-rearing and college costs—parents on average voluntarily gave a total of $25,000 more to each child than they got back.

The lesson: An economic perspective on fertility is not useless, but it is much less intellectually satisfying than advertised. For an extra helping of disillusion, note that the decline of family size has not been smooth. In the middle of the century, the United States had the legendary baby boom: The total fertility rate soared from a little more than two kids in the early Thirties to a little less than four kids in the late Fifties. America's total fertility rate bottomed out in the mid-Seventies at 1.7 kids. At the time, women earned 60 percent as much as men, and only 45 percent worked; now they earn 80 percent as much as men, and 60 percent work. If women's foregone earnings and career options were decisive, children would now be rarer than ever. Instead, American fertility rebounded back to replacement.

THE TRIUMPH OF HINDSIGHT BIAS

> There is no shortage of popular explanations to ac-
> count for the drop in fertility. In Athens, it's common to
> blame the city's infamous air pollution; several years
> ago a radio commercial promoted air-conditioners as a
> way to bring back Greek lust and Greek babies.
>
> —Russell Shorto, "No Babies?"

Human beings tend to rationalize the past as inevitable. Psychologists call this *hindsight bias*. Case in point: Since we know that family size has fallen, we instinctively treat this decline as the only possible outcome. Every major social change seems like yet another reason for parents to want fewer kids than they used to.

What happens if we strive to overcome hindsight bias? Let's pretend we don't know how the story turned out, then mentally review the last fifty years. On reflection, modern parents have serious self-interested reasons to want bigger families than ever.

TECHNOLOGY VASTLY IMPROVED

Think how much work a child was back when moms had to launder diapers by hand and cook every meal from scratch. Parents shopped in a dozen different stores to feed and dress their families. It's remarkable that our great-grandparents chose to have any children at all. Compare that to the modern world of disposable diapers, washer-dryers, microwaves, dishwashers, WalMart, and Amazon. I can see progress between 2002 and 2010; my third son's Kiddopotamus swaddling blankets are far superior to his brothers' old-fashioned rectangular wraps. Raising kids is not yet easy, but it's way easier than it used to be.

WE'RE MUCH RICHER

Our real incomes have more than tripled since the 1950s. Back in the bad old days, parents might literally worry about "having another mouth to feed." Now most of us have the resources to feed, clothe, and shelter the Brady Bunch. Today's parents have money to throw at problems great and small. Need a night out—or help around the house? There's much more to spare for babysitters, nannies, and housecleaners. Too tired to cook? Restaurant budgets are much bigger than they were in the bad old days. Need a little peace and quiet? You're more likely to find them in a McMansion than a duplex.

FINANCIAL BENEFITS ARE PROBABLY NO WORSE THAN BEFORE

A stubborn believer in the kids-as-pensions theory might admit that kids were never a good investment but insist that they're now deeper money pits than ever. They are probably wrong. In the old days, elders died too young to receive much of their "pension." When Social Security began, thirty-year-olds could expect to survive to age sixty-eight. Today the average thirty-year-old makes it to about eighty. So even if parents get a lower level of annual support from their children than they used to, they collect for many more years.

NONFINANCIAL BENEFITS ARE LONGER LASTING AND BETTER THAN EVER

Thanks to rising life spans, modern parents enjoy their children's *non*financial assistance for many more years. Your kids rarely buy you a palace in your old age or even pay your bills. But they usually include you in their lives and help with emergencies great and small. When trust is an issue, kids are a better bet than hired help—and the more bets you place, the better your odds. One careful study of elder care found that each additional child substantially cut the chance of ending up in a nursing home.

Back when people died at sixty, this flow of services didn't last long. Now you can expect to collect for decades. Furthermore, in our rapidly advancing world, the younger generation's time is more valuable to elders. Two hundred years ago, parents didn't need their kids' help to upgrade to high-definition TV or install the latest version of Windows.

Once we get past our hindsight bias, the downsizing of the family is deeply puzzling. In terms of objective conditions, there's never been a better time to have a lot of kids. If you asked parents in the Fifties to imagine raising their four children with the help of the technology and wealth that we take for granted, they probably would have cheered. Why are so few couples taking advantage of this historic opportunity?

VALUES, SELF-IMPOSED RULES, AND FORESIGHT

I fear the disapproval of Gary Becker. I want my idol to like me. Still, given his legendary candor, I have to think that he prefers heresy to insincerity. My confession: Although I'm familiar with standard enlightened self-interest stories about the incredible shrinking family, three nonstandard factors strike me as more important: changes in values, changes in self-imposed rules, and changes in foresight.

CHANGES IN VALUES

If you look at the General Social Survey, the decline of marriage and religion explains much of the last four decades' fall in family size. The simplest interpretation is that values changed: Marriage, religion, and "bringing souls into the world" are intertwined, and average Americans take none as seriously as they used to.

A connection between changing values and smaller families isn't a reason—selfish or otherwise—to have more kids. This book tries to show you better ways to get what you care about, not tell you what to care about. I acknowledge changing values to avoid overstating my case. Intellectual error explains much of the decline in family size, but not the whole story.

CHANGES IN SELF-IMPOSED RULES

Thanks to the growth of technology and wealth, parenting has never been less laborious or more affordable. If objective conditions were decisive, the modern family would be bigger than ever. Still, we can partly salvage the self-interest story of declining family size by casting a wider net. Instead of stubbornly searching for countervailing objective conditions, let's redirect our attention to *subjective* conditions—the burdens we impose on ourselves.

With modern resources, almost anyone can be a good parent by the standards of 1950. But we don't want to be good by the standards of the Fifties; we want to be good by the standards of today. During the last half century, we picked up a list of *self-imposed* rules—of "stuff we gotta do." These rules are awfully strict. As we've seen, the time that parents spend on child care is way up, even though more moms have jobs and families are smaller. Imagine combining the standards of today with the family size of yesterday.

I could almost sell this to Gary Becker, but there's one sticking point: My story is self-interested, but not enlightened. Given all the rules, small families are the prudent choice for Today's Typical Parents. But that's not saying much. The rules are a choice—and child neglect is not the only alternative. What do parents, or kids, get out of these rules? According to twin and adoption studies, not much.

CHANGES IN FORESIGHT

When I was a child, people often accused others of "breeding like rabbits." The picture's not pretty: Rabbits get pregnant four times a year, have litters of half a dozen, nurse their young for only minutes a day, and boot them out of the nest after a month. The point of the rabbit analogy is that we expect more from human beings. We ought to use our heads to calculate how many children we can comfortably support and take care not to exceed that number. If you don't use your head, you will not only be a bad parent and a burden on society, but you will also ruin your life.

You don't hear the rabbit analogy much anymore. At least in developed countries, people have too much foresight to breed like rabbits. Many babies remain the fruit of impulsive, unprotected sex, but few parents stick to the rabbit strategy once they have one or two unplanned children. Look at thirty-something American moms who never married: 45 percent have just one child, and 26 percent have two. Married moms in their thirties, in contrast, are much more likely to have two kids (41 percent) rather than one (22 percent).

This brings us to my last un-Beckerian explanation for smaller families: Changes in foresight. While impulsive, unprotected sex feels as good as ever, we are more likely to look ahead a few years and count the costs. Do you want to spend your twenties having fun and advancing your career—or changing diapers for crying kids? Do you want to spend your thirties with a kid or two, plus time for other pursuits—or so many kids that you don't have a minute to yourself? In the past, we took the path of least resistance—ignoring future costs in favor of immediate sexual pleasure. As civilization has progressed, more of us have found the foresight to resist—or defuse—our biological urges.

A LITTLE FORESIGHT IS A DANGEROUS THING

If you're reading this, you're probably a person who plans ahead. Instead of acting on impulse, you're *reading a book* about how many kids to have. Natalists often argue that foresighted folks like you are the reason so many cradles are empty. Why do you have to overthink everything? If everyone were like you, we would have gone extinct ages ago! Their story, crudely put, is that the human race can only continue with the help of bad judgment and strong liquor.

Their story is not mine. Moderate increases in foresight are an important cause of lower fertility. But *moderate* foresight and *high* foresight lead to very different family plans.

If human beings had zero foresight, we would have lots of unprotected sex, and plenty of kids. If we foresaw *only* the initial downside of kids—nothing but sleepless nights, temper tantrums, and dirty diapers—we'd be childless, if not celibate. Unfortunately, this is what usually passes for foresight today—weighing short-run pleasure against a few years' worth of negative consequences. True foresight, however, is about calmly optimizing a *lifetime's* worth of good and bad.

The early years are often rough. Many moms agree with Angelina Jolie that pregnancy "makes you feel round and supple, and to have a little life inside you is amazing," but others find pregnancy a mixed blessing—or necessary evil. After the delivery, both parents endure trying months. An infant is a lot of work even if you're easy on yourself. I just gave my baby a 2:00 AM stroll to calm him down, and my bedtime is hours away.

If you have more than one child, your troubles multiply. Caring for two youngsters often feels more than twice as stressful. As a veteran of the twins' night shift, I speak from experience. When one baby wakes up while you're feeding another, you're in a no-win situation: One cries if you interrupt the feeding, the other cries if you don't. *Moderate* foresight tells you to stop having kids. If one infant makes you tired and cranky, why have another?

High foresight has a simple response: Infancy is a passing phase, but children last a lifetime. Costs fall: The older kids get, the easier they are to care for. Last week, we left our seven-year-olds home alone for the first time; before long, they'll be babysitting their little brother. Benefits increase over time, too. Kids who walk and talk are more fun than newborns who sleep and cry.

Now gaze further into the future. Once your kids are teenagers, you'll rarely feel like you need a moment to yourself. You'll have to pressure them to spend time with *you*. When they're grown, all your children will likely be a plus. You'll enjoy their company and take pride in their accomplishments but no longer bear the responsibility. As an added bonus, every child is another chance for grandchildren.

In the winter, strangers are often shocked to see me wearing shorts. "Aren't you cold?" they shout. If I'm outside and it's forty degrees, I'm freezing, but I don't base my whole decision on the outside temperature. My office runs warm. During January, I'm only outside five minutes a day. When I decide what to wear, I maximize my *average* comfort. I'd rather be thirty degrees too cold for five minutes than ten degrees too hot for eight hours, so I stick with shorts.

Choosing the best number of kids is a lot like deciding what to wear on a winter day. You make one decision, then live with the consequences. The child-free often see this as an argument against kids, but it cuts both ways. People who want kids they can't have are just as "trapped" as people who have kids they don't want. In fact, irreversibility cuts in favor of kids. As we've seen, regret is *ab*normal for people who have kids, and normal for people who missed their chance.

I admit that a perfectly foresighted person could choose a life of childlessness. If your sole dream is to wander the earth, kids will only slow you down. And perfect foresight almost certainly leads to fewer kids than zero foresight. The thought of eight kids scares me, too. The claim I stand by: *Typical* parental feelings paired with *high* foresight imply more kids than *typical* parental feelings paired with *moderate* foresight.

Since the effect of kids on parental well-being changes over time, what precisely does enlightened self-interest advise? For starters, heavily discount the way you feel now. Your feelings are important, but from a purely selfish point of view, your feelings today are no more important than your feelings half a century from now. Instead of dwelling on the present, judiciously estimate the lifetime consequences of Plans A through Z, then pick the plan with the highest overall score. One good rule of thumb is to figure out the optimal number of kids to have during each of the major stages of your life—then set your target number of children equal to your average answer.

Suppose you're thirty. Selfishly speaking, you conclude that the most pleasant number of children to have during your thirties is one. During your forties, your optimal number of kids will rise to two—you'll have more free time as your kids assert their independence. By the time you're in your fifties, all your kids will be busy with their own lives. At this stage, wouldn't it be nice to have four kids who periodically drop by? Finally, once you pass sixty and prepare to retire, you'll have ample free time to spend with your grandchildren. Five kids would be a good insurance policy against grandchildlessness.

If you apply my "take the average" rule of thumb to this example, the best number of kids is three. Five kids would be foolish; you'd sacrifice the rest of your life for a great retirement. It would be similarly foolish to have one child in your thirties, declare your life perfect, and schedule a vasectomy. Foresight implores you to strike a balance between too many kids in your early years and too few later on.

A time-worn tactic to discourage teen pregnancy is to give students a fake baby (a doll, an egg, whatever) and make them take care of it for a week. The more temperamental the faux infant, the better: Advanced models cry and scream unless their guardians meet expectations. The point is to give a little extra foresight to those who need it most—to show teens what they can expect next year if they have unprotected sex today. If you take this educational exercise literally, however, its lesson is that babies are more trouble than they're worth. The experiment isn't an argument against teens having kids; it's an argument against kids, period. And it's a deeply misleading argument, because infancy doesn't last long.

Maybe the only way to reach teens is with a noble lie, but I prefer an honest approach. Like: Having a child is a serious decision. But if you take the decision seriously enough, you won't just avoid pregnancy until you're ready for kids. You'll also start having kids before it's too late to have as many as you want. Or: Plan ahead before you have a child. But don't just plan on dirty diapers and lost sleep. Remember to look forward to your kids' hilarious questions, trips to Disneyland, and Christmas with your grandchildren.

You've probably heard the maxim "A little knowledge is a dangerous thing." When it comes to kids, a little foresight is a dangerous thing, too. Looking a few years ahead, it's tempting to conclude that the best number of children is one, or none. But from a bird's-eye view of your whole life, a zero-to-one child policy usually looks like a big mistake.

FORESIGHT AND FERTILITY: FRIENDS NOT FOES

Natalist attacks on the excessive foresight of civilized man bother me in two ways. First, I take them personally. I happen to be a person of foresight. I started pondering retirement long before I got my first real job. (My current plan is to work till I drop.) Second, and more important, the critique of foresight buys into the view that kids are a bad deal.

Exhausted parents of young children who vow "never again" normally have selfish motives. But are they good at being selfish? Maybe in the midst of their temporary misery, they calmly computed the lifetime consequences of another child and found that it's not worth it. If they really have such stoic detachment, great. But real human beings are more likely to be myopic—to let the negatives right before their eyes unduly tilt their decision. When your toddler is driving you crazy, you have to struggle to remember that he'll only be two once.

How myopic are parents? Judging by their body language, they focus almost wholly on the here and now. When they imagine the short-term consequences of another kid, they often visibly recoil; but if you mention the consequences twenty or thirty years hence, they apathetically roll their eyes. Maybe they've thought through their middle age and retirement so carefully that the topic bores them. Maybe they're keeping their deliberations secret to spite me. More plausibly, however, they're too short-sighted to put "How many kids will I want when I'm sixty?" on their List of Things to Wonder About.

If I had telepathy, I could check my suspicions. Since I don't, I'll never conclusively prove that parents are myopic to my own satisfaction, much less anyone else's. From a social scientist's point of view, this is a frustrating limitation. From your point of view, however, it's not relevant, because *you can measure your myopia by looking inside yourself*. You know whether you've gazed all the way to the horizon. You know whether you've calmly weighed the lifetime consequences of another child.

If you've been there and done that, wonderful. If you haven't, I'm not trying to make you feel guilty. I'm appealing to your prudence. If you were good at being self-interested, "How many kids will I want when I'm sixty?" would interest you as much as "How many kids do I want right now?" If your answers to these two questions are not the same, balancing your present and future interests is no sacrifice. It's common sense. Splitting the difference is as selfish as waking up a little early to pack yourself a lunch.

6
...

YOUR KIDS ARE GOOD FOR YOU—
BUT ARE THEY GOOD FOR THE WORLD?

> There came to me the memory of reading a eulogy
> delivered by a Jewish chaplain over the dead on the bat-
> tlefield at Iwo Jima, saying something like, "How many
> who would have been a Mozart or a Michelangelo or an
> Einstein have we buried here?" And then I thought,
> Have I gone crazy? What business do I have trying to
> help arrange it that fewer human beings will be born,
> each one of whom might be a Mozart or a Michelangelo
> or an Einstein—or simply a joy to his or her family and
> community, and a person who will enjoy life?
>   —Julian Simon, *The Ultimate Resource 2*

WE USUALLY LIMIT OUR NUMBERS OUT OF SELF-INTEREST—OR TO
be more precise, perceived self-interest. When a couple has an unwanted pregnancy, they feel sorry for themselves, not for the world.
Still, self-interest isn't the whole story. Some of us have fewer kids
than we'd like to avoid being selfish. Another baby might make you
happier, but it's wrong to think only of yourself. Shouldn't I be pushing altruism, instead of refining selfishness?

My answer is a definite maybe. If having more kids were bad for
the world, the book in your hands would be awfully irresponsible. I'd

be a cheerleader for evil. Even if all my earlier arguments held water, my book would be encouraging bad behavior because it happens to feel good. If more kids were good for the world, however, I'd have no cause for shame. When self-interest and the general interest coincide, preaching prudence is a public service.

The crucial question, therefore, is: Does the birth of another baby make the world better—or worse? If creating one more life has bad overall consequences, then the unselfish should ignore my selfish reasons to have more kids—and everyone should hope I stay silent. Overpopulation burdens the selfish and unselfish alike. But if creating one more life has good overall consequences, everyone should be glad to see me promoting enlightened self-interest—and consistency seems to require even altruists to follow my advice.

GIVING BIRTH: AT LEAST YOU'RE DOING THE KID A FAVOR

> You and your intellect would not be here,
> If Mother's traits had all been fine, my dear.
> And it's most fortunate for you that she,
> Was not wed solely to philosophy.
> Relent, and tolerate in me, I pray,
> That urge through which you saw the light of day.
> And do not bid me be like you, and scorn,
> The hopes of some small scholar to be born.
>
> —Jean-Baptiste Molière, *The Learned Ladies*

Considering how cute babies are, it's amazing how much we blame them for. Whether we're worrying about poverty or the environment, we're quick to point fingers at people who still haven't learned to talk. Yet the accusations don't stop there. When people weigh whether to have a baby, many openly doubt whether the *baby* benefits. One of the most common questions about reproducing is: Would it be fair to the child?

Sometimes prospective parents worry that their motives are suspect: Do I want a child for the right reasons? Am I having a child out of loneliness? To hold my marriage together? To please my parents? Other times, they wonder whether their qualifications are substandard: Do I have the money to support a child? Am I too old? Too young? Will my job leave enough time for my child? Am I nurturing enough? Once we doubt our motives or qualifications, many of us can't help but wonder if we would be wronging a child by bringing him into the world.

What's funny about these doubts is that virtually no one feels that it was unfair for their parents to have *them*. While we waste a lot of time blaming our parents for our problems, almost no one tells himself: "My parents were wrong to have me. They should be ashamed of themselves!"

The more specific the doubts, the weirder they sound. Many prospective parents fret, "It's not fair to have a child when we're having trouble making ends meet," or "It's not fair to have a child out of loneliness." Can you imagine someone saying, "My whole life has been a mistake because I grew up poor," or "My parents had me out of loneliness; it would be better never to have been born"? These are flimsy reasons to regret your own existence. If they wouldn't come close to convincing you that your life was a mistake, aren't they equally flimsy reasons against passing the gift of life along to someone else?

Almost everyone—children of flawed parents included—is glad to be alive. The upshot is that, contrary to popular worries, almost anyone who decides to reproduce is doing the child a favor. Fretting about "fairness" is looking a gift horse in the mouth. No one asks to be born, but almost everyone would if they could.

We like to think that every child deserves the best, but almost no real human being lives up to this standard. We're the imperfect children of imperfect parents. If it's unfair to have a child without giving him the best, the only way to avoid treating your children unfairly is to remain childless. Be glad your parents held themselves to a looser standard; otherwise you wouldn't be here to read this.

If you're still unsure, consider: How bad would your life have to be before you'd wish you'd never been born? You'll probably need ultra-grim scenarios to answer the question. If a medical condition condemned me to a lifetime of horrible pain, if my parents were too poor to save me from immediate starvation, or if it were customary to savagely beat me just for fun, I'd regret having seen the light of day. Perhaps you have a longer list of nightmares. Still, wouldn't your life have to be vastly below average before you'd wish to erase your whole existence?

In the graphic novel *It's a Bird*, a writer named Steve shows how Huntington's disease, a dreadful hereditary condition, has haunted his family. He finally realizes that his father "doesn't want to admit to himself that he might have doomed his own children . . . simply by having them." Steve finally tells his dad to forget his regrets: "I'd rather have known my family, and fallen in love with Lisa, and written my stories, and then come down with Huntington's . . . if that turns out to be my fate . . . than not to have lived, and missed all that."

There's no need to dwell on nightmares come true; they're happily as rare as they are disturbing. Yet asking yourself, "How bad would my life have to be before I'd wish I'd never been born?" teaches a profound lesson: *At least one person benefits tremendously from virtually every birth—the new baby.* The baby benefits if the parents have him out of loneliness, or to hold their marriage together. The baby benefits if the parents are poor, or workaholics, or carry Huntington's disease in their genes. Turning the gift of life into a curse is quite a challenge.

Prospective parents ought to do right by their children. But unless you foresee that your child's life will be a full-blown tragedy, stop worrying about the fairness of creating life. How can it be unfair to give your child a gift that's way better than nothing? When you wonder whether a new life will make the world a better place, don't forget that being born means the world to someone.

KIDS AND POVERTY: WHY PROSPERITY AND POPULATION GO TOGETHER

> Every generation has perceived the limits to growth that finite resources and undesirable side effects would pose if no new recipes or ideas were discovered. And every generation has underestimated the potential for finding new recipes and ideas. We consistently fail to grasp how many ideas remain to be discovered . . . Possibilities do merely not add up; they multiply.
>
> —Paul Romer, "Economic Growth"

Whenever a baby is born, at least *someone* has a reason to rejoice. What about the rest of us? Should we join the party, or mutter that the birth of another human being is nothing to be happy about? In practice, we tend to celebrate every particular baby, but grumble about the consequences of babies in general.

The classic grumble is that population growth leads to poverty. When a stranger crashes a party, the invited guests get smaller slices of cake. Similarly, the argument runs, the birth of a new baby, eager for his cut of the world's resources, helps impoverish those of us who are already here.

This complaint is true in a trivial sense: Babies rarely hold steady jobs but still have to eat. A birth adds a consumer to the world without adding a producer, so as a matter of arithmetic, any child's arrival reduces average consumption. Still, your infant's unemployment hardly gives neighbors, countrymen, or the world much reason to complain. Unless your family is on welfare, it's your problem, not theirs. Parents, not society, give up fancy vacations to pay for diapers, formula, and Onesies.

In any case, babies don't stay unemployed forever. Those who see more people as a source of poverty are missing half the story: Over the course of their lives, human beings do not just consume, they also *produce*. Kids eventually grow up and pull their own weight. The world economy is not like a party where everyone splits a birthday cake; it is more like a potluck where everyone brings a dish.

If this seems like wishful thinking, consider: The total number of people on earth *and* the average standard of living skyrocketed over the last two centuries. The world has never been more populous or more prosperous than it is today. Never. By historic standards, almost everything is cheap. You may wince at the price of gas, but have you looked inside a WalMart lately? They're practically giving stuff away.

These would be amazing coincidences if population growth were an important cause of poverty. Indeed, it makes you wonder: Is our population a *cause* of our prosperity?

The answer is almost certainly yes. The main source of progress is *new ideas*. We are richer today than we were 100 years ago because we learned so much. We learned ways for one farmer to feed hundreds of people, we learned how to fly, we learned how to make iPhones. As Nobel Prize–winning economist Robert Lucas puts it, the world's expanding prosperity is "mainly an ongoing intellectual achievement, a sustained flow of new ideas."

The magic of ideas is all around us. As a little boy, I typed my first words on my mom's electric typewriter and corrected mistakes by hand. Now I use Microsoft Word, and I haven't touched a bottle of Liquid Paper in twenty years. If you put this book down for a moment, the fruit of new ideas is probably right in front of your eyes. If you're wearing contact lenses or had Lasik surgery, the fruit of new ideas is actually *on* your eyes.

The sweetest thing about ideas is how cheap they are to share. A million people—or 7 billion—can enjoy the latest discovery almost as easily as a solitary hermit. In fact, ideas often become *more* useful when more people use them. The Internet was so-so when only one person in 100 had a modem; now we can't live without it.

Our future depends on new ideas. So how would you respond to a precocious five-year-old who asks: "Where do new ideas come from?" You don't have to dodge the question out of embarrassment. Feel free to blurt out the scandalous truth: New ideas come from *people*—especially smart, creative people. When you get more people, you get more smart, creative people; and when you get more smart, creative people, you get more new ideas. In the words of economist Julian Simon, "the human imagination" is "the ultimate resource."

If seven castaways wash up on a desert island, how many will be creative geniuses? On *Gilligan's Island*, the answer is one (remember "the Professor"?), but few groups of seven random strangers would be so well-endowed. As the population of the island grows from seven to 7,000 or 7 million, the chance that Thomas Edison, Bill Gates, Beethoven, or the Professor resides there sharply improves. Once you hit a population of 7 *billion*—as Earth soon will—the island will be home for 7,000 innovators who are literally one in a million.

Now consider: If you had the right stuff to change the world, you might not bother. The market has to be big enough to make creativity worthwhile. If, like the Professor, you have only seven potential customers counting yourself, most innovations won't pay. Suppose the Professor could spend a year of his life working on an idea worth $1 per person. As long as he's stuck on the island, he'll be working for $7 a *year*. He'd be better off picking coconuts. If the Professor could escape the island and bring his idea to a world market of 7 billion customers, though, it would amply repay a lifetime of research.

It takes a whole planet to sustain the progress that we take for granted. You need smart, creative people to get new ideas, but they're not enough. You also need armies of customers to turn creativity into a paying job. Creative geniuses are the most dramatic characters in the story of progress. Without a cast of billions of extras, however, the story would be less exciting. Indeed, without the extras, there would be no story to tell.

When you look at languages, the link between population and creation is obvious. There are a lot more books, movies, and TV shows in English than Romanian. One major reason has to be that English speakers vastly outnumber Romanian speakers. There's a lot more English-speaking talent—writers, directors, actors. But just as important, there's a much bigger market for works in English. Legions of foreign directors move to Hollywood to win a global audience—and a bigger paycheck.

For English versus Romanian, the advantages of the larger community are obvious. The world of today is better than the world of yesterday for the same reason: We belong to a much larger community than our ancestors did. The result is the modern world, where great new ideas pop up nonstop.

If you make a kindergarten's worth of children, you might impoverish *yourself* for a while. But your fertility does not impoverish the world. Maybe your child will be one of the smart, creative people who enrich us all. Even if your child isn't the next Edison, though, he will almost surely grow up to be a productive member of society whose dollars inspire smart, creative people around the world to do their thing. Either way, your fertility is enriching your fellow man, not pushing him into poverty.

YOU DON'T HAVE TO RAISE THE AVERAGE TO PULL YOUR WEIGHT

Eighty percent of success is showing up.

—Woody Allen

When asked, "Does the birth of another baby make the world better—or worse?" I suspect that many secretly answer, "It depends on the baby." If he grows up to be a scientist, they think the world's better off. If he grows up to be a janitor, they think the world's worse off. The implicit dividing line, apparently, is that people make the world a better place if and only if they *raise average income*. If our average income is $50,000 a year, the birth of a future janitor supposedly impoverishes us by pulling down the average.

To modern ears, this "eugenic" perspective sounds true but cruel—like pointing out that someone is fat or ugly. But it's usually not even true. Eugenicists mistake arithmetic for injury. A "burden on society" isn't someone who produces less than average; it's someone who consumes more than he produces. The birth of a future janitor is nothing to worry about as long as he'll be self-supporting and peaceful. The vast majority of janitors are.

When Danny DeVito enters a room, he reduces its occupants' average height. But he doesn't cause anyone to "lose height." Shortness isn't contagious. Neither is low income. A janitor earns less than average, but his existence doesn't impoverish his fellow citizens.

Does the world really need another janitor? Absolutely. If janitors weren't useful, employers wouldn't pay them $20,000 for a year of their time. Many think there's no place for unskilled workers in the high-tech economy of the future, but *someone* has to do their jobs. When there aren't enough unskilled workers to wash dishes and collect garbage, skilled workers pick up the slack—and their other talents go to waste. If Bill Gates spent half his time cleaning his own office, making his own meals, and watching his own kids, he'd discover far fewer new ideas to enrich us all.

KIDS AND CHOICE: WHY EVEN MISANTHROPES PAY TO LIVE IN MANHATTAN

> No, all you say I'll readily concede:
> This is a low, dishonest age indeed;
> Nothing but trickery prospers nowadays,
> And people ought to mend their shabby ways.
> Yes, man's a beastly creature; but must we then
> Abandon the society of men?
>
> —Jean-Baptiste Molière, *The Misanthrope*

Imagine you're an introvert, a loner, or an outright misanthrope. You're trying to decide where to live. Two possibilities come to mind. The first is Hays, Kansas; population, about 20,000. The second is New York City; population, about 8 million. In Hays, you can buy a decent house for under $100,000. In New York, that's the cost of a closet.

If you're the opposite of a "people person," the decision seems like a no-brainer: Hays is a lot less crowded and a lot cheaper. Yet the total number of introverts, loners, and misanthropes in New York far exceeds the number in Hays. After all, it has 400 times as many people. Antisocial New Yorkers presumably know that places like Hays exist. So why do they pay exorbitant rents to live near millions of strangers?

"Choices" is the obvious answer—choices about where to work, live, eat, shop, and play. In Hays, you soon run out of stuff to do. Before long, you're bored and wonder why the locals didn't leave long ago. New York, in contrast, is the legendary city that never sleeps. Despite its drawbacks, the Big Apple's got something for everyone—misanthropes included.

A New York misanthrope might be tempted to quip, "This city would be perfect if it weren't for all the people." But the quote is self-refuting. New York doesn't have more people and more choices than Hays by coincidence. The extra people *cause* the extra choices. Stores need customers, firms need workers, and hobbies need enthusiasts. The more people there are, the more stores, firms, and hobbies have the customers, workers, and enthusiasts they need to flourish. As the number of choices goes up, so does their diversity. Options too obscure or eccentric to make the cut in Hays pass the market test in New York City.

Fans of urban living might simply conclude that the city is better than the country. But an analogous argument applies globally: Population growth makes the whole world more like New York, and less like Hays. Physical proximity is not essential. As long as there's communication and trade, more population means more choices. A football fan in Hays is hours from the nearest NFL stadium, but thanks to tens of millions of fans around the world, he can watch games on TV and read about his favorite athletes in the newspaper.

The Internet is the clearest illustration of the dependence of choice on population. Think about all your options: If you can imagine a product or activity, it's probably a Google search away. With almost 2 billion users worldwide, there is a critical mass for the most obscure interests. In third grade, I was literally the only fan of Greek mythology I knew. Now, thanks to the vast population of cyberspace, I could talk about Zeus and Hercules all day long.

KIDS AND RETIREMENT:
WHO'S GOING TO CARE FOR THE CHILD-FREE

In narrowly financial terms, as we've seen, kids have always been a bad investment. You shouldn't be surprised; after all, children have no legal obligation to repay their parents. Yet in most advanced countries, the young *are* legally obliged to support old-age programs like Social Security and Medicare. You can disown your parents, but still have to pay your taxes.

Selfishly speaking, there's a crucial difference between requiring children to support their parents and requiring the nation's young to support the nation's old. If your kids had to support you, they would virtually be money in the bank. Programs like Social Security and Medicare don't work that way. Your benefits don't depend on your fertility. When the child-free retire, they collect as much as the Duggars.

Governments could conceivably change the benefit formula to reward fertile families. Until they do, however, having kids is effectively a charitable donation to future retirees and the taxpayers bound to support them. The selfish can neglect these future benefits when they plan their families, but altruists should give early and often.

Big families have subsidized retirement since the dawn of government retirement programs. But as family size shrinks, every child counts more. When the average family had four children, families with one more child did roughly 25 percent extra to support the elderly. Now that the average family has about two children, families with one more child do roughly 50 percent more to support future retirees. In Hong Kong, where families average less than one child, two-child families contribute more than *twice* the usual amount. If you care about tomorrow's retirees, or the workers expected to support them, having another kid is a good way to lend a hand—and the smaller families get, the more every hand counts.

When the elderly depend on programs like Social Security and Medicare, it's easy to see how fertility helps future retirees: Children are the taxpayers of tomorrow. But retirees' well-being would depend on fertility even if governments stayed out of the retirement business. Imagine if we stopped having kids altogether. In three generations, everyone would exceed the retirement age—and a lifetime of retirement savings wouldn't buy much. To get by, most of the elderly would have to spend their seventies working for people in their eighties.

This nightmare won't happen, but we're moving in its direction. In 1940, the United States had almost ten working-age adults (age twenty to sixty-four) to shoulder the burden of every retiree (age sixty-five and up). Now it's about five workers per retiree. In about fifteen years, it will be only three. In other words, the average American worker used to support 10 percent of a retiree, now supports 20 percent of a retiree, and will soon support 33 percent of a retiree. If you care about the elderly, ponder that before you decide that your family is complete.

By the way, thanks to unusually high fertility and immigration, the United States is doing better than most advanced countries. Japan, to take one of the worst cases, already has fewer than three working-age adults (age fifteen to sixty-four) for every retiree (age sixty-five and up). By 2030, they expect only two workers per retiree. To cope, the Japanese will have to make tough choices—like sharply raising their retirement age.

Many communities across the United States now advertise themselves as "fifty and better" or "sixty and better." Families with younger members need not apply. While I respect seniors' right to live among their own kind, they're kind of insulting the hand that feeds them. Kids may be noisy and mischievous, but ultimately they're the people who make retirement possible. Seniors might not want large families in their neighborhood, but they should definitely want large families in their society.

KIDS AND THE ENVIRONMENT:
DON'T THROW THE BABY OUT WITH THE BATHWATER

Crowing about the riches of the modern world occasionally back-fires. Many grant the point, then retort, "Our standard of living is the problem." As they see it, the environment is going from bad to worse *because* we are simultaneously prosperous and populous. As biologist Paul Ehrlich argues, it is precisely because people in the United States are rich that "the addition of each person to the American population, whether by birth or immigration, is many times the disaster for the world as a birth in Kenya or Bangladesh."

While this rhetoric won't convince many to embrace childlessness, it does inspire admiration of greens who practice what they preach. Take the case of Toni Vernelli. At the age of twenty-seven, she had herself sterilized to protect the planet. "Having children is selfish," she explained. "Every person who is born uses more food, more water, more land, more fossil fuels, more trees and produces more rubbish, more pollution, more greenhouse gases, and adds to the problem of overpopulation." Is she right? Would you really be doing the planet a favor if you chose to be childless? If so, wouldn't I have to be a jerk to discourage readers from following in Vernelli's footsteps?

The effect of population on the environment is more complex than the effect of population on the economy. Powerful arguments show that more people make us richer. Mankind's long-run effect on the planet is less clear-cut. Still, it's important to remember that claims about the environment are factual questions. If we angrily dismiss those who question whether we're heading for disaster, we might wind up taking drastic actions for no good reason. Drastic actions like . . . sterilizing ourselves.

As it turns out, Vernelli should have been more skeptical. Many—though not all—of the problems on her list don't add up. Basic economics says that scarcity means high prices and abundance means low prices. But despite Vernelli's widely shared fears that we're running out of things like food and fuel, resources have been getting *cheaper* for the last century and a half. Not every day or every year, of course—prices bounce around. We went through a rough patch a few years ago—remember $4 gas? Yet adjusting for inflation, average commodity prices have fallen about 1 percent per year since the time of the Civil War.

The one clear exception is people's time, also known as "labor." Time has been getting pricier for centuries. Everyone nowadays has labor-saving machines, but only the wealthy can still afford personal servants. Strange though it sounds, if we're "running out" of anything, it's people.

While resource depletion is only one of many environmental concerns, there is some good news on other fronts, too. Most notably, air and water quality in the Western world improved substantially in recent decades. Around the globe, there's a standard two-stage pattern: As countries go from dirt poor to poor, pollution gets worse; as countries go from poor to rich, pollution gets better.

Shrinking environmental problems are admittedly still problems, and there is usually some bad news mixed with the good. Air is getting more pleasant to breathe, but most scientists say that our emissions of carbon dioxide cause global warming. I don't deny that putting another person on the planet will mildly aggravate some problems. Population does have *some* negative side effects.

So should we thank the Toni Vernellis of the world after all? Not so fast. If the birth of a human being has a lot of positives and a few negatives, the constructive response isn't to denounce "people." The constructive response is to *selectively target* the negatives. Name specific problems, and figure out the cheapest way to handle them.

Selective targeting requires more imagination than mass sterilization, but it's worth the extra mental effort. If you want to do something about man-made global warming, you don't have to reduce the number of human beings on the planet. You just have to get humanity to reduce its carbon emissions. A carbon tax is one simple way to get from here to there. To discourage emissions, make emissions more expensive, then sit back and watch lifestyles and technology adapt. The same principle applies to virtually any population problem you can imagine. Don't like congestion at rush hour? An electronically collected toll is a straightforward way to get traffic moving again.

Improving the environment without cutting population is not wishful thinking. We've been doing it for decades. Resources are more abundant. Air and water are cleaner. Problems remain, but the smart path to a better world isn't restraining our numbers. It's targeting specific problems by raising the price of bad behavior. To sterilize yourself because your son or daughter will eventually drive a car is truly a case of throwing the baby out with the bathwater.

ONE MORE KID: GOOD FOR YOU, GOOD FOR THE WORLD

Self-interest and concern for others are often compatible. People who have good manners get ahead *and* make the world more pleasant. The same goes for people who have more kids. Pathological cases aside, the parents are better off, and so is the rest of the world. The kids are better off; they get the gift of life. Economic growth is faster; more people mean more ideas, the fuel of progress. Choices are more abundant; the more people there are, the more options the market offers. Retirees are better off; it's hard for the elderly to call it quits without a lot of younger workers to pick up the slack and serve the early bird specials. Contrary to doomsayers, natural resources have been getting more abundant for over a century, and air and water quality have improved for decades. Population admittedly has some bad effects on the environment, but restraining our numbers to solve them is like using a sword to kill a mosquito. Bad incentives, not people, are the fundamental environmental problem. Better incentives, not fewer people, are the fundamental solution.

I know my account sounds one-sided. When you're stuck in traffic or can't find a parking space at the mall, who isn't tempted to hiss, "If only there weren't so many people around here"? Nevertheless, the good effects of population far outweigh the bad. If there weren't a lot of people in your area, there might not *be* a mall; there might not even be a road. Idealizing the past is easy, but you wouldn't want to live in the uncrowded world of 1910. Ten years from now, you probably won't even want to return to the world of today—and no matter how much you complain about the crowds, you won't move to Hays, Kansas.

7
■ ■ ■

SELFISH GUIDELINES FOR
WANT-TO-BE GRANDPARENTS

> If I had known grandchildren were this much fun
> I would have had them first.
>
> —Unknown

YOU CAN HAVE TOO MANY CHILDREN, BUT NOT TOO MANY grandchildren. Like your kids, they're cute, they're playful, and they bring hope. Unlike your kids, you can send them home when you've had enough. It's the deal of a lifetime. Maybe that's why there are over a million Google hits for "child-free," but only a couple thousand for "grandchild-free."

The catch is that you can't make your own grandchildren. You have to rely on your kids to create the next generation while you're still young enough to enjoy it. If you're tired of waiting for your kids to give you some grandchildren to spoil, what can you do?

On the surface, grandchildren are a matter of luck: Some parents get lots, others get none. While luck plays a role, here are some tips to tilt the odds in your favor. The sooner you get started, the easier it is to make a difference—but late is better than never.

PRIVATIZING NATALISM

After natalists finish lamenting low birthrates, they usually get on a soapbox and demand that the government "do something about it." There are two big reasons why I refuse to join their chorus. First, while I agree that more kids make the world a better place, I oppose social engineering—especially for such a personal decision. When people are deciding how many children to have, government ought to mind its own business. Second, libertarian scruples aside, asking politicians to solve your problems is a waste of time. The government won't listen to you. If you want the job done right, you have to do it yourself.

The main weakness of traditional natalism is that it's scary. Once we admit that more kids are a good thing, aren't we on a slippery slope with a contraception ban at the bottom? Quite the contrary. The heart of the natalist position is that more children are good, not that government intervention is effective or morally acceptable. The value of kids and the role of government are two separate issues. Natalism can and should be privatized.

Unlike the typical government, I won't oversell the effectiveness of my advice. My first guideline for getting more grandkids demonstrably works well. The other guidelines are merely plausible hypotheses. They are difficult to scientifically test, which is probably why no one has tested them. Still, they're common sense, there's suggestive evidence in their favor, and there's not much downside. While I can't prove they're effective, I am willing to bet on them—and plan to use them myself.

GUIDELINE #1: HAVE MORE KIDS

In modern societies, the most reliable way to get a lot of grandchildren is to have a lot of children. While success is not guaranteed—one retiree I know has five grown children but only one granddaughter—research confirms the obvious. The most comprehensive study ever done looks at the entire Danish population born during 1968 and 1969. It finds that Danes with more siblings have more children. The General Social Survey confirms the same pattern in the United States: People with more brothers and sisters have more sons and daughters.

It's tempting to infer that doubling your number of children *more* than doubles your expected number of grandchildren. That's too optimistic. Fertility runs in families because of nature, not nurture, so doubling your number of children only doubles your expected number of grandchildren. Still, that's nothing to sneeze at, and there's a free bonus: Every child is an insurance policy against getting no grandkids at all. If each of your offspring has a 20 percent chance of childlessness, you can reduce your probability of grandchildlessness to 4 percent by having two kids, and 0.16 percent by having four. If you want to continue the chain letter of life, be sure to mail a lot of copies.

Of course, this strategy only works for aspiring grandparents who are still young enough to have more kids. If you start craving grandchildren at your retirement party, your window of opportunity has probably closed. If you can take advantage of this strategy, though, why not consider it?

When our parents nag us for grandchildren, their words usually fall on deaf ears. Because this book is about selfish reasons to have more kids, I won't try to make you feel guilty about ignoring their pleas. I'll just point out that by the time you reach your parents' age, you'll probably want more grandchildren, too. You should take steps to satisfy your future desire while you're still young enough to make a difference.

HOW GOVERNMENTS GOOSE THE STORK

Having more kids is not a foolproof way to get more grandkids, but it definitely tilts the odds in your favor. Unfortunately, most of us don't start thinking about grandchildren until our children grow up. If you're ready to become a grandparent, you're probably not in the market for a thirty-year plan. You want *fast-acting* ways to make your grandparental dreams come true.

At this point, it would be convenient to forget twin research. Convenient, but dishonest. Back in the "Parent's Guide to Behavioral Genetics," we explored the main twin studies of family size. All found that differences in parenting have little or no effect on children's fertility. In other words, the techniques that parents typically use to influence their children's fertility are roughly equally effective—or equally ineffective. If you want to boost your kids' fertility, you need to go off the beaten path and try an unconventional approach.

This advice is normally vacuous. Searching for effective unconventional parenting strategies is usually like searching for a needle in a haystack. But fertility is an exception. Governments often try to influence childbearing—and researchers who study their policies know some approaches that clearly work. Government preaching and nagging seem about as futile as parental preaching and nagging. When government rewards parents with money and other tangible benefits, however, storks fly.

The single most impressive experiment: In the late Eighties, Quebec began sending cash bonuses to new parents, and gradually increased these bonuses over the next decade. From May 1992 to September 1997, Quebec's parents got Can$500 for their first child, two payments of Can$500 for their second child, and twenty payments of Can$400 (Can$8,000 in total) for each additional child. The program was then abolished. The main researcher who studied Quebec's program concluded that Can $1,000 in first-year benefits—just over 700 American dollars at the time—increased the probability of having a child by 16.9 percent. Families eligible for the full Can$8,000 payment plan were 25 percent more likely to have another child. The response was much stronger for women who were married and/or over twenty-five years old.

Another research team looked at the effect of paid parental leave in Austria. Under Austrian regulations, an employee on parental leave received roughly 340 Euros per month from the government, plus the right to return to her previous job. Before July 1, 1990, a parent could take one year of official leave after the birth of a child. From July 1, 1990, until 1996, the time limit was doubled to two years. Then the limit was cut to a year and a half. Researchers took advantage of this policy seesaw to measure the effect of the 1990 experiment—and found that twelve extra Austrians were alive for every 100 women of childbearing age. Other researchers argue fairly convincingly that "family-friendly" policies—paid parental leave, subsidized child care, and so on—partly explain relatively high birth rates in Sweden and other Nordic countries.

Personally, I oppose "family-friendly" subsidies and regulations. But you don't have to support these programs to learn from them—and if you do support them, you don't have to win over public opinion to act on them. Quebec and Austria convince people to have more babies with the right incentives. So can you.

Unless you're fabulously wealthy, there's not much that you as an individual can do to raise your *nation's* birthrate. Yet there is plenty that you as an individual can do to raise your *family's* birthrate. Instead of preaching and nagging, people who want more grandkids should replicate successful natalist experiments on a smaller scale.

GUIDELINE #2: BECOME THE IN-LAWS FROM HEAVEN

Many grandparents already offer their children generous assistance. So why don't twin studies detect an effect of parenting on fertility? I could be wrong, but I see a crucial difference between the programs of Quebec or Austria and the behavior of generous, helpful grandparents: Successful natalist programs give parents *assistance without interference*. Grandparents rarely offer their children the same deal. Within the family, assistance and interference come as a package. To get grandparents' help, people have to tolerate their unwanted input. For all too many parents, that's a Faustian bargain—and the origin of expressions like "the in-laws from hell."

To run successful natalist programs at the family level, you need to defy grandparental stereotypes. Promising assistance without interference is a good start. The problem is convincing your children and their spouses that you mean business. Winning their trust won't be easy; how do they know that you won't start meddling as soon as you get your grandchildren? There's no perfect solution, but building a reputation is largely a matter of time and consistency—so you might as well start today. Your mission: Convince the next generation that you are the *in-laws from heaven*.

What are the in-laws from heaven like? My two-word slogan is *quietly useful*. Tread lightly. Don't bundle your babysitting or other assistance with unwanted advice about how to raise your grandchildren or run the household. If you don't know whether your advice is unwanted, here's a blunt but wise rule of thumb: If someone wants your advice, they will *ask* for it. Whether or not your kids and kids-in-law say this to your face, they're probably thinking it. When you were a new parent, I bet you were thinking the same thing.

The Golden Rule tells us to "Do unto others as you would have them do unto you." It's good advice, but not enough to ensure family harmony. The late economist Bernie Saffran taped a rebuttal to his office door: "Do *not* do unto others as you would have them do unto you. They may have different tastes." His point: Nice is not enough. The Golden Rule is kind, but not respectful. If you want your kids and kids-in-law to appreciate your help, treat them as *they* would like to be treated.

I understand if my advice makes you angry. If you're a family elder, maybe you feel like it's your turn to get your way. Perhaps you feel like your respect has to be earned—and your daughter-in-law hasn't earned it. If you're handing out money and babysitting, maybe you think you're entitled to a say in your grandchildren's upbringing. But even if you're completely right, being completely right won't get you more grandchildren. Your interference could be off-putting enough to keep your next grandchild from being born in the first place. With so much at stake, is it really so hard to drop the hard line?

Avoiding petty interference is one thing, but it hurts to stand idly by when you believe that your grandchildren's welfare is in danger. Just keep matters in perspective. If your grandchildren's parents are severely abusing them, don't just speak up; take action. Otherwise, think twice before intervening. Keep thoughts like "You're raising him wrong" and "You're spoiling him rotten" to yourself. Remember the central lesson of twin and adoption research: Even if your kids are moderately bad parents, your grandchildren will probably still turn out fine. Before you speak up, ask yourself: Would adoption agencies consider your grandkids' parents fit to adopt? If so, correcting their deviations from your ideal of parenting is imprudent. The parents probably won't listen, they certainly won't like it, and they might feel too stressed to give you another grandchild.

GUIDELINE #3: TACTFULLY REWARD YOUR KIDS FOR EACH GRANDCHILD

For the sake of argument, suppose you're comfortable with the idea of spending money to get more grandchildren. As Troy McClure, *The Simpsons'* hammy documentary narrator, might say, "So, you've decided to design your own natalist program." How should you proceed? If you show up at your children's homes and ask them to name their price, they'll probably think you're crazy. In the best-case scenario, they'll interpret your offer as: In exchange for your support, they agree to endure your . . . eccentricities.

To get the most bang for your buck takes more tact. Don't suddenly offer explicit bribes. Build a solid reputation for hands-off helpfulness before any grandchildren come along. After laying that foundation, casually communicate that you've only shown them the tip of the iceberg. If and when grandchildren come along, you'll happily step up your contribution.

One serious snag to worry about: Even in a loving family, it's hard to convince others that your help comes with no strings attached. Perhaps this is why government checks so clearly affect childbearing. People know that no matter how many checks they cash, the government won't pop in to critique their parenting.

For trust issues like this, actions speak louder than words. If you're ready to help financially, the best way to prove that there are no strings attached is to make one-shot gifts. No matter what you say, a monthly check feels contingent. It's more convincing to celebrate the birth of each new baby with an early inheritance—and the suave excuse, "This will all be yours eventually, anyway." True, you're giving up control, but as computer geeks say, "That's a feature, not a bug." Grandparents' money talks louder when they surrender control. Or to be more precise, when you surrender control over your grandchildren's upbringing, you get *extra* control over a more important outcome: their number.

You don't have to be Bill Gates to strategically design wills, trusts, and one-shot gifts. A middle-class income is more than enough. Compared to the out-of-pocket cost of raising a child to adulthood, the baby bonuses in Quebec and Austria were small. They worked anyway. Since most people intrinsically desire children, modest incentives are often enough to convince them to have an extra baby.

You don't need to openly tell your children that their inheritance partly depends on how many grandchildren they give you. Don't hurt anyone's feelings. Just give generously to your children each and every time they enlarge your family. Then write a will that gives each of your children equal shares of whatever's left.

Another diplomatic way to reward fertility is to set up trusts for your grandchildren—and make your children the trustees. The parents will eventually use the trust to pay for expenses like college that otherwise would have come out of their own pockets. You're effectively giving more to the children who gave more to you. Yet officially, you're treating your children equally.

Can natalist incentives work too well? No matter how impatient you are for grandchildren, you probably don't want your kids to drop out of high school or college to have a baby—and you almost certainly wouldn't want to encourage it. In practice, fortunately, you needn't worry. The Quebec experiment found little or no effect of baby bonuses on young and unmarried women; it was older and married women who had the extra kids. Young, single women tend to get pregnant by mistake, so modest prizes aren't enough to change their minds. Older, married women, in contrast, are already interested in kids, so a little money is often all it takes to sway them. If you're still nervous about bad incentives, make it clear that you only reward parents for responsible pregnancies. If you think it unfair to penalize a grandchild for his parents' mistakes, take the money you would have given his parents under ideal circumstances and hold it in trust on your grandchild's behalf.

One last thought: Retirees are often much wealthier than they see themselves. If you own your home outright, you're semi-rich—and if you think you can't spend a house, you're mistaken. Almost any bank will let you cash out some of its value with a home equity loan. Some sell reverse mortgages—you sign your home over to the bank in exchange for a monthly check and free rent. Look before you leap into unfamiliar financial strategies, but keep an open mind. What's better—the abstract knowledge that you've paid off your mortgage or the concrete fact that you have a new grandchild to spoil?

SELFISH SAINTS

> Man has almost constant occasion for the help of his brethren, and it is in vain for him to expect it from their benevolence only. He will be more likely to prevail if he can interest their self-love in his favour, and show them that it is for their own advantage to do for him what he requires of them . . . It is not from the benevolence of the butcher, the brewer, or the baker, that we expect our dinner, but from their regard to their own interest.
>
> —Adam Smith, *The Wealth of Nations*

We usually picture selfish people as pushy, inconsiderate, loud, mean, and miserly. Want-to-be grandparents who follow my selfish guidelines are none of above. They're practically saints. How can I begin by condoning selfishness and end by recommending respect, tact, and generosity?

My answer: Pushy, inconsiderate, loud, mean, and miserly people are *bad at being selfish*. While they're acting on selfish impulses, they fail to carefully weigh how other people will respond to their behavior. They're like restaurants with bad food and bad service. Once word gets around, no one wants anything to do with them.

Grandparents' main problem, though, isn't that they're bad at being selfish, but *bad at being nice*. When grandparents tell their children how to raise their kids, they're trying to help. Where do they go wrong? By acting on their *un*selfish impulses, instead of carefully weighing how other people will respond. As a result, they provoke ill will despite their helpful intentions. And for what? The long-run effect of grandparenting has to be even weaker than the long-run effect of parenting.

In the end, Selfish Guidelines for Want-to-Be Grandparents look a lot like *Un*selfish Guidelines for Want-to-Be Grandparents. The crucial factor is foresight, not intentions. Without foresight, you'll either be a selfish jerk or an unselfish annoyance. Either way, you'll antagonize your kids and kids-in-law. With foresight, you will show respect, tact, and generosity even if, deep down, it's all about you. Playing the in-law from heaven paves the way for your grandchildren to enter the world. When you see the face of your next grandchild, you'll be glad you did the right thing.

8
...

LIFE-GIVING SCIENCE: WHAT IT MEANS FOR YOU

> My son is now sixteen years old . . . The boy is beyond smart. I'm quite sure he's way beyond genius. It was never my intention to "cultivate" this particular aspect of his existence—I was happy simply to have my own and only child, however he or she would turn out.
>
> Nor does it particularly matter to me now that he's in line for valedictorian, has a vast knowledge of computers, technology, international finance, geopolitics, and other subjects he's grown interested in entirely on his own . . .
>
> Did I do anything wrong or immoral? I don't think so.
> —Anonymous mother of a "Nobel sperm bank" baby

THE CLASSIC SOLUTION TO INFERTILITY IS TO FIND SOMEONE ELSE to be fertile with. Since antiquity, inability to sire or bear a child has been a major cause of divorce, adultery, and polygamy. In the Bible, Abraham's "barren" wife, Sarah, urges him to marry Hagar to continue his family line. Henry VIII changed the religion of England because his wife couldn't give him a son and the pope wouldn't give him an annulment.

Despite its pedigree, the classic solution to infertility leaves much to be desired. For the fertile, it is a bad solution. You have to sacrifice your partner to become a parent. For the infertile, it is no solution at all. The breakup leaves you not just childless, but alone. Luckily, there is now a better way. New life-giving technology allows many of us to beat infertility. Millions have children—and millions are alive today—because scientists figured out how to improve on Mother Nature.

When Apple first announced the iPhone, the world was thrilled. My colleague Russ Roberts named it "the most beautiful toy yet" and enthused, "Apple hits a home run. No, a grand slam. Actually, a five-run homer, the kind you're not supposed to try to hit." Two months after the iPhone's release, however, users were out for blood. Apple's crime: cutting the price by $200. This is how we normally greet progress—an exciting honeymoon, followed by constant ingratitude.

For reproductive progress, strangely, our reactions reverse: We skip the honeymoon but gradually learn to love it. New advances initially horrify both public and pundits. The public shakes its head; pundits split hairs to prove that the latest technology is an unprecedented affront to human dignity. Governments often answer their repugnance with regulation and bans. Yet before long, entrepreneurs dig a bunch of loopholes, and a new market blossoms. A decade or two later, public and pundits forget they ever objected—yet consumers of the once "repugnant" services feel grateful every time their miracle children blow out the candles on another birthday cake.

Critics often belittle the users of new reproductive technology as narcissistic or selfish. But why is a person who turns to science any more selfish than someone who gets pregnant the old-fashioned way? Still, the critics accidentally make a useful point: Selfishly speaking, reproductive technology makes it easier to get the children we want. Kids who would have been too costly to have in 1950 are often a good deal today. Technological progress is another selfish reason to have more kids.

When I hail these benefits for parents, critics often accuse me of moral blindness. How can I neglect the welfare of the *children* created by artificial means? But I'm not "neglecting" children's welfare. I just find it painfully obvious that *being alive is good for them*. While we can imagine lives so awful that they aren't worth living, being a miracle baby is hardly hell on earth.

Yes, the child of assisted reproductive technology probably carries a little extra emotional baggage. When single women conceive via artificial insemination, their children often wonder why they don't have a dad. When children born from donor eggs grow up, some yearn to find their biological mothers. Still, these drawbacks are dwarfed by the gift of life. Who would seriously say, "I was raised by a single mom; I wish I was never born," or "Unless I find my real dad, my life won't be worth living"?

In *Jurassic Park*, Jeff Goldblum's character protests the resurrection of the dinosaurs. The project is arrogant and reckless: "Your scientists were so preoccupied with whether or not they could, they didn't stop to think if they should." When we hear about new reproductive technology, most of us share his unease. I say that instead of assuming the worst, we should take Goldblum's advice literally. Let's find out what science can do for parents, then "stop to think" how we should respond.

USING TECHNOLOGY TO GET MORE KIDS

In the United States, one cycle of in vitro fertilization costs about $12,000—and that's when the mother uses her own egg and carries her own baby. It sounds expensive, yet it's infinitely cheaper than it used to be. In 1970, in vitro was beyond the reach of billionaires, for the technology did not exist. The surprising lesson is that innovation *reduces* the true price of babies by turning what money can't buy into what money can buy.

The smart response is to check whether the price has fallen far enough to make another kid a good deal for you. For some technologies—like fertility drugs—weighing costs and benefits is simple: Do they improve your chances of conception enough to outweigh the effort and expense? The pros and cons of other technologies, however, are more complex, so let's take a quick tour of what's available now—and what's next. If the help you seek is outside your price range, don't despair. The world gets better all the time. Most of the products we take for granted—meat, cars, air-conditioning, computers, cell phones, you name it—were once luxuries. In ten years, you too might enjoy the reproductive choices that the rich already take for granted.

ARTIFICIAL INSEMINATION (AI)

Doctors have used AI to overcome male fertility problems for over a century. In 1987, the Office of Technology Assessment estimated that thanks to AI, 65,000 babies—35,000 from their mother's husband's sperm, the rest from donor sperm—were born in the United States during the previous twelve months. The government hasn't collected numbers since, but there are two big reasons to think that so-called baster babies are more common than ever. First, medical norms against selling AI to unmarried women and lesbians are all but dead. Second, the out-of-pocket cost dropped from about $1,000 in 1987 to $400 today. Counting inflation, that's almost 80 percent less.

The obvious selfish benefit of AI: It helps men overcome *biological* obstacles to fatherhood. If their sperm is viable but has trouble reaching the egg, AI makes conception much more likely. The subtler selfish benefit: It helps women overcome *social* obstacles to motherhood. Women married to infertile men don't have to resort to divorce or adultery. Unmarried women don't have to find a suitable father. Lesbians don't have to find a man at all. If any of these conditions were deal breakers for you, AI is a compelling reason to sign your name on the dotted line.

IN VITRO FERTILIZATION (IVF)

Louise Brown, the world's first test-tube baby, was born in 1978. Since then, this revolutionary solution to male and female infertility has exploded. Specialists know how to create an embryo in a petri dish, freeze it for years, implant it in any functioning uterus, and get a healthy baby. According to the latest report from the Centers for Disease Control, the number of babies born in the United States using IVF and similar techniques rose from about 21,000 in 1996 to almost 55,000 in 2006. During this decade, success rates per cycle steadily rose from 22 percent to 30 percent. For about twice the regular price, some clinics give money-back guarantees—if you don't get a baby, you don't pay. Partly thanks to regulations and lawsuits, the price in the First World remains high, but low-cost IVF clinics are springing up in poorer countries. Doctors in

Africa—where 10–30 percent of women are infertile—already offer "no-frills" IVF for about $300 a cycle.

Biologically, IVF is much more versatile than AI. It treats both male and female infertility and works for men with low-quality sperm. IVF also allows you to have kids on your own terms. You can reproduce with the person you love—or go solo using donor sperm. If you're a woman who wants to delay childbearing, you can do the first stages of IVF, freeze the embryos, and implant them years later when you feel ready. With an egg donor, the process allows post-menopausal pregnancy. IVF does not eliminate the trade-offs that parents face, but it does make their trade-offs more flexible.

Another perceived benefit, at least for some women, is the high rate of twins. If you implant more than one embryo, you stand a good chance of completing your family with a single pregnancy. The downside is that multiples are less healthy due to prematurity and low birth weight. "Octomom" Nadya Suleman's heaviest baby weighed three pounds, one ounce. Her last octuplet to come home spent almost three months in the hospital. And statistically speaking, the Sulemans were lucky. Multiples have much higher infant mortality rates than singletons: Five times higher for twins, ten times higher for triplets, eighteen times higher for quads.

As a father of twins, I feel like I dodged a bullet. Yet the numbers aren't as bad as they sound. A twin born today is about as safe as the average baby born in 1950. A quadruplet born today is over 50 percent safer than the average baby born in 1900. When Alfred Khoury, a doctor at a high-risk maternity ward, warns, "If Nature thought it was appropriate for homo sapiens to have litters, Nature would not have selected against it," he lacks historical perspective. Nature now selects against quads less brutally than it used to select against every child born.

In any case, IVF is moving away from octomoms. Parents are responding to higher success rates by implanting fewer embryos. Between 1996 and 2006, the fraction of successful cycles that ended in triplets or more fell from 7 percent to 2 percent. In a decade or two, we will probably remember "litters" of underweight babies only as a symptom of how primitive IVF once was.

SURROGACY

Surrogacy contracts have radically changed during the last two decades. The original idea was for a fertile man and his infertile partner to hire another woman to impregnate using AI. After the baby's birth, the surrogate would give her biological child to his biological father and partner to raise.

Modern contracts usually cut surrogates out of the genetic loop. Ninety-five percent of surrogates now get pregnant using IVF. Customers prefer a division of labor: The egg donor and the baby carrier are typically two different women. Most women who hire a surrogate prefer to donate the egg themselves, so kids born to surrogates today are often the biological children of *both* of the parents who rear them.

If you're lucky, a relative, friend, or random benefactor will agree to carry your baby for free. If you're not so lucky—or don't want to impose—you'll need a commercial surrogate. They're pretty expensive. In the United States, the all-inclusive cost of a surrogate pregnancy—IVF, the surrogate's fee, medical expenses, miscellaneous—is about $75,000. If you already plan to use IVF, the upcharge for a surrogate is about $20,000. Sticker shock is understandable, but you don't have to pay cash. If you were hiring a contractor, you'd probably borrow against your home. You might finance your surrogate pregnancy the same way. Surrogates aren't for everyone. But it is in your own best interest to weigh the option with an open mind.

After warming up to the idea of surrogacy, one naturally wonders, "Is there a cheaper way?" Yes. It's called "fertility tourism." The booming economy of India has quickly become the market leader. Quality is high, and prices are roughly one-third the U.S. level. The all-inclusive surrogacy package that costs $75,000 in the United States runs you about $20,000 in India. As fertility tourism evolves—and more low-income countries enter the market—deals will probably keep getting better.

There are plenty of good reasons not to outsource your pregnancy to India, but don't let guilt keep you away. By Indian standards, surrogates are very well paid. Your patronage gives them—and their children—a far better life. A profile of a typical surrogate in Delhi:

Separated from her husband, she found that her monthly wages of 2,800 rupees, about $69, as a midwife were not enough to raise her 9-year-old son. With the money she earned from the first surrogacy, more than $13,600, she bought a house. She expects to pay for her son's education with what she earns for the second, about $8,600 . . . "I will save the money for my child's future," she said.

Third World poverty is heartbreaking, but use your head: Fertility tourists are part of the solution, not the problem.

Selfishly speaking, surrogacy is more than another fertility treatment. It's practically magic: Women no longer have to choose between pregnancy and childlessness. And while many women treasure their pregnancies, the experience definitely gets mixed reviews. If you love kids but dread pregnancy, surrogacy is a historic opportunity to painlessly create life.

ARTIFICIAL WOMBS?

Fertility tourism has a bright future for the next couple of decades. But how many surrogates will be on the market after countries like India join the developed world? In fifty years, perhaps our daughters will tell our granddaughters, "Back in my day, we outsourced our pregnancies to India," and the granddaughters will impatiently reply, "Mom, outsourcing just isn't affordable anymore."

Surrogacy is an amazing advance, but it merely redistributes pregnancy. The long-term solution for women who see pregnancy as a burden is the creation—and mass production—of artificial wombs. Science fiction? Imagine people's skepticism in 1950 if you told them that they would see the day when one woman would give birth to another's child.

Artificial womb research remains a tiny field, but early experiments are promising. In the late Nineties, Japanese researchers managed to keep premature goat fetuses alive for weeks in an artificial womb. Much more impressive results came a few years later, when Hung-Ching Liu, director of Cornell University's Reproductive Endocrine Laboratory, successfully implanted human embryos in an artificial womb. Embryos grew for up to ten days; then Liu pulled the plug on the experiment to comply with federal regulations. Next, she switched to mouse embryos—and almost got one to term.

Law and outrage have made it hard to extend Liu's research, but science has repeatedly overcome law and outrage before. The artificial womb probably won't make it any easier for you to have another child but might make it easier for you to have another grandchild. Stay tuned.

USING TECHNOLOGY TO GET DIFFERENT KIDS

> Mother after mother said the same thing to me: she had picked the Repository because it was the only place that let her select what she wanted.
>
> —David Plotz, *The Genius Factory: The Curious History of the Nobel Prize Sperm Bank*

The great paradox of parenting is that we yearn to change the people we unconditionally love. Accepting our kids as they are is easier said than done. Deep down, most of us prefer to unconditionally love a certain kind of child. I'd love my sons even if they were jocks, but I want them to be nerds like me.

Today's Typical Parents cope by trying to remold the kid they've got into the kid they want. Yet twin and adoption research leaves little hope for this orthodox approach. If you want to change your kids, you'd better start before conception. The low-tech method is as old as humanity itself: mate selection. Choose a partner who has the traits you want to see in your kids. Heredity is no guarantee, but it's a mighty force of nature.

Alas, this mighty force is sometimes your enemy. What if you've got a genetic disease that you *don't* want to pass on? Heredity is also unreliable: Your child can inherit Tay-Sachs or sickle-cell anemia even if you and your partner show no symptoms. Or what if you long for a baby girl? Sex ratio doesn't run in families, so picking a partner with lots of sisters and no brothers won't change your chances.

For most of human history, we had to play the genetic lottery or remain childless. Yet in recent decades, scientists have discovered new ways to rig the lottery in our favor. As they learn how to give us children, they also learn how to give us children with—or without— specific traits. These high-tech advances are another selfish reason to have more children: If you're not quite ready to take your chances on one more kid, a little extra control over the type of kid you get should change your mind.

Once again, it's tempting to object, "Never mind the parents. What about the welfare of the children?" But trait selection is better for kids, too. Compatibility is a two-way street: When parents get kids they really want, kids get parents who really want them. More important, trait selection reassures parents—which leads them to be more generous with the gift of life. Parents who want this control might seem depraved, but don't be so quick to condemn them. If it's okay to rig the genetic lottery by marrying Mr. Right, why is it wrong to rig the genetic lottery by visiting Dr. Know? If it's okay to refuse to have *any* children, why is it wrong to refuse to have children of a certain kind?

In practice, people object most stridently to the *idea* of trait selection. They're more open to specific practices. If two Tay-Sachs carriers use genetic screening to ensure a healthy baby, few call them monsters. Such cases are so compelling that most critics retreat to the slippery slope argument. So let's look at specifics and see where the slippery slope leads.

GENETIC SCREENING

The simplest innovation is trait selection: Before you start a family with someone, peek at each others' genes, then decide whether to move forward. In the future, these genetic tests might be packed with details, but for now they're mainly used to avoid hereditary diseases. If you and your partner both carry genes for Tay-Sachs, sickle-cell anemia, or cystic fibrosis, one in four of your children will have the disorder. If you don't like those odds, the low-tech solution is to find another partner.

Fortunately for romantics, there are two high-tech alternatives to seeing other people. The first is prenatal testing: Get pregnant, then test the fetus. The disturbing drawback is that when prenatal tests detect a problem, abortion is usually the only recourse. The second alternative is preimplantation genetic diagnosis. As long as you're already using IVF, doctors can look at your embryos' genes before they decide which—if any—embryos to implant. If you don't want your children to have sickle-cell anemia, keep affected embryos away from your womb. The same goes for gender: If you want a girl, implant only female embryos.

For parents, the selfish advantages of high-tech genetic screening are plain. No one wants their children to be born with a terminal illness. The thought is enough to scare high-risk parents into childlessness. Technological reassurance makes parents better off—and entices them to create life that otherwise would not have seen the light of day.

ARTIFICIAL INSEMINATION AND EGG DONATION

Mate selection is the classic way to get the kids you want, but has one big limitation: The people with the traits you want your kids to have might not want to have kids with you. Donor sperm and eggs vastly expand your options. Only a handful of women can marry Nobel Prize winners, but in the Eighties and Nineties, Robert Graham's "Nobel sperm bank" made it possible for any fertile woman to bear their children. His bank closed in 1999, but the vibrant industry Graham inspired now lets every woman pick a well-educated, healthy, handsome father for her children. The out-of-pocket cost is barely worth mentioning. The Fairfax Cryobank will inseminate you for $355, with a $100 upcharge for PhD sperm. If you want the donor's personality test results, you pay another $19; for a childhood picture, add $16.

Donor eggs are far more expensive. If you use a traditional agency, expect to pay your egg donor $5,000–$10,000. In the eyes of these agencies, anything more is "unethical." Other firms scoff at this informal price ceiling. Elite Donors' wealthy clients typically pay ten times as much. As I write, they're offering $75,000 for a "very attractive" donor of "proven intelligence"—ideally an Ivy League graduate, though 1350 on your SATs keeps you in the running.

Sperm and egg markets aren't on the radar of most fertile couples. They want kids with each other, not impressive strangers. If you're already open to sperm or egg donation, however, the bustling marketplace has much to offer. While you probably can't afford to give your kids your ideal biological mother, you can already give them your ideal biological father for the price of an iPhone.

SPERM SORTATION

Several moms I know don't want another kid because—their words—"It might be a boy." While they'd like a daughter, they dread the prospect of another wild son rampaging through the house. As a boy, I could take offense, but I'd rather introduce moms to an easy, affordable way to get what they want: sperm sortation.

Sperm sortation is AI with a twist. Before implantation, doctors use a process called flow cytometry to segregate "boy sperm" and "girl sperm." If you want a boy, sperm sortation boosts your odds to 75 percent; if you want a girl, to 90 percent. Compared to IVF, it's cheap—about $3,000 per cycle at top U.S. clinics. If you don't care about your child's gender, save your money. But if you dream of playing football with your son or shopping for a wedding dress with your daughter, sperm sortation is an affordable way to make your dream much more likely to come true.

GENETIC ENGINEERING (GE)?

Twin and adoption studies show that genes affect almost every item on the Parental Wish List. Specialists can already look at embryos' genes in order to decide which ones to implant. Only one last obstacle stands between us and so-called "designer babies": figuring out *which* genes matter for each wish. Solid answers may be decades away, but human genetic engineering requires no more scientific breakthroughs—just persistence. The first customers will be wealthy eccentrics, but in a few decades, GE will be affordable and normal. Without strict government prohibition, I predict that our descendants will be amazingly smart, healthy, and accomplished.

Most people find my prediction frightening. Some paint GE as a pointless arms race; it's individually tempting, but society is better off without it. Others object that GE would increase inequality; the rich will buy alpha babies, and the rest of us will be stuck with betas. But there's something fishy about these complaints: If better *nurture* created a generation of wonder kids, we would rejoice. Suppose you naturally conceived an amazingly smart, healthy, and accomplished child. Would it bother you? If your neighbors had such a child, would you forbid your children to play with him? If your neighborhood were full of wonder kids, would you move away?

On my office wall, I have a picture of my dad at his high school graduation, towering a foot above his grandparents. Such height differences were common at the time because childhood nutrition improved so rapidly. I doubt that the grandparents who attended that graduation saw height as an "arms race" or griped that rich kids were even taller. They were happy to look up to their descendants—and we'd feel the same way. Deep down, even technophobes want their descendants to surpass them. They just think that picking embryos is a vile way to make it happen.

Moderate defenders of genetic engineering often distinguish between good GE that prevents disease and disability, and bad GE that increases intelligence, beauty, athletic ability, or determination. The theory is that good GE helps kids lead better lives, but bad GE merely panders to parents' vanity. The logic is hard to see. We praise parents who nurture their kids' health, intelligence, beauty, athletic ability, or determination because we know they're *all* good traits for kids to have.

In the wrong hands, GE could admittedly do great damage. A totalitarian government could use GE to root out individuality and dissent. But if government abuse is the real danger, the smart line to draw in the sand isn't government prohibition. It's reproductive freedom. Insist that parents, not governments, decide if, when, and how to make babies.

The selfish advantages of GE are obvious. Parents have wishes; GE is a genie that grants them. Would you want to live in such a world? Consider the kinds of wishes most parents share: Health, intelligence, happiness, success, character, appreciation. Who doesn't hope that the future holds more of these? If you fear a gray uniformity, remember that most parents also yearn to transmit their controversial values to the next generation. As long as parents have reproductive freedom, then, GE will help *preserve* diversity of religion, politics, tradition, and interests. Our descendants will be more impressive and fortunate than us, but they'll still disagree on the Big Questions and the Good Life.

THE CASE OF CLONING

> Should we not assert as a principle that any so-called great man who did consent to be cloned should on that basis be disqualified, as possessing too high an opinion of himself and of his genes? Can we stand an increase in arrogance?
>
> —Leon Kass, "Making Babies—the New Biology and the 'Old' Morality"

If reproductive progress is so great, why not allow human cloning? Over 85 percent of Americans—and 100 percent of George W. Bush's Council on Bioethics—favor a ban. But frankly, laymen and experts need to be more open-minded. Reproductive advances almost always disgust us—until we see the life and hope they bring.

If you think clones are contrary to nature, think twice. Identical twins are naturally occurring clones—two humans who have all their genes in common. Since clones already walk among us, we don't have to idly philosophize about the psychological and social dangers of cloning. We can look—and see that cloning's opponents don't know what they're talking about. The Council on Bioethics warns, "A cloned child . . . is at risk of living out a life overshadowed in important ways by the life of the 'original.'" Yet identical twins rarely agonize over their supposed lack of individuality. Instead, they feel grateful for their special bond. When people ask how my identical twin sons get along, I answer, "I've never seen anything like it. They are literally 'brotherly.'"

Unlike most opponents of cloning, at least the Council on Bioethics *tries* to explain why cloning is worse than twinning:

> Identical twins . . . are born together, before either one has developed and shown what his or her potential—natural or otherwise—may be. Each is largely free of the burden of measuring up to or even knowing in advance the genetic traits of the other . . . But a clone is a genetic near-copy of a person who is already living or has already lived . . . Everything about the predecessor . . . will appear before the expectant eyes of the cloned person, always with at least the nagging concern that there, notwithstanding the grace of God, go I.

Even if this were true, life with a mild inferiority complex remains much better than no life at all. But the council's "measuring up" argument actually shows that clones have a *lighter* cross to bear than twins. Suppose two identical twins grow up together. If one is less successful than the other, what's his excuse? With the same genes, upbringing, place, and time, personal responsibility is almost inescapable. An underachieving clone, in contrast, can always plausibly tell his predecessor, "I grew up in a totally different era; the rules changed; the world doesn't work the way it did when you were my age."

You could say that human cloning is so far in the future that self-ishly speaking, we might as well ignore it. I'm more optimistic. Look at how far IVF has come over the last four decades. In twenty years, cloning might be a great option for infertile women in their forties and fifties. Even if it takes centuries to perfect the process, though, the *idea* of cloning challenges our prejudices. If it is good to create human life, why is it bad to create it in an unfamiliar way?

BETTER LIVING THROUGH BIOLOGY

When my wife and I told the world that we were expecting twins, the standard reaction was, "Oh, did you use fertility treatments?" Total strangers weren't afraid to ask. I was surprised but took no offense. The nosy questions helped me appreciate the full value of applied reproductive science. It has given life to millions of children, and children to millions of parents—and undermined the age-old stigma of infertility in its spare time.

We can't yet make everyone fertile, or every child healthy, but we're getting there. You'd think the whole world would be celebrating the triumphs of life-giving science and adding, "The best is yet to come." We're not. People whose lives have been touched by advances in reproductive technology are grateful, but bystanders keep looking the gift horse in the mouth: "It's touching to see new parents holding a 'miracle baby' in their arms, but what about the broader consequences? What about the welfare of the children, the threat to our humanity, the exploitation of surrogates, the com-modification of life?"

But the broader consequences of scientific progress do not take away from its glory. They add to it. Here is the quick and dirty case for past, present, and future advances in reproductive technology:

1. *It is good to exist.* The clearest beneficiary of any life-giving technology is the child himself, who will almost certainly be glad to be alive. Aren't you? Miracle babies have no reason to love their lives any less.

2. *Trade is mutually beneficial.* Sperm donors, egg donors, and surrogates are not victims. They are consenting adults who help others for a mixture of meaning and profit, just like doctors, teachers, engineers, and chefs. Low-income donors and surrogates aren't "exploited." By their standards, they have great jobs that let them build better lives for themselves and their families.

3. *Third parties gain, too.* In the long run, higher population makes us richer, not poorer. In the words of Julian Simon, human minds are "the ultimate resource." Progress depends on new ideas, and new ideas come from people. Yes, it's *conceivable* that a baby will grow up to be the next Hitler. The very existence of civilization shows, however, that the average baby grows up to be a creator, not a destroyer.

Like Jeff Goldblum in *Jurassic Park*, the opponents of reproductive technology are quick to call others arrogant and reckless. They should look in the mirror. Their stubborn search for dark linings in every silver cloud reeks of arrogance. Who are they to grumble against technologies to which millions of families owe their children—and millions of children owe their lives? But the opponents' intolerance is even worse than their pessimism. They don't want to persuade others to avoid "unnatural" technologies. They want to turn their flimsy complaints into worldwide bans. Since they would rather be childless than resort to AI, IVF, surrogacy, or cloning, everyone on earth should be forced to make the same choice. If that isn't reckless and arrogant, what is?

9

BE FRUITFUL AND MULTIPLY:
FOUR CHATS ON KIDS, PARENTING,
HAPPINESS, AND SELF-INTEREST

> Excepting suicide, the most serious decision in life
> should be to have a child; however, not to have a
> child, if one is capable of having children, should
> perhaps be an even more serious decision.
> —Thomas Szasz, *The Untamed Tongue*

THE BEST WAY TO UNDERSTAND A POSITION IS TO ARGUE ON ITS
behalf. You learn as you speak. Sometimes you find that objections
are stronger than you realized; other times you discover that they're
weaker than they looked. You may end up abandoning the position—
or improving it and returning to the fray. Critics don't just keep you
honest; they show you the light.

Now that you've heard my main arguments, it's time to wrestle
with some critics. The following exchanges are admittedly staged.
I'm the only real character; the rest are composites. But each repre-
sents a popular reaction to my position, and all the arguments are
drawn from life.

THE CAST

BRYAN.............................*Mr. "Selfish Reasons to Have More Kids"*
Number of Kids: 3

BECKY.........................*Single career woman and my toughest critic*
Number of Kids: 0

STEVE...*Frazzled dad*
Number of Kids: 1

CHRISTINE...*Semi-sympathetic mom*
Number of Kids: 2

IVAN..*Skeptical social scientist*
Number of Kids: 0

MARY...*Supermom*
Number of Kids: 5

CHAT #1: HOW CAN YOU THINK THAT PARENTS DON'T MATTER?

BRYAN: So what do you think about my key premise: A lot of parental unhappiness is unnecessary because a lot of parental "investment" doesn't pay?

CHRISTINE: I see your point, but aren't you exaggerating? Genes definitely make a difference—some kids are tougher to raise than others. That doesn't mean that parents shouldn't try to promote all that stuff on your "Parental Wish List."

BRYAN: Health, intelligence, happiness, success, character, values, and appreciation.

CHRISTINE: Yeah. Are you saying that parents shouldn't tell their kids to brush their teeth, eat their dinner, and go to school?

IVAN: Good question. To be blunt, I think that Bryan's survey of twin and adoption research verges on irresponsible. There is *lots* of evidence that environment matters. He should objectively summarize instead of cherry-picking.

BRYAN: Hold on, Ivan. My review of the twin and adoption evidence comes with a loud and clear warning: What you find depends on where you look. Almost all twin and adoption studies are set in developed countries. Families that adopt are usually middle class, and always want children. It would be irresponsible to read these studies, then tell the world that child abuse does no lasting damage or that your child will turn out equally well if he grows up in the Third World. But I say no such thing. I'm more than willing to believe that horrible families cause sickness, stupidity, unhappiness, failure, and vice.

CHRISTINE: So what exactly are you saying?

BRYAN: That the child-rearing strategies that parents frequently use in countries like the United States, Sweden, and Australia end up producing surprisingly similar adults. I'm not talking about freakish parents who never tell their kids to brush their teeth, eat their dinner, or go to school.

IVAN: So as long as the typical adoption agency would consider you a fit parent, the details don't matter?

BRYAN: Basically. Parenting has a pretty big effect on how much your kids appreciate you. That's important to me—and I bet most parents feel the same way. Parents also have a few large, superficial effects. They powerfully influence their kids' religious affiliation and political party—but not their deeper religious and political orientation.

CHRISTINE: What else?

BRYAN: Many studies also find small parental effects for other items on the Parental Wish List, though plenty find no effect at all. But even if pushy parenting makes a slight difference, it's not worth it. Your chance of transforming your child's adult health, intelligence, happiness, success, character, or values is slim. Your chance of hurting how your child feels about you—his appreciation—is very real.

IVAN: If that's your view, then I still say that your presentation is irresponsible. Who cares if there's a range over which parental differences don't matter much? Most of the world falls well below those standards. If international development experts took you seriously . . .

BRYAN: That's why I've clearly labeled this a book about parenting, not a book about international development. I don't tell international development experts that they're fearmongering when they advise people in the Third World to boil their water. Why should they object when I tell parents in the First World to cut themselves some slack?

CHRISTINE: Is it possible that you put too much stock in twin and adoption research because you happen to be the father of identical twins?

BRYAN: Personal experience did affect my views, but not the way you suggest. I was interested in twin and adoption research years before I became a dad. Raising twins didn't change my confidence in the science; my sons were about as alike as the research predicted. But having kids made me appreciate the *practical relevance* of behavioral genetics. The point of medical research is to help doctors. Shouldn't the point of twin and adoption research be to help parents?

CHRISTINE: I've never actually read one of these studies. I honestly don't know enough about statistics to judge their trustworthiness. When they go against common sense, isn't that a big strike against them?

IVAN: I'm with Bryan here. You can't rely on common sense, Christine. Common sense tells us that the earth is flat.

BRYAN: Hold on, Ivan—I'm with Christine. If a study you don't understand contradicts your firsthand experience, it's reasonable to doubt the study. My position is that twin and adoption studies are in harmony with common sense.

CHRISTINE: Your version of common sense must differ from mine. My common sense tells me that parenting matters a lot.

BRYAN: Mine tells me that parenting matters a lot *in the short run*. If I put my kids in the naughty corner for fighting, I can usually count on an hour or two of peace—not a lifetime. That's common

sense, too—and when twin and adoption studies distinguish between short- and long-run effects, that's what they find.

CHRISTINE: I like to believe that if I nag my kids enough when they're
young, my lessons will stick.

BRYAN: There are times when I'd like to believe that, too. If common
sense tells us anything, though, it's that the truth and what we'd
like to believe are often very different. Twin and adoption research shows that kids aren't like clay that parents mold for life.
They're more like flexible plastic that responds to pressure but
pops back into shape when the pressure goes away.

CHRISTINE: So even when I see I've made a difference, I should expect
it to wear off? How depressing.

BRYAN: Not necessarily. I find it liberating to accept that my sons will
grow up to be their own men and make their own choices.
They'll all probably be successful in their own ways. Now that I
know that their future is largely out of my hands, I feel like we
can relax and enjoy our journey together.

BECKY: Let's back up. You're both giving Bryan too much credit. All of
his so-called genetic effects have environmental explanations.
Identical twins are more alike than fraternal twins because their
parents and other people treat them more alike. Adoptees do
worse because parents favor their biological children. Haven't
you seen *Cinderella*?

BRYAN: I agree that these objections are worth pursuing—and I'm
pleased to report that they've already been pursued.

BECKY: [sarcastically] Really.

BRYAN: [enthusiastically] Yes, really! Researchers have checked
whether twins are more similar in intelligence or personality
when their appearance or childhood environments were more
similar. With a few exceptions, they aren't. They've also taken advantage of the fact that families occasionally have false beliefs
about what kind of twins they've got. If similarity of treatment
caused resemblance, then identical twins who falsely believe
they're fraternal should be less similar. They're not.

BECKY: What about adoptees?

BRYAN: Your Cinderella story has two big problems. First, parents
invest at least as much in their adopted children as they do in

their biological children. One study of families with both kinds of children found that parents give their adoptees *more* educational and financial assistance.

BECKY: All right, the Cinderella reference was overly harsh.

BRYAN: But there's a deeper problem. For the sake of argument, suppose parents affect success, and parents treat adopted children worse than biological children. We would naturally expect adopted children to be less successful. Still, it's a lot better to be adopted by a rich, well-educated family, right?

BECKY: Obviously.

BRYAN: That's not what adoption studies find. In practice, kids adopted by more successful families do about as well as kids adopted by less successful families. Your story can't explain this. Mine can.

CHAT #2: KIDS AND HAPPINESS

STEVE: Can we come back to "enjoying the journey"? It sounds terrible, but I can't honestly say that I enjoy being a dad. I'm exhausted. If I were totally selfish, I never would have had kids. Now that I know what's involved, I'm too selfish to want any more.

BRYAN: It sounds terrible, but you're probably blaming your kid for your own mistakes. I bet I could find a lot of ways to make your life easier without hurting your kids. For starters, how many activities is your kid involved in?

STEVE: [counting] Let's see. Soccer, ballet, Tae Kwon Do, and catechism.

BRYAN: Which is your daughter's least favorite?

STEVE: Probably ballet. She whines every time we tell her to go get ready.

BRYAN: Great. Cancel ballet. Stay home and take a nap while she watches TV. I just made your life better.

STEVE: That's no way to raise a kid.

BRYAN: Says who? She doesn't like going to ballet, you don't like taking her, and the job prospects for ballerinas aren't that great anyway. I'm not telling you to cancel all of her activities in favor of TV—just to make a judicious adjustment.

STEVE: I probably wouldn't even get to take the nap. Before long, she'd be running around screaming.

BRYAN: Have you tried . . . discipline?

STEVE: I'm so tired that I don't have the energy for discipline. It's easier to let her have her way.

BRYAN: In that case, canceling ballet is better than I thought. Instead of taking a nap, use the energy you save to invest in discipline. It will more than pay for itself.

STEVE: Maybe for some kids, but my daughter is trouble.

BRYAN: How is that an argument *against* discipline? The more trouble your kids are, the more you have to gain. Suppose parents can cut their kids' bad behavior in half by laying down the law. Parents with model children would hardly notice the difference— but you sure will.

MARY: Is this how dads really think? It's pretty disturbing. My five children are enrolled in thirteen different activities, and I'm not complaining. Being a parent is about giving your all, not cutting corners and taking naps.

STEVE: [sigh] You're right, Mary. When I see parents like you, I feel pretty guilty. I know I could be doing a better job.

BRYAN: I don't see why either of you should feel guilty. Mary's a great mom, but her schedule isn't for everyone. Steve loves his daughter and takes good care of her. He gave her the gift of life. What has he got to feel guilty about?

MARY: That lack of discipline will hurt her later in life. She won't have the skills she needs to excel in school or work. Who knows? She might even end up pregnant or in trouble with the law.

BRYAN: Highly unlikely. Twin and adoption studies find little or no long-run effect of parents on education, income, criminality, or teen pregnancy. Still, I second Mary's advice. Steve needs to use more discipline—not because lack of discipline hurts his daughter later in life, but because lack of discipline hurts Steve right now. His daughter makes him feel like a prisoner in his own home. Steve has to stand up for himself.

MARY: I hate to bring this up in front of Steve, but if parents don't matter, why are my five kids so much better behaved than his one?

STEVE: I suppose I should blame myself. Still, I can't help thinking that I was dealt a tougher hand than you were, Mary.

BRYAN: You're both partly right. Mary's kids don't walk all over her because, unlike Steve, she won't stand for it. While Mary's discipline has little effect on her kids' future success, it definitely improves their current behavior. Nevertheless, discipline isn't a panacea, even in the short term. Personality is partly hereditary—and I'll bet that Steve was a more difficult child than you were, Mary.

MARY: I still don't like your attitude, Bryan. You're encouraging people to be bad parents.

BRYAN: Do you have to be a bad parent to seek an easier path?

MARY: If you're as lazy as you sound, why did you bother having kids in the first place?

BRYAN: You say "lazy." I say "balanced." I had kids because I love kids. I make time to play board games with my friends because I enjoy that, too. If my kids are too young to appreciate a movie I'd like to see, I catch it on my way home from work. Why should parenting take over my entire life?

STEVE: I think my wife would kill me if I did stuff like that.

MARY: Maybe she should. It sounds like Bryan just dumps his "excess" parenting responsibilities on other people. Someone has to pick up the tab for your carefree lifestyle. I suspect it's your wife.

BECKY: Thanks for finally pointing this out, Mary. Raising kids is *inevitably* a lot of work—and it's interesting that Bryan barely mentions that women do almost all of it. That's why I plan to stay child-free.

BRYAN: I officially object. You both talk as if couples share a fixed pie of happiness—the only way for dad to get more is to give mom a smaller slice. That's false. Real families are far from perfect, so there's plenty of room for improvement. I'm a parental entrepreneur on the lookout for ways to make family life less work and more fun. If I pinpoint a waste of time, and my wife and I split the savings, we're both better off.

BECKY: Give me a break. Your arguments are just ammunition for men who want to keep women barefoot and pregnant. If you

really cared about your wife—or any woman for that matter—
you wouldn't be pressuring them to have more kids.

BRYAN: You're fretting about a gender conflict that doesn't really exist. Average desired family size for men and women is virtually identical. Women are *more* likely than men to say that having kids is "one of the most important things" to them. If I'm giving ammunition to people who want more kids than their partner, let me point out that about half of these people are women.

BECKY: None of that changes the fact that women suffer all the pain and perform most of the thankless labor. We have every reason to be suspicious when a man offers to "pinpoint a waste of time" and "split the savings." What does your split look like? 60–40 in your favor? 90–10?

BRYAN: I don't know why you're so suspicious of me, Becky. Scoff if you must, but if I had an extra hour of leisure to hand out, I'd give it to my wife. She needs it more than I do—and as the saying goes, "If mamma ain't happy, ain't nobody happy."

STEVE: It sounds like you haven't completely converted your wife to your position.

BRYAN: Who has?

STEVE: I think you've accidentally exposed a fatal flaw in your advice: It's useless unless both parents accept it. The odds of that happening are slim at best.

BRYAN: My advice definitely works better if both parents accept it, but one parent can still make a difference. Couples compromise. Your spouse won't let you follow my advice all the time, but you can still tip the scales toward happiness.

MARY: Well, if you converted my husband, I wouldn't compromise. I'd veto every one of your ideas. It's up to me to put my kids' interests first. Which reminds me: Don't many of the twin and adoption studies that you're hiding behind report that parents have *small* effects on their kids?

BRYAN: Some of them. According to the Korean adoption study, for example, Mary's firstborn child will finish six fewer months of education because she gave him four siblings.

MARY: That's seems like a small price to pay for the blessing of four brothers and sisters.

BRYAN: I agree, but I bet that many parents would feel like you failed to put your son's interests first.

MARY: They're entitled to their opinion. My point is that there's nothing unscientific about the way I raise my kids. I'm willing to endure a lot of pain in order to give my kids small gains, so your whole argument backfires. My effort is less fruitful than I thought? Then I'll have to try harder.

BRYAN: Why would you do that to yourself? When your children grow up and have kids of their own, do you want their lives to be as tough as yours?

MARY: When it's their turn to be parents, sure.

BRYAN: Fine, let's run with that. No one denies you're a great mom, Mary, but I have to ask: Do you ever lose your temper with your kids?

MARY: I'm only human. Raising five kids is no picnic.

BRYAN: Okay, given all your experience as a mom, I'm curious. According to the Ask the Children survey, two of kids' most common wishes are for their parents to be "less tired" and "less stressed." Overall, kids gave their parents good marks, but more than 40 percent gave moms and dads grades of C, D, or F for controlling their tempers. Do you buy these results?

MARY: I suppose. Parents aren't great actors. It's a lot easier for parents to do right by their kids than to pretend they're enjoying themselves.

BRYAN: Suppose one of your kids gave you an F for losing your temper. How would you handle it?

MARY: I'd try to improve.

BRYAN: Yeah, but aren't you already making a serious effort?

MARY: Like I said, I'm only human.

BRYAN: Me too. Apparently the most realistic way for a parent to seem happier is actually to *be* happier.

MARY: Your point being?

BRYAN: One of the best ways to improve your parenting is to make yourself happier. So even if you put your kids' interests first, you should give some of my advice a chance.

CHAT #3: FROM HAPPIER PARENTING TO MORE KIDS

BECKY: Is it just me, or is Bryan's whole argument painfully hard to follow? He admits that parents are less happy than the child-free. He talks about a bunch of twin and adoption studies. Then he tells everyone that it's okay to be selfish, so they should have a ton of kids. Bryan may have crafted the worst argument I ever heard.

IVAN: I agree that it's got some holes, but I think I'm able to follow his logic.

BRYAN: Care to walk us through the main steps as you understand them?

IVAN: Sure. You begin by claiming that parents are only slightly less happy than the childless—and you've got statistics to back you up.

BRYAN: Right.

IVAN: Then you point out that parents today hold themselves to much higher standards than they used to. You've got hard data for that, too.

BRYAN: So far, so good.

IVAN: Then you recommend ways for parents to make their lives easier—with nothing more than common sense to back you up?

BRYAN: Time diaries confirm that parents enjoy an hour of recreation more than an hour of child care. But I haven't run a big experiment showing that parents become happier when they spend more time doing things they enjoy. Seems like a lot of work to prove the obvious.

IVAN: That's the first weak link in the chain. Your next big step is all the twin and adoption research, which supposedly shows that parenting doesn't matter.

BRYAN: You're overstating my case. What twin and adoption research shows is that parenting matters a lot less than most parents think.

IVAN: You don't actually measure "what most parents think," do you?

BRYAN: Nope. Twin and adoption research clearly goes against the grain.

IVAN: You don't directly measure parenting styles either?

BRYAN: Twin and adoption studies rarely bother. One of their main advantages is that they capture *all* the effects of parenting.

IVAN: Still, it's conceivable that some rare parenting strategies are highly effective.

BRYAN: "Magic bullets" are theoretically possible, but I see no reason to believe they're real. In any case, suppose we knew that some magic bullets were out there. What good would that do for parents until we actually pinpoint them? Existing research, in contrast, already offers a life-changing lesson: Downtrodden parents can end many painful sacrifices guilt-free.

BECKY: Enough already. Suppose we grant Bryan everything. How would any of this show that women should turn themselves into baby factories?

IVAN: I'm pretty sure he never said that.

BRYAN: You're a good listener, Ivan. To repeat, my claim is that parents should have *more* kids than they originally planned. I never said, "Whoever has the most kids, wins."

BECKY: Then why do you have so much respect for Mary? What's so great about moms with five kids?

BRYAN: Mary's doing the world a favor. Her five kids make the world a better place, and she deserves our gratitude. But that's not central to my argument. Want to wrap this up, Ivan?

IVAN: Sure. The last step in your argument is that the "price" of high-quality kids is less than parents imagine, so selfishly speaking, they should buy more.

BECKY: Are you going to let him get away with that, Ivan?

IVAN: From a social scientist's point of view, the last step in Bryan's argument is the least debatable. It's a straightforward application of what economists call the law of demand. When a store marks its merchandise 20 percent off, don't you buy more, Becky?

BECKY: Yes, but we're talking about babies, not clothes.

IVAN: The same principle applies. When stuff gets cheaper, prudence tells us to stock up.

BRYAN: Well said, Ivan. Before you correct me, though, let me add two caveats. First, if a good is indivisible—like a car or a baby— a 20 percent price cut might not be enough to make you buy one more. Second, if you *dislike* a product, the price doesn't matter. I hate pickles so much that I wouldn't eat them even if they were free.

Okay, now that you've correctly explained my argument, I've got one question for you: Are you convinced?

IVAN: [laughs] Every step in your argument would require a lifetime of research to establish. You're about to turn forty. Spend a few more centuries on this project, then ask me again.

BRYAN: [laughs] You're forgetting one thing: I don't have to do the basic research myself. I'm happy to stand on the shoulders of giants.

IVAN: Even so, you can't see very far. None of the research you rely upon is fully convincing.

BRYAN: Even if this were pure research, I'd say your standards are unreasonably high. And I'm not doing pure research. I'm trying to give scientifically literate advice.

IVAN: I still think you rely too heavily on your own introspection, and not enough on science.

BRYAN: Introspection pops up in a lot of my arguments, I'll grant you that. When you're giving personal advice, however, it's okay for introspection to play a larger role than in pure research. Introspection is a great way to check whether a factor is important *for you*. If your introspection disagrees with mine, discount my advice. However, if your introspection agrees with mine . . .

IVAN: Hmm.

BRYAN: Okay, now I've got a challenge for you. You're planning on having kids, right?

IVAN: Yeah.

BRYAN: So how do you plan to raise them? Will any of my arguments affect your decisions?

IVAN: I guess. What you're saying is less stupid than most of the other stuff people say about parenting.

BRYAN: So you understand my argument, and it's persuasive enough to sway your behavior. You know what, Ivan? Being "less stupid than most of the other stuff" is good enough for me.

CHAT #4: KIDS AND SELFISHNESS

CHRISTINE: You make some decent points, but I don't like how you package them. I don't see why selfish people would have kids in the first place.

BRYAN: Selfish people have kids for the same kinds of reasons that selfish people buy HDTVs or trips to Japan. Maybe kids are fun, interesting, or cool. Maybe parents want a challenge.

CHRISTINE: Fine, but what about all the drawbacks of parenthood? Why do you try to convince us to have more kids, instead of neutrally listing pros and cons?

BRYAN: I don't want to insult my readers' intelligence by reminding them of the obvious. Every potential reader of this book knows that babies cry, kids cost money, and teenagers are surly. When people decide how many kids to have, I assume that they've already factored this knowledge into their decision. My goal is to give readers non-obvious information—and this information happens to weigh heavily in favor of more kids.

CHRISTINE: What about the happiness research showing that kids make people less happy?

BRYAN: I think this finding is already widely accepted. Young adults delay childbearing because they want to have fun. Parents complain loudly about their sacrifices. Television and movies aimed at adults rarely make parenting look easy.

CHRISTINE: If it's so obvious, why discuss happiness research at all?

BRYAN: To lay the ground for two non-obvious points. First, the size of the effect is surprisingly small. Given all the unnecessary toil parents impose upon themselves, the measured effect of kids on well-being is better than expected. Second, it's not hard to flip the direction of such a small effect. People can have the pride and joy of being a parent without surrendering the pride and joy of being an adult.

CHRISTINE: Suppose I didn't want to have kids. How would you change my mind?

BRYAN: The book isn't called *Selfish Reasons to Have Kids*—it's called *Selfish Reasons to Have* More *Kids*.

CHRISTINE: Yes, but one is more than zero, right?

BRYAN: Fair enough. I guess I'd begin by asking whether the person likes kids.

CHRISTINE: If not?

BRYAN: I'd point out that over two-thirds of people who don't have kids live to regret it. Then I'd drop the subject. I can't sell air conditioners to Eskimos. If kids simply don't appeal to you, there's not much more to say.

CHRISTINE: On the other hand, if I like kids, but think the price too steep . . .

BRYAN: Then I'd give you my whole spiel: Today's Typical Parents *artificially* inflate the price of kids, needlessly worry, and neglect the long-run benefits of larger families. If you avoid these mistakes, kids are a good deal.

CHRISTINE: So you wouldn't advise *everyone* to have kids?

BRYAN: Correct. If you know the facts and still don't want kids, I'm the last person to bug you about it. However, I do insist that even unwanted children are almost always glad to be alive and make the world a better place. "I don't feel like it" is the only solid reason to be child-free. The many variations on "unfair to the child" and "bad for the world" sound nobler but rarely stand up to scrutiny.

CHRISTINE: This seems kind of mean, but when I go to the mall, I often think, "Some people should have fewer kids."

BRYAN: If the kids are future ax murderers, I'll agree with you. Fortunately, few people are that awful. You don't have to be a straight-A student to enjoy your life and pull your weight. You can be average. You can be well below average.

CHRISTINE: [wincing] So you're not worried that . . . not-so-smart people . . . are . . . outbreeding . . . smart people?

BRYAN: Nope. I freely admit that some people are smarter and contribute more to human progress than others. But you don't need to be smart to be a valuable human being. If a person is glad to be alive and self-supporting, we should be happy for him.

STEVE: Still, aren't your arguments more relevant for people who are smart, well-educated, and successful?

BRYAN: Since you asked: Yes. Elite parents hold themselves to especially high—and therefore especially wasteful—standards.

STEVE: So elites have more unnecessary unhappiness to lose?

BRYAN: Exactly. If Today's Typical Parent is making kids twice as painful as they need to be, Today's Elite Parent might be making kids five times as painful as they need to be.

CHRISTINE: Elite parents also have a lot more money to throw at their problems.

BRYAN: Indeed. I'm amazed at how many elite parents with young children endure chronic sleep deprivation instead of hiring some help. Do they really think their kids won't get into Harvard because a nanny spoke Spanish to them when they were three months old?

STEVE: Would you add that, thanks to the power of heredity, elite parents are more likely to be pleased with their kids?

BRYAN: That's plausible, but I'd put it a little differently: If you're proud of yourself and your partner, you'll probably be proud of your kids, too.

STEVE: So it's about being self-satisfied, not being elite.

BRYAN: Exactly. The science of nature and nurture says that as long as you raise your kids in a vaguely normal way, they'll turn out a lot like you. If you want your kids to be different from you, this is bad news—and a reason to have fewer kids. As long as you want your kids to resemble you, however, this is good news—and a reason to have more kids. And how many of us don't want our kids to resemble us?

CHRISTINE: That's depressing for people who want to adopt.

BRYAN: If you're adopting in order make a little copy of yourself, science offers little hope. However, if your goal is to make a huge difference in a child's life, behavioral genetics has a recipe for success: Adopt from the Third World. Remember: Twin and adoption studies only show that nurture effects are small inside of rich countries. Moving a child from Third World poverty to First World comfort is a totally different story. When you rescue a child from an orphanage in China, Haiti, Romania, Bangladesh, or Malawi, you're almost guaranteeing him a much better childhood—and a much better adulthood.

Conclusion

> Ultimately, low birth rates are a cultural and ethical problem, a sign of a world-wide spiritual crisis. Having children is simply not viewed as a fulfilling life project anymore by many couples. Only when young men and women turn away from consumerism and individualism will birth rates begin to climb beyond replacement levels.
>
> —Michael Cook, "Clutching at Straws to Reverse the Birth Dearth"

A DECADE BEFORE I BECAME A DAD, AN EPISODE OF DENNIS PRAGER'S talk show left a lasting impression on me. Marrying well was the theme of the day. To expose singles' mixed-up priorities, Prager read a random personal ad that mentioned an interest in backpacking. Then he pounced. I quote from memory: "If you ever have kids, you're not going to have any time left for *backpacking*!"

The largely middle-aged audience—most of them parents, I'm sure—roared with laughter and approval. But this is no laughing matter. When we think about parenthood, we don't picture our children's smiling faces or a game of family dodgeball. Instead, we picture life devoid of relaxation or independence. I doubt Prager meant that kids were a bad deal overall, but it sure sounded that way. You're having kids? Then no more backpacking for you. No more doing *anything* you like.

I don't deny that some parents immiserate themselves for their children's sake. What I reject is the widely shared assumption that conflict between kids and happiness is *unavoidable*. It's natural for antinatalists to equate the first couple of kids with servitude—and any more with slavery. What amazes me is how readily natalists agree. You'd expect them to downplay parental misery. Instead, most race to concede its inevitability—and tell us to be less calculating and selfish.

At least to my ears, natalists' pleas against prudence are pretty lame. Arguing against foresight with a straight face isn't easy. Imagine the public service campaign: "You think too much. Just have a baby." Appeals to duty are less laughable: "Your parents sacrificed their happiness to have you. Now it's your turn." But aspiring grandparents have tried guilt since the dawn of man. It's hard to imagine that strangers' nagging will succeed where relatives' nagging failed. The child-free don't want to sacrifice their lifestyles, and parents feel like they've already sacrificed enough.

This book takes a different approach. I don't defend acting on impulse; I'm a big fan of planning ahead. I don't preach a duty to be fruitful and multiply; I expect sermons to fall on deaf ears. Instead, I appeal to enlightened self-interest. While kids *can* make their parents unhappy, the choice between kids and happiness is largely self-imposed. My goal isn't to attack consumerism and individualism but to join forces with them—to show that kids are a better deal than they seem.

Today's Typical Parents aren't miserable, but they've turned parenting into a chore—and act as if happier paths are impossible or abusive. They're mistaken. Kids are not like tropical fish that only flourish in a carefully controlled environment. Twin and adoption studies find that the long-run effects of parenting are shockingly small. As long as you don't do anything crazy, your kids will probably turn out fine. Contrary to Dennis Prager, you can be a great parent and an avid backpacker. Rather than trying to raise the perfect child, you should enjoy the journey together. Maybe your kid will turn out to be a backpacker just like you.

If I convince you of nothing more, I'll be happy. But since I never burned my bridges to consumerism and individualism, I can cross them to reach my conclusion. As a consumer, how do you change your behavior when a product gets cheaper or better or easier to purchase? You buy more. You go back. You tell your friends. You post a five-star review on Amazon. If kids are the product, consumer logic still applies: Buy more as the deal gets sweeter. When you make parenting less work and more fun, consumerism and individualism become reasons to have more kids—not to stop, or stop before you start.

Books on "to be or not to be a parent" rarely have a bottom line. They list pluses and minuses but refuse to give readers a straight answer. *Selfish Reasons to Have More Kids*, in contrast, bears a straight answer on its cover. This raises an awkward question for me: Wouldn't an agnostic approach show a lot more respect for individual choice than telling people what to do?

Not really. Way back in the Introduction, I explicitly limited my advice to people who are at least mildly interested in being a parent. What do I say to people who don't like children? Nothing. Traditional natalism, with its strong sense that everyone should bear children for the common good, is pushy. I'm not. If you know the real trade-offs yet prefer a life of speed dating and exotic travel, it's not my place to pester you. Once you buy into the idea of kids, however, I can give definite advice and respect your choices at the same time.

I don't claim that you should have any specific number of children. That depends on your priorities. I'm an overgrown kid at heart, so it's no wonder that fatherhood agrees with me. Tonight I'm taking my kids to meet the author of the *Scooby-Doo* chapter books. How cool is that? If you'd rather taste wine at an art gallery, I can see why you'd want fewer kids than I do. Still, whatever your priorities happen to be, my arguments are reasons to have more kids than you initially planned.

MOST IDEAS *DON'T* HAVE CONSEQUENCES; THESE DO

The depressing thing about exciting ideas is that most of them go nowhere. To see your ideas in action, you often have to convince millions of your fellow citizens that they're worth trying. In practice, that's almost impossible. My other book, *The Myth of the Rational Voter: Why Democracies Choose Bad Policies*, spotlights clever reforms that the man on the street will probably never consider. Almost everyone who's pondered a free market in human kidneys admits that it's a great way to make sick people healthy and poor people rich, but no politician who values his career would try to sell this policy to the American public.

If *Selfish Reasons to Have More Kids* convinces you, however, you don't have to convert millions of your fellow citizens to act. If you can persuade one person—your partner—the two of you can go full steam ahead. Other parents may disapprove, but forget about them. They're too exhausted by their own parenting to pay much attention to yours.

If you can't fully persuade your spouse, welcome to the club. Although my wife and I have three children together, she still thinks I'm a little crazy. That's okay. If I expected to convert her to my way of thinking, I would be crazy. I count myself lucky to have persuaded my wife to try *some* of my ideas. We rarely enroll our kids in activities they don't enjoy. We barely monitor the content of their video games. We had a third child—and finally started ignoring his 2:00 AM tantrums. If my wife thinks that any of these are her ideas, even better.

A TALE OF TWO SONOGRAMS

I'll never forget my wife's first sonogram. The technician stared at the monitor while she asked my wife boilerplate questions about her medical history.

"How long have you been pregnant?"

"About twelve weeks."

"Morning sickness?"

"A little."

"Any family history of genetic diseases?"

"No."

"Any history of twins?"

"No."

"Well, you're having twins."

My eyes bugged out. I was pretty sure a twin hoax would be a firing offense, but I still stammered, "You wouldn't joke about something like that? . . ." When the tech showed me the screen, my eyes bugged out a little more. There they were: two tiny bodies with massive heads. As I drove back to work, I was pale white. Two kids—what were we going to do?

Seven years later, my wife was pregnant again. This time, I *hoped* for twins. I proposed baby names in pairs. The thought of triplets didn't faze me. Before the sonogram technician turned on the machine, I asked for an ASAP answer to our burning question: Are there more multiples in our future? Five minutes later, we had our answer: No. We were going to be a family of five, not six or seven. I was delighted to have another healthy child on the way but couldn't help but feel slightly disappointed.

Why was I so afraid of twins the first time around—and so hopeful the next? What did I learn between the two pregnancies? In part, I gained self-knowledge. I expected to like playing with my kids, but I didn't realize that taking care of them would be so satisfying. When the twins outgrew their 2:00 AM feeding, I kind of missed it.

Yet most of what I figured out between the sonograms was not about my personality, but about the link between science and life. Before I became a dad, the conflict between my book learning and modern parenting was purely academic. After I became a dad, the conflict suddenly became very practical. Belief in the power of nurture inspired other parents to make painful sacrifices for their children—and dread the thought of another baby. Wouldn't it stand to reason, then, that my *dis*belief in the power of nurture ought to inspire me to avoid painful sacrifices for my children— and welcome the thought of another baby?

Although parents rarely had solid answers to my questions, it seemed rash to dismiss their firsthand experience. Maybe parents saw crucial facts that researchers missed. By the time our twins were toddlers, however, I realized that I didn't need to discount anyone's experiences. Parents heavily influence their kids in many ways; they see it with their own eyes. Their mistake is to assume that their influence lasts a lifetime, instead of fading out as their kids grow up.

Once I reconciled my book learning with my firsthand experience, I had a lot to reconsider—starting with our first fateful sonogram. My knee-jerk reaction was dead wrong. I should have been thrilled to get two kids for the price of one. While my wife and I could have made ourselves miserable by mindlessly doubling all the standard parental sacrifices, we compromised on a more relaxed approach. We spent money to make our lives easier. We didn't struggle to put our twins in the best preschool or peewee chess championship. We let them watch TV. Twins were a little tiring at first, but I kept my 2:00 AM double feedings in perspective. The extra start-up costs were modest—and these kids would be ours for the rest of our lives.

That's why I went to our second big sonogram hoping for twins. Would four kids ruin our lives? That was up to us. How would we handle another set of twins? The same way we handled the first set: Work a little harder for a year or so—and remember that parenting is graded pass/fail. When the sonogram showed a healthy singleton, I had to fight the temptation to tell my wife, "Better luck next time." I counted my blessings, but never felt relieved.

I can tell you what I learned between those two sonograms while standing on one foot: There's no substitute for reasonable expectations. If you imagine that your children's future is in your hands, and single-mindedly do "whatever is best for your kids," then one child is more than enough to ruin your life. But once you accept that your children's future is largely up to them and remember that your happiness counts, too, an unplanned set of twins is no big deal. Before long, you'll probably think they're the best thing that ever happened to you. I know we did.

NOTES

INTRODUCTION

1   *In 1976, 20 percent of women:* "Supplemental Table 2, Distribution of Women 40 to 44 Years Old by Number of Children Ever Born and Marital Status: Selected Years, 1970 to 2006," U.S. Census Bureau, 2008.

1   *the Greeks blame air pollution:* Russell Shorto, "No Babies?" *New York Times Magazine,* June 29, 2008.

3   *parental effort is at an all-time high:* See, for example, Suzanne Bianchi et al., *Changing Rhythms of American Family Life* (New York: Russell Sage Foundation Publications, 2006).

4   *A small army of researchers has compared adoptees to their relatives:* For introductions to twin and adoption research, see, for example, Nancy Segal, *Entwined Lives: Twins and What They Tell Us About Human Behavior* (New York: Plume, 1999); Judith Harris, *The Nurture Assumption: Why Children Turn out the Way They Do* (New York: Free Press, 1998); and David Rowe, *The Limits of Family Influence* (New York: Guilford Press, 1994).

6   *Children under five years old are almost five times as safe:* See *Vital Statistics of the United States 1950,* Volume 3, Mortality Data, Table 57, U.S. Department of Health, Education, and

Welfare, 1953, available at www.nber.org/vital-statistics/
historical/vsus_1950_3.pdf; and "National Vital Statistics
Reports, Deaths, Final Data for 2005," Centers for Disease
Control and Prevention, 2008, Table 11, available at www.cdc
.gov/nchs/data/nvsr/nvsr56/nvsr56_10.pdf.

8   *Back in 1940, America had almost ten workers per retiree:*
      "Social Security Area Population Projections: 1997," Social
      Security Administration, Figure 8, available at www.ssa.gov/
      OACT/NOTES/pdf_studies/study112.pdf; "Table V.A2—Social
      Security Area Population as of July 1 and Dependency Ratios,"
      Social Security Administration 2002, available at www.ssa
      .gov/OACT/TR/TR02/lr5A2–2.html.

8   *Air and water quality have improved:* For good introductions,
      see Julian Simon, *The Ultimate Resource 2* (Princeton: Prince-
      ton University Press, 1996), pp. 241–257; and Bjorn Lomborg,
      *The Skeptical Environmentalist: Measuring the Real State of
      the World* (Cambridge: Cambridge University Press, 2001),
      pp. 163–177, 189–205.

8   *Carbon dioxide emissions . . . are still on the rise:* "Millennium
      Development Goals Indicators: Carbon Dioxide Emissions,"
      United Nations Statistics Division, 2010, available at mdgs.un
      .org/unsd/mdg/SeriesDetail.aspx?srid=749.

9   *About 80 percent of Americans twenty-five and older:* General
      Social Survey, 2008. Variable identifier CHILDS.

10   *a chapter for every reason you've heard* not *to have a child:*
      Diana Dell and Suzan Erem, *Do I Want To Be a Mom? A
      Woman's Guide to the Decision of a Lifetime* (New York:
      McGraw-Hill, 2003).

CHAPTER 1

14   Do I Want to Be a Mom? *ominously warns:* Dell and Erem, *Do
      I Want To Be a Mom?* p. 1.

14   *in 1976,* Newsday *commissioned the highest-quality survey:*
      "91% Would Have Children (Take That, Ann Landers)," *News-
      day,* June 13, 1976. For a discussion of the background behind
      the *Newsday* survey and the famous Ann Landers survey that
      inspired it, see David Bellhouse, "Ann Landers Survey on Par-

enthood," available at Nicholas R. Miller Web page, userpages .umbc.edu/~nmiller/POLI300/stat353annlanders.pdf.

15 *In 2003, Gallup asked childless adults:* Frank Newport, "Desire to Have Children Alive and Well in America," Gallup Poll, April 19, 2003, available at www.gallup.com/poll/9091/ desire-children-alive-well-america.aspx. A common objection to these results is that infertility inflates the measured regret of the childless. True enough, but by the same logic, unplanned pregnancies inflate *parents'* measured regret. It is also worth pointing out that people are often infertile *because* they waited too long to have kids.

15 *surveys have spent decades asking . . . "How happy are you?":* For good introductions, see Daniel Gilbert, *Stumbling on Happiness* (New York: Knopf, 2007); and Arthur Brooks, *Gross National Happiness* (New York: Basic Books, 2008).

15 *Before you join the "children make us miserable" chorus:* This is how blogger Will Wilkinson sums up the happiness research: "Children Make Us Miserable," available at www.willwilkinson.net/flybottle/2008/04/04/children-make-us -miserable, August 4, 2008.

15 *every child makes you about 1 percentage point less likely:* 1.3 percentage points, to be precise. You can check all of my General Social Survey results online at the Survey Documentation and Analysis Archive, available at sda.berkeley.edu/ cgi-bin/hsda?harcsda+gss08. First, define VERYHAPPY (which equals 1 if HAPPY=1, and 0 otherwise) and MARRIED (which equals 1 if MARITAL=1, and 0 otherwise). Then regress VERYHAPPY on MARRIED, AGE, ATTEND, and CHILDS.

16 *Otherwise identical people who have one child instead of none:* To check this result, define ZEROKIDS (which equals 1 if CHILDS=0, and 1 otherwise). Then regress VERYHAPPY on MARRIED, AGE, ATTEND, ZEROKIDS, and CHILDS. The estimated effect of the first child on the probability of being very happy is the coefficient on CHILDS minus the coefficient on ZEROKIDS.

16 *many things in a parent's life that bring great joy:* Brooks, *Gross National Happiness*, p. 66.

17   *Nobel laureate Daniel Kahneman . . . study of working moms:*
Daniel Kahneman et al., "A Survey Method for Characterizing
Daily Life Experience: The Day Reconstruction Method,"
Science 306 (5702) (December 2004), pp. 1776–1780.

17   *"an act of parenting makes most people about as happy as":*
Daniel Gilbert, "Does Fatherhood Make You Happy?" *Time,*
June 11, 2006.

17   *"When researchers ask parents what they enjoy":* "The Joys of
Parenthood," *Economist,* March 27, 2008.

17   *Yet even he looks at these very numbers and concludes:* Brooks,
Gross National Happiness, p. 67.

18   *Child care isn't a picnic, but it beats a paying job:* Also worth
noting: A similar study (Mathew White and Paul Dolan, "Ac-
counting for the Richness of Daily Activities," *Psychological
Science* 20 (8) (August 2009), pp. 1000–1008) asked participants to rate how pleasurable and *rewarding* their activities
were. Spending time with your children turns out to be below
average in pleasure but above average in reward.

18   *"When people think about their offspring":* Gilbert, *Stumbling
on Happiness,* p. 242.

18   *"Although parenting has many rewarding moments":* Ibid.,
p. 244.

20   *Back in 1965, when the typical mom was a housewife:* Bianchi
et al., *Changing Rhythms of American Family Life,* p. 63.

20   *Stay-at-home moms went from about:* Ibid., p. 76.

20   *Parents in 2000 spent about 25 percent fewer hours with each
other:* Ibid., p. 104.

22   *"Sleep is a negotiation":* Joshua Gans, *Parentonomics: An
Economist Dad Looks at Parenting* (Boston: MIT Press, 2009),
p. 26.

23   *It works, but it's harsh:* For a good survey, see Jodi Mindell et
al., "Behavioral Treatment of Bedtime Problems and Night
Wakings in Infants and Young Children," *Sleep* 29 (10) (2006),
pp. 1263–1276.

23   *The Ferber method . . . works wonders, too:* Mindell et al.,
"Behavioral Treatment of Bedtime Problems and Night
Wakings."

24   *"Find one thing you've pushed your kids to do":* Lenore Skenazy, *Free-Range Kids: Giving Our Kids the Freedom We Had Without Going Nuts with Worry* (San Francisco: Jossey-Bass, 2009), p. 124.

27   *They call it "behavioral parent training":* See Anne Shaffer et al., "The Past, Present, and Future of Behavioral Parent Training: Interventions for Child and Adolescent Problem Behavior," *Behavioral Analyst Today* 2 (2) (April 2001), pp. 91–106; Michelle Wierson and Rex Forehand, "Parent Behavioral Training for Child Noncompliance: Rationale, Concepts, and Effectiveness," *Current Directions in Psychological Science* 3 (5) (October 1994), pp. 146–150; Anthony Graziano and David Diament, "Parent Behavioral Training: An Examination of the Paradigm," *Behavioral Modification* 16 (1) (January 1992), pp. 3–38.

27   *Experiments typically find that the average child of the trained parents:* Wendy Serketish and Jean Dumas, "The Effectiveness of Behavioral Parent Training to Modify Antisocial Behavior in Children," *Behavior Therapy* 27 (2) (Spring 1996), pp. 171–186. See also Sheila Eyberg et al., "Evidence-Based Psychosocial Treatments for Children and Adolescents with Disruptive Behavior," *Journal of Clinical Child and Adolescent Psychology* 37 (1) (January 2008), pp. 215–237.

27   *The main weakness of the training:* Shaffer et al., "The Past, Present, and Future of Behavioral Parent Training."

27   *A central criticism of behavioral parent training:* See, for example, Judith Harris, *No Two Alike* (New York: W. W. Norton, 2007), pp. 130–135.

28   *Yet when Skenazy bragged about his odyssey:* For Skenazy's full story, see *Free-Range Kids*, pp. xiii–xvi.

29   *"Volunteer to watch the kids who are waiting":* Ibid., pp. 58, 102, 143.

31   *Using money to make parenting easier:* I separately regressed VERYHAPPY on MARRIED, AGE, ATTEND, ZEROKIDS, and CHILDS on the bottom and top halves of REALINC. For the bottom half of the income distribution, ZEROKIDS has a coefficient of .061, versus .030 for the top half. (The

coefficients on CHILDS were the same: .006.) One tempting explanation for this pattern is simply that higher-income people are more careful to avoid unwanted pregnancies. Remember, however, that these results already control for age and marriage—which are presumably the main predictors of whether or not a pregnancy is wanted.

33 *Overall, parents did pretty well:* Ellen Galinsky, *Ask the Children: What America's Children Really Think About Working Parents* (New York: William Morrow, 1999), pp. 46–47.

CHAPTER 2

40 *When a couple raises the child of a perfect stranger:* The main caveat is that some adoption agencies use "selective placement"—they try to match adoptees with families similar to their biological families in socioeconomic status, religion, and more. When you compare adoptees to their adopted families, selective placement makes nurture effects look larger and nature effects look smaller than they really are. When you compare adoptees to their biological families, selective placement makes nurture effects look smaller and nature effects look bigger than they really are. For further explanation, see Joseph Horn, "The Texas Adoption Project: Adopted Children and Their Intellectual Resemblance to Biological and Adoptive Parents," *Child Development* 54 (2) (April 1983), pp. 268–275.

42 *If parents' income, education, marital status, parenting philosophy, religion:* A few studies split this blanket "nurture effect" into more specific components, such as parental influence, sibling influence, and special twin environments. But most data sets do not have enough information to disentangle these effects.

42 *you could just as well say "none of the above":* I owe the "none of the above" label to Judith Harris's *The Nurture Assumption.* Harris's *No Two Alike* critiques leading accounts of unique environment and offers her own.

47 *One looked at almost 3,000 pairs of Danish twins:* Anne Herskind et al., "The Heritability of Human Longevity: A Population-

Based Study of 2872 Danish Twin Pairs Born 1870–1900," *Human Genetics* 97 (3) (March 1996), pp. 319–323.

47   *Yet the Danish twin study found:* Ibid., p. 319.

47   *Another study looked at the mortality of about 9,000 Swedish twins*: Anatoli Yashin et al., "Half of the Variation in Susceptibility to Mortality Is Genetic: Findings from Swedish Twin Survival Data," *Behavior Genetics* 29 (1) (January 1999), pp. 11–19.

47   *A study of over 3,000 elderly Danish twins:* Kaare Christensen et al., "A Danish Population-Based Twin Study on General Health in the Elderly," *Journal of Aging and Health* 11 (1) (February 1999), pp. 49–64.

47   *Another team of researchers looked at about 2,500 Swedish twins:* Pia Svedberg et al., "Age and Sex Differences in Genetic and Environmental Factors for Self-Rated Health: A Twin Study," *Journal of Gerontology* 56 (3) (May 2001), pp. 171–178.

47   *A smaller study of older female Finnish twins:* Raija Leinonen et al., "Genetic Influences Underlying Self-Rated Health in Older Female Twins," *Journal of the American Geriatrics Society* 53 (6) (June 2005), pp. 1002–1007.

47   *notable exception comes from the Swedish Adoption/Twin Study of Aging:* Jennifer Harris et al., "Age Differences in Genetic and Environmental Influences for Health from the Swedish Adoption/Twin Study of Aging," *Journal of Gerontology* 47 (3) (May 1992), pp. 213–220.

48   *In the Swedish Adoption/Twin Study of Aging, twins raised together:* Ibid., pp. 216–217.

48   *A major survey article on the genetics of obesity:* John Hewitt, "The Genetics of Obesity: What Have Genetic Studies Told Us About the Environment?" *Behavior Genetics* 27 (4) (July 1997), pp. 353–358, cites several studies finding a lack of parental influence even for young children; Kelly Klump et al., "Age Differences in Genetic and Environmental Influences on Eating Attitudes and Behaviors in Preadolescent and Adolescent Female Twins," *Journal of Abnormal Psychology* 109 (2) (May 2000), pp. 239–251, find an effect of shared environment for eleven-year-olds but not seventeen-year-olds.

48   *A major study of adult Swedish twins looked at gingivitis:* L. A. Mucci et al., "Environmental and Heritable Factors in the

Etiology of Oral Diseases: A Population-Based Study of Swedish Twins," *Journal of Dental Research* 84 (9) (September 2005), pp. 800–805.

49 *A study of over 3,000 male twins from the Vietnam Era Twin Registry:* William True et al., "Common Genetic Vulnerability for Nicotine and Alcohol Dependence in Men," *Archives of General Psychiatry* 56 (7) (July 1999), pp. 655–661.

49 *another study of the same group of twins found that nurture mattered:* Ming Tsuang et al., "Genetic and Environmental Influences on Transitions in Drug Use," *Behavior Genetics* 29 (6) (December 1999), pp. 473–479.

49 *A study of Australian twins found:* A. C. Heath et al., "Genetic and Environmental Contributions to Alcohol Dependence Risk in a National Twin Sample: Consistency in Findings of Women and Men," *Psychological Medicine* 27 (6) (November 1997), pp. 1381–1396.

49 *Researchers using the Virginia 30,000 sample:* Hermine Maes et al., "Genetic and Cultural Transmission of Smoking Initiation: An Extended Twin Kinship Model," *Behavior Genetics* 36 (6) (2006), pp. 795–808.

49 *One team studied the tobacco, alcohol, and drug use:* Cong Han et al., "Lifetime Tobacco, Alcohol and Other Substance Use in Adolescent Minnesota Twins: Univariate and Multivariate Behavioral Genetic Analyses," *Addiction* 94 (7) (July 1999), pp. 981–993.

49 *other studies conclude that parents don't affect drinking:* Matt McGue, "The Behavioral Genetics of Alcoholism," *Current Directions in Psychological Science* 8 (4) (August 1999), p. 113.

49 *adoptees drank like their adopted siblings:* Matt McGue et al., "Parent and Sibling Influences on Adolescent Alcohol Use and Misuse: Evidence from a U.S. Adoption Cohort," *Journal of Studies on Alcohol* 57 (1) (January 1996), pp. 8–18.

49 *study of over 1,000 Koreans adopted by American families:* Bruce Sacerdote, "How Large Are the Effects from Changes in Family Environment? A Study of Korean American Adoptees," *Quarterly Journal of Economics* 122 (1) (January 2007), p. 143.

50   *One misreported study about "the Mozart effect":* Marina
      Krakowsky, "Discredited 'Mozart Effect' Remains Music to
      American Ears," *Stanford Graduate School of Business News*
      (February 2005).

50   *The Minnesota Study of Twins Reared Apart reunited almost
      100:* Thomas Bouchard et al., "Sources of Human Psycholog-
      ical Differences: The Minnesota Study of Twins Reared
      Apart," *Science* 250 (4978) (October 1990), p. 223. The first
      test was the Wechsler Adult Intelligence Scale. The second
      test was a composite of the Raven Progressive Matrices and
      the Mill-Hill Vocabulary Test.

50   *If you did better than 80 percent of the population on both tests:*
      Ibid., p. 226.

50   *"Growing up in the same family does not contribute to simi-
      larity":* Robert Plomin et al., "Variability and Stability in Cog-
      nitive Abilities Are Largely Genetic Later in Life," *Behavior
      Genetics* 24 (3) (1994), p. 214.

50   *tested about 1,600 reared-together adult twins from the Dutch
      Twin Registry:* Daniëlle Postuma et al., "Genetic Contribu-
      tions to Anatomical, Behavioral, and Neurophysiological In-
      dices of Cognition," in Robert Plomin et al., eds., *Behavioral
      Genetics in the Postgenomic Era* (Washington, DC: American
      Psychological Association, 2002), p. 143.

51   *In 1975, the Colorado Adoption Project began studying 245
      adopted babies:* Robert Plomin et al., "Nature, Nurture, and
      Cognitive Development from 1 to 16 Years: A Parent-Offspring
      Adoption Study," *Psychological Science* 8 (6) (November 1997),
      pp. 442–447.

51   *The Texas Adoption Project . . . also found no effect of up-
      bringing on the IQs:* John Loehlin et al., "Heredity, Environ-
      ment, and IQ in the Texas Adoption Project," in Robert
      Sternberg and Elena Grigorenko, eds., *Intelligence, Heredity,
      and Environment* (Cambridge: Cambridge University Press,
      1997), p. 123.

51   *If you're happier than 80 percent of people, your fraternal twin:*
      David Lykken, *Happiness: The Nature and Nurture of Joy and
      Contentment* (New York: St. Martin's Press, 2000), p. 57.

52 *"Nearly 100 percent of the variation in the happiness set point":* Ibid., p. 58.

52 *Twins raised apart were more alike in happiness:* Ibid., p. 56.

52 *The single most impressive study interviewed almost 8,000 twins:* K. S. Kendler et al., "A Population-Based Twin Study of Self-Esteem and Gender," *Psychological Medicine* 28 (6) (June 1998), p. 1406.

52 *further research using the Minnesota Twin Registry concludes:* Deborah Finkel and Matt McGue, "Sex Differences and Non-additivity in Heritability of the Multidimensional Personality Questionnaire Scales," *Journal of Personality and Social Psychology* 72 (4) (April 1997), pp. 929–938.

54 *In 2004–2005, economist Bruce Sacerdote tracked down:* Sacerdote, "How Large Are the Effects from Changes in Family Environment?"

54 *Another major study of over 2,000 Swedish adoptees:* Anders Björklund et al., "The Origins of Intergenerational Associations: Lessons from Swedish Adoption Data," *Quarterly Journal of Economics* 129 (3) (August 2006), p. 1013.

54 *The most remarkable examined about 2,000 pairs of American twins:* Jere Behrman and Paul Taubman, "Is Schooling Mostly 'In the Genes'? Nature-Nurture Decomposition Using Data on Relatives," *Journal of Political Economy* 97 (6), pp. 1425–1446.

55 *Researchers who looked at about 2,500 Australian twins:* Paul Miller et al., "Genetic and Environmental Contributions to Educational Attainment in Australia," *Economics of Education Review* 20 (3) (June 2001), pp. 211–224; see also Paul Miller et al., "What Do Twin Studies Reveal About the Economic Returns to Education? A Comparison of Australian and U.S. Findings," *American Economic Review* 85 (3) (June 1995), pp. 586–599.

55 *An early study of Norwegian twins found strong family effects:* A. C. Heath et al., "Education Policy and the Heritability of Educational Attainment," *Nature* 314 (6013) (April–May 1985), pp. 734–736.

55 *Researchers using the Minnesota Twin Family Registry and the Finnish Twin Cohort Study:* Karri Silventoinen et al., "Heri-

tability of Body Height and Educational Attainment in an International Context: Comparison of Adult Twins in Minnesota and Finland," *American Journal of Human Biology* 16 (5) (September–October 2004), pp. 544–555.

55   *One team combined thousands of observations from earlier studies:* George Vogler and David Fulker, "Familial Resemblance for Educational Attainment," *Behavior Genetics* 13 (4) (July 1983), pp. 341–354.

56   *A more recent study of Australian twins reports moderate nurture effects:* Laura Baker et al., "Genetics of Educational Attainment in Australian Twins," *Behavior Genetics* 26 (2) (March 1996), pp. 89–102.

56   *An early study of about 500 Australian twins reported little or no effect of upbringing:* C. E. Gill et al., "Further Evidence for Genetic Influences on Educational Achievement," *British Journal of Educational Psychology* 55 (3) (November 1985), pp. 240–250. This study did, however, note that only the top 34 percent of students took the exam and argued that nurture would matter more for the bottom two-thirds of the ability distribution.

56   *A research team investigating the attitudes of almost 700 Canadian twins:* James Olson et al., "The Heritability of Attitudes: A Study of Twins," *Journal of Personality and Social Psychology* 80 (6) (June 2001), p. 850.

56   *The most impressive evidence . . . comes from the U.S.-based National Longitudinal Study of Adolescent Health:* François Nielsen, "Achievement and Ascription in Educational Attainment: Genetic and Environmental Influences on Adolescent Schooling," *Social Forces* 85 (1) (September 2006), pp. 193–216.

57   *In Sacerdote's Korean adoption study, biological children from richer families:* Sacerdote, "How Large Are the Effects from Changes in Family Environment?" p. 142.

57   *The Swedish adoption study mentioned earlier finds small effects:* Björklund et al., "The Origins of Intergenerational Associations," p. 1013.

57   *Identical twins turn out to be almost exactly twice as similar in labor incomes:* David Cesarini, "Decomposing the Genetic

Variance in Income: The Role of Cognitive and Noncognitive Skill," MIT Working Paper, 2010.

57   *A study of over 2,000 Australian twins finds the same thing:* Miller et al., "What Do Twins Studies Reveal About the Economic Returns to Education?" p. 590.

58   *In the U.S. Twinsburg Study:* Samuel Bowles and Herbert Gintis, "The Inheritance of Inequality," *Journal of Economic Perspectives* 16 (3) (Summer 2002), p. 16.

58   *A study of American full and half siblings using the National Longitudinal Survey of Youth:* David Rowe et al., "Herrnstein's Syllogism: Genetic and Shared Environmental Influences on IQ, Education, and Income," *Intelligence* 26 (4) (November 1998), p. 419.

59   *If you make a list of the traits that almost all parents want to instill:* See, for example, Ralph Piedmont, *The Revised NEO Personality Inventory: Clinical and Research Applications* (New York: Plenum Press, 1998); and Robert Hogan et al., eds., *Handbook of Personality Psychology* (New York: Academic Press, 1997). The agreeableness umbrella also covers some seemingly *un*desirable cognitive traits such as "illogical" and "emotional."

60   *One of the earliest studies of nature, nurture, and character:* C. S. Bergeman et al., "Genetic and Environmental Effects on Openness to Experience, Agreeableness, and Conscientiousness: An Adoption/Twin Study," *Journal of Personality* 61 (2) (June 1993), pp. 159–179.

60   *A survey article published in* Science *a year later:* Thomas Bouchard, "Genes, Environment, and Personality," *Science* 264 (5166) (June 1994), pp. 1700–1701.

60   *One team looked at almost 2,000 German twins:* Rainer Riemann et al., "Genetic and Environmental Influences on Personality: A Study of Twins Reared Together Using the Self- and Peer Report NEO-FFI Scales," *Journal of Personality* 65 (3) (September 1997), pp. 449–475.

60   *Studies of 1,600 American twins and 600 Canadian twins:* John Loehlin et al., "Heritabilities of Common and Measure-Specific Components of the Big Five Personality Factors," *Journal of Research in Personality* 32 (4) (December 1998),

pp. 431–453; Kerry Jang et al., "Heritability of the Big Five Personality Dimensions and Their Facets: A Twin Study," *Journal of Personality* 64 (3) (September 1996), pp. 577–591.

60 *you might prefer the Swedish approach:* Cesarini, "Decomposing the Genetic Variance in Income."

61 *If your parents were higher in conscientiousness and agreeableness than 80 percent of the population:* John Loehlin, "Resemblance in Personality and Attitudes Between Parents and Their Children," in Samuel Bowles et al., eds., *Unequal Chances: Family Background and Economic Success* (Princeton: Princeton University Press, 2005), p. 198.

61 *In 1984,* Science *published a study of almost 15,000 Danish adoptees:* Sarnoff Mednick et al., "Genetic Influences in Criminal Convictions: Evidence from an Adoption Cohort," *Science* 224 (4651) (May 1984), pp. 891–894.

62 *In 2002, a study of antisocial behavior in almost 7,000 Virginian twins:* Kristen Jacobson et al., "Sex Differences in the Genetic and Environmental Influences on the Development of Antisocial Behavior," *Development and Psychopathology* 14 (2) (Spring 2002), p. 412.

62 *a major review of fifty-one twin and adoption studies reported:* Soo Rhee and Irwin Waldman, "Genetic and Environmental Influences on Antisocial Behavior: A Meta-Analysis of Twin and Adoption Studies," *Psychological Bulletin* 128 (3) (May 2002), pp. 512–513.

63 *A major study of over 7,000 adult Australian twins:* Brian D'Onofrio et al., "Understanding Biological and Social Influences on Religious Affiliation, Attitudes, and Behaviors: A Behavior Genetic Perspective," *Journal of Personality* 67 (6) (December 1999), pp. 953–984.

64 *Another study of almost 2,000 women from the Virginia Twin Registry:* Kenneth Kendler et al., "Religion, Psychopathology, and Substance Use and Abuse: A Multimeasure, Genetic-Epidemiologic Study," *American Journal of Psychiatry* 154 (3) (March 1997), p. 325.

64 *One early study of almost 2,000 adult Minnesota twins reared together and apart:* Niels Waller et al., "Genetic and Environmental Influences on Religious Interests, Attitudes, and

Values: A Study of Twins Reared Apart and Together," *Psychological Science* 1 (2) (March 1990), pp. 138–142.

64   *A recent follow-up found similar results:* Thomas Bouchard et al., "Genetic Influence on Social Attitudes: Another Challenge to Psychology from Behavior Genetics," in Lisabeth DiLalla, ed., *Behavior Genetics Principles: Perspectives in Development, Personality, and Psychopathology* (Washington, DC: American Psychological Association, 2004), pp. 92–95.

64   *Parents have almost no effect on adult church attendance:* D'Onofrio et al., "Understanding Biological and Social Influences on Religious Affiliation, Attitudes, and Behaviors." They did, however, find that twins had a noticeable effect on *each other's* church attendance.

64   *Another major study of American and Australian church attendance:* K. M. Kirk et al., "Frequency of Church Attendance in Australia and the United States: Models of Family Resemblance," *Twin Research* 2 (2) (June 1999), pp. 99–107.

65   *If you're more religious than 80 percent of people:* Laura Koenig et al., "Genetic and Environmental Influences on Religiousness: Findings for Retrospective and Current Religiousness Ratings," *Journal of Personality* 73 (2) (April 2005), pp. 471–488.

65   *When about 600 female Minnesota twins took the same test:* Laura Koenig et al., "Stability and Change in Religiousness During Emerging Adulthood," *Developmental Psychology* 44 (2) (March 2008), pp. 532–543.

65   *In the Virginia 30,000 study, both identical and fraternal twins:* Peter Hatemi et al., "Is There a 'Party' in Your Genes?" *Political Research Quarterly* 62 (3) (September 2009), Tables 3, 5.

65   *Party identification works the same way in Australia:* Peter Hatemi et al., "The Genetics of Voting: An Australian Twin Study," *Behavior Genetics* 37 (3) (May 2007), pp. 435–448.

65   *The Virginia 30,000 study found that parents have little effect on the* strength: Hatemi et al., "Is There a 'Party' in Your Genes?" Table 5.

66   *parents have little influence over whether people bother to vote:* James Fowler et al., "Genetic Variation in Political Participa-

tion," *American Political Science Review* 102 (2) (May 2008), pp. 233–248.

66 *Parents may slightly affect how conservative you are:* For details, see Thomas Bouchard and Laura Koenig, "Genetic and Environmental Influences on the Traditional Moral Values Triad—Authoritarianism, Conservatism, and Religiousness—as Assessed by Quantitative Behavior Genetic Methods," in Patrick McNamara, ed., *Where God and Science Meet,* vol. 1 (Westport, CT: Praeger Publishers, 2006); Thomas Bouchard and Matt McGue, "Genetic and Environmental Influences on Human Psychological Differences," *Journal of Neurobiology* 52 (1) (January 2003), pp. 27–29; Lindon Eaves et al., "Comparing the Biological and Cultural Inheritance of Personality and Social Attitudes in the Virginia 30,000 Study of Twins and Their Relatives," *Twin Research* 2 (2) (June 1999), pp. 62–80; Hatemi, "The Genetics of Voting"; John Alford et al., "Are Political Orientations Genetically Transmitted?" *American Political Science Review* 99 (2) (June 2005), pp. 153–167; Olson et al., "Heritability of Attitudes"; N. G. Martin et al., "Transmission of Social Attitudes," *Proceedings of the National Academy of Sciences* 83 (12) (June 1986), pp. 4364–4368.

67 *including studies of over 1,000 Swedes raised apart and together:* Bergman et al., "Genetic and Environmental Effects on Openness to Experience, Agreeableness, and Conscientiousness"; Riemann et al., "Genetic and Environmental Influences on Personality"; Loehlin et al., "Heritabilities of Common and Measure-Specific Components of the Big Five Personality Factors"; Jang et al., "Heritability of the Big Five Personality Dimensions and Their Facets."

67 *The average adoption study finds a small but reliable effect of parenting:* Loehlin, "Resemblance in Personality and Attitudes Between Parents and Their Children," p. 198.

67 *The first included over 3,000 women:* M. P. Dunne et al., "Genetic and Environmental Contributions to Variance in Age at First Sexual Intercourse," *Psychological Science* 8 (3) (May 1997), pp. 211–216.

67 *A follow-up roughly doubled the sample size:* Mary Waldron et al., "Age at First Sexual Intercourse and Teenage Pregnancy

in Australian Female Twins," *Twin Research and Human Genetics* 10 (3) (June 2007), pp. 440–449.

68   *Another research team used the National Longitudinal Survey of Youth:* Joseph Rodgers et al., "Nature, Nurture and First Sexual Intercourse in the USA: Fitting Behavioural Genetic Models to NLSY Kinship Data," *Journal of Biosocial Science* 31 (1) (January 1999), pp. 29–41.

68   *Girls' parents are more likely to take extreme measures:* If fear of teen pregnancy merely increased the *average* effort of parents of girls, there would be no reason to expect differences in nurture to matter more. But as long as fear of teen pregnancy also increases the *variation* in parents' effort, we should expect a larger nurture effect.

68   *While the Australian study of almost 7,000 female twins found:* Waldron et al., "Age at First Sexual Intercourse and Teenage Pregnancy in Australian Female Twins."

68   *A study of about 2,000 female Swedish twins born in the Fifties:* Petra Olausson et al., "Aetiology of Teenage Childbearing: Reasons for Familial Effects," *Twin Research* 3 (1) (March 2000), pp. 23–27.

68   *Less than a third of Americans believe that premarital sex is always wrong:* General Social Survey 2008. Variable identifier PREMARS1.

68   *if you were in the 80th percentile, you could expect your adopted sibling:* J. Bailey et al., "Do Individual Differences in Sociosexuality Represent Genetic or Environmentally Contingent Strategies? Evidence from the Australian Twin Registry," *Journal of Personality and Social Psychology* 78 (3) (March 2000), pp. 537–545.

69   *A second study of 1,600 female twins in the United Kingdom:* Lynn Cherkas et al., "Genetic Influences on Female Infidelity and Number of Sexual Partners in Humans: A Linkage and Association Study of the Role of the Vasopressin Receptor Gene (*AVPR1A*)," *Twin Research* 7 (6) (December 2004), pp. 649–658.

69   *Psychologists used to label homosexuality:* See Ronald Bayer, *Homosexuality and American Psychiatry: The Politics of Diagnosis* (New York: Basic Books, 1981).

69   *identical twins are more alike in their sexual orientation than fraternal twins:* Khytam Dawood et al., "Genetic and Environmental Influences on Sexual Orientation," in Yong-Kyu Kim, ed., *Handbook of Behavior Genetics* (New York: Springer, 2009), p. 271. High-quality recent studies that confirm the standard findings include Katarina Alanko et al., "Common Genetic Effects of Gender Atypical Behavior in Childhood and Sexual Orientation in Adulthood: A Study of Finnish Twins," *Archives of Sexual Behavior* 39 (1) (February 2010), pp. 81–92; and Niklas Långström et al., "Genetic and Environmental Effects on Same-Sex Sexual Behavior: A Population Study of Twins in Sweden," *Archives of Sexual Behavior* 39 (1) (February 2010), pp. 75–80.

69   *adopted brothers of gay men and adopted sisters of gay women:* Dawood et al., "Genetic and Environmental Influences on Sexual Orientation," p. 271.

69   *A large Swedish twin study . . . confirms a small nurture effect:* Långström et al., "Genetic and Environmental Effects on Same-Sex Sexual Behavior."

69   *"The princess realized that in the process of getting to know each other":* Leo Tolstoy, *Anna Karenina* (New York: Barnes and Noble, 1993), p. 42.

70   *A study of over 4,000 Minnesota twins, most in their thirties and forties:* Wendy Johnson et al., "Marriage and Personality: A Genetic Analysis," *Journal of Personality and Social Psychology* 86 (2) (February 2004), pp. 285–294.

70   *A long-running study of almost 6,000 men from the World War II Twin Registry:* Susan Trumbetta et al., "Marriage and Genetic Variation Across the Lifespan: Not a Steady Relationship?" *Behavior Genetics* 37 (2) (March 2007), pp. 362–375. However, moderate family influence strangely reemerged when the twins were sixty and seventy.

70   *A research team asked 1,000 female Swedish twins and their spouses:* Eric Spotts et al., "Genetic and Environmental Influences on Marital Relationships," *Journal of Family Psychology* 18 (1) (March 2004), pp. 107–119.

70   *An early study using the Minnesota Twin Registry found large effects of genes:* Matt McGue and David Lykken, "Genetic

Influence on Risk of Divorce," *Psychological Science* 3 (6) (November 1992), pp. 368–373.

70   *Heredity matters a lot, upbringing doesn't matter at all:* Victor Jockin et al., "Personality and Divorce: A Genetic Analysis," *Journal of Personality and Social Psychology* 71 (2) (August 1996), pp. 288–299.

70   *A major study of Danish twins born 1870–1910:* Hans-Peter Kohler et al., "Is Fertility Behavior in Our Genes? Findings from a Danish Study," *Population and Development Review* 25 (2) (June 1999), pp. 253–288.

70   *Upbringing had a tiny influence on when Danes tried to start a family:* Joseph Rodgers et al., "Behavior Genetic Modeling of Human Fertility: Findings from a Contemporary Danish Twin Study," *Demography* 38 (1) (February 2001), p. 36.

70   *A different team of researchers looked at about 2,000 American twins:* Joseph Rodgers and Debby Doughty, "Genetic and Environmental Influences on Fertility Expectations and Outcomes Using NLSY Kinship Data," in Joseph Rodgers et al., *Genetic Influences on Human Fertility and Sexuality* (New York: Springer, 2000).

71   *Siblings gave fairly similar answers whether or not they were biologically related:* Kirby Deater-Deckard et al., "A Genetic Study of the Family Environment in the Transition to Early Adolescence," *Journal of Child Psychology and Psychiatry* 40 (5) (July 1999), p. 772. The survey also found, however, that parents had little effect on how their children perceived their families' achievement orientation.

71   *The first questioned about 1,200 Minnesota twins:* Matt McGue et al., "Perceptions of the Parent-Adolescent Relationship: A Longitudinal Investigation," *Developmental Psychology* 41 (6) (November 2005), pp. 971–984.

71   *They confirmed that parents continue to have moderate effects on how their young adult children:* Susan South et al., "Adolescent Personality Moderates Genetic and Environmental Influences on Relationships with Parents," *Journal of Personality and Social Psychology* 94 (5) (May 2008), pp. 899–912.

72   *The Swedish study discovered moderate nurture effects for seven out of eight measures:* Robert Plomin et al., "Genetic Influence

on Childhood Family Environment Perceived Retrospectively from the Last Half of the Life Span," *Developmental Psychology* 24 (5) (September 1988), p. 743.

72   *Other studies of German, Canadian, and Swedish twins:* Christian Kandler et al., "Genetic and Environmental Mediation Between Measures of Personality and Family Environment in Twins Reared Together," *Behavior Genetics* 39 (1) (January 2009), pp. 24–35; Philip Vernon et al., "Environmental Predictors of Personality Differences: A Twin and Sibling Study," *Journal of Personality and Social Psychology* 72 (1) (January 1997), pp. 177–183; Paul Lichtenstein et al., "Remembered Parental Bonding in Adult Twins: Genetic and Environmental Influences," *Behavior Genetics* 33 (4) (July 2003), pp. 397–408.

72   *"Extraordinary claims require extraordinary evidence":* Carl Sagan, *Cosmos*, Episode 12, "Encyclopedia Galactica."

73   *I take advantage of two mathematical facts implied by standard behavioral genetic models:* See, for example, Robert Plomin et al., *Behavioral Genetics* (New York: Worth Publishers, 2008), pp. 374–402.

74   *Suppose the trait in question is education:* Baker et al., "Genetics of Educational Attainment in Australian Twins," *Behavior Genetics* 26 (2) (March 1996), pp. 89–102.

74   *If they report only correlations for identical versus fraternal twins:* See, for example, Plomin et al., *Behavioral Genetics*, p. 382.

CHAPTER 3

77   *prominent behavioral geneticists looked at major adoption studies of IQ:* Matt McGue et al., "Behavioral Genetics of Cognitive Ability: A Life-Span Perspective," in Robert Plomin and Gerald McClearn, eds., *Nature, Nurture, and Psychology* (Washington, DC: American Psychological Association, 1993), pp. 64, 67. For an unusually large twin study (11,000 subjects from four nations) of declining parental influence on IQ, see C. Haworth et al., "The Heritability of General Cognitive Ability Increases Linearly from Childhood

to Young Adulthood," *Molecular Psychiatry* (June 2009), available at www.nature.com/mp/journal/vaop/ncurrent/full/mp200955a.html.

78   *The Colorado Adoption Project provides an especially vivid illustration:* Plomin et al., "Nature, Nurture, and Cognitive Development."

78   *"Adopted children resemble their adoptive parents slightly in early childhood":* Ibid., p. 442.

78   *One study of over 5,000 Swedish twins:* David Cesarini, "The Effect of Family Environment on Productive Skills, Human Capital, and Lifetime Income," MIT Working Paper, 2010.

78   *there are noticeable nurture effects for children younger than fifteen:* Jacobson et al., "Sex Differences in the Genetic and Environmental Influences on the Development of Antisocial Behavior," p. 409.

78   *A major review of twin and adoption studies of antisocial and criminal behavior:* Rhee and Waldman, "Genetic and Environmental Influences on Antisocial Behavior: A Meta-Analysis of Twin and Adoption Studies," p. 514.

79   *Parents influence when their daughters* start *having sex:* J. Bailey et al., "Do Individual Differences in Sociosexuality Represent Genetic or Environmentally Contingent Strategies?" See also Cherkas et al., "Genetic Influences on Female Infidelity and Number of Sexual Partners in Humans."

79   *The cleanest study asked over 500 Minnesota twins questions:* Koenig et al., "Genetic and Environmental Influences on Religiousness."

82   Because there's a lot more to "the environment" than the family: For further discussion, see Harris, *No Two Alike.*

83   *If this assumption is wrong, standard models oversell the effect of nature:* See D. A. Grayson, "Twins Reared Together: Minimizing Shared Environmental Effects," *Behavior Genetics* 19 (4) (December 1989), pp. 593–604.

83   *Cutting-edge studies of the* children *of twins find bigger effects:* See, for example, Brian D'Onofrio et al., "Intergenerational Transmission of Childhood Conduct Problems: A Children of Twins Study," *Archives of General Psychiatry* 64 (7) (July 2007), pp. 820–829. ; Brian D'Onofrio et al., "A Children of Twins

Study of Parental Divorce and Offspring Psychopathology,"
Journal of Child Psychology and Psychiatry 48 (7) (July 2007),
pp. 667–675; Brian D'Onofrio et al., "A Genetically Informed
Study of the Intergenerational Transmission of Marital Instability," *Journal of Marriage and Family* 69 (3) (August 2007),
pp. 793–809 ; and Stacy Lynch et al., "A Genetically Informed
Study of the Association Between Harsh Punishment and Offspring Behavioral Problems," *Journal of Family Psychology* 20
(2) (June 2006), pp. 190–198. The interpretation of children
of twins studies remains problematic. As one prominent paper admits, "the Children of Twins Design does not control for
genetic risk from the spouse of twins" (D'Onofrio et al., "A
Genetically Informed Study of the Intergenerational Transmission of Marital Instability," p. 806). For further discussion, see Lindon Eaves et al., "Revisiting the Children of
Twins: Can They Be Used to Resolve the Environmental Effects of Dyadic Parental Treatment on Child Behavior?" *Twin
Research and Human Genetics* 8 (4) (August 2005), pp. 283–
290.

83   *Twins come from all walks of life:* See, for example, Eric
Turkheimer et al., "Socioeconomic Status Modifies Heritability of IQ in Young Children," *Psychological Science* 14 (6) (November 2003), pp. 623–628. Twin studies based on national
registries don't have this problem, but countries with national
registries tend to have less inequality than the United States.

85   *the median American went to church "several times a year":*
General Social Survey, 2008. Variable identifier ATTEND.

85   *parents suffer from what psychologists call the illusion of con-
trol:* See, for example, Nathanael Fast et al., "Illusory Control:
A Generative Force Behind Power's Far-Reaching Effects,"
Psychological Science 20 (4) (April 2009), pp. 502–508.

87   *For personality traits, however, spouses are barely alike:* See
David Lykken and Auke Tellegen, "Is Human Mating Adventi-
tious or the Result of Lawful Choice? A Twin Study of Mate
Selection," *Journal of Personality and Social Psychology* 65 (1)
(July 1993), pp. 56–68; Robert Krueger et al., "Assortative
Mating for Antisocial Behavior: Developmental and Method-
ological Implications," *Behavior Genetics* 28 (3) (March

1998), pp. 173–186; J. Rushton, "Genetic Similarity, Human Altruism, and Group Selection," *Behavioral and Brain Sciences* 12 (3) (1989), pp. 503–559; Sven Wilson, "The Health Capital of Families: An Investigation of the Inter-Spousal Correlation in Health Status," *Social Science and Medicine* 55 (7) (October 2002), pp. 1157–1172; and Ulrich Schimmack and Richard Lucas, "Marriage Matters: Spousal Similarity in Life Satisfaction," *Schmollers Jahrbuch* 127 (1) (January 2007), pp. 105–111. Admittedly, low personality correlations could instead show that many seek mates who *differ* from them. But when some traits are widely seen as better than others, why would opposites attract?

87   *Over 13 percent of the children in Malawi:* For child mortality in Malawi, see *World Population Prospects: The 2006 Revision* (New York: United Nations, 2007), Table A.19. Madonna successfully appealed the initial rejection of her adoption petition. See Larry McShane, "Madonna Malawi Adoption Request Rejected By Court," *New York Daily News*, April 3, 2009; and Raphael Tenthani, "Malawi Welcomes Madonna Adoption," *BBC News*, June 13, 2009.

87   *Merely moving an adult Nigerian to the United States:* Michael Clemens et al., "The Place Premium: Wage Differences for Identical Workers Across the U.S. Border," Washington, DC: Center for Global Development Working Paper, 2008.

87   *There are even waiting lists for domestic adoption of special needs children:* Heidi Lindh, "Characteristics and Perspectives of Families Waiting to Adopt a Child with Down Syndrome," *Genetics in Medicine* 9 (4) (April 2007), pp. 235–240.

88   *"So you mean it doesn't matter how I treat my child?":* Harris, *The Nurture Assumption*, p. 341.

CHAPTER 4

94   *They're straight out of the original document:* If you're curious about the details, see the Appendix to Chap. 4: Where the Mortality Tables Come From.

100 *Whenever Gallup asks, "Is there more crime in the U.S.":* Lydia Saad, "Perceptions of Crime Remain Curiously Negative," available at www.gallup.com/poll/102262/perceptions-crime -problem-remain-curiously-negative.aspx, October 22, 2007.

100 *In 2008, it estimated a violent crime rate of 19.3 per 1,000:* Michael Rand, "Criminal Victimization, 2008," *Bureau of Justice Statistics Bulletin* (September 2009), Table 3, available at bjs.ojp.usdoj.gov/content/pub/pdf/cv08.pdf. The NCVS does not measure murder because (a) it is based on interviews with victims, and (b) murder is almost always reported anyway.

101 *But according to police reports, kids under twelve are* much *safer:* David Finkelhor and Richard Ormrod, "Characteristics of Crimes Against Juveniles," Office of Juvenile Justice and Delinquency Prevention (2000), available at www.ncjrs.gov/ pdffiles1/ojjdp/179034.pdf.

101 *The best source on child abduction:* Andrea Sedlak et al., "National Estimates of Missing Children: An Overview," Office of Juvenile Justice and Delinquency Prevention (2002), available at www.ncjrs.gov/pdffiles/ojjdp/196465.pdf.

103 *no child has* ever *been killed or seriously injured by Halloween treats:* See Joel Best, *Threatened Children: Rhetoric and Concern About Child-Victims* (Chicago: University of Chicago Press, 1993), and his more recent update, "Halloween Sadism: The Evidence," University of Delaware Library Institutional Repository (2008), available at dspace.udel.edu:8080/dspace/ handle/19716/726.

104 *"Once you can picture an eight-year-old":* Skenazy, *Free-Range Kids*, p. 43.

104 *One of psychologists' most effective treatments for anxiety:* See David Richard and Dean Lauterbach, eds., *Handbook of Exposure Therapies* (Burlington, MA: Academic Press, 2006).

106 *During 1950, 14,650 soldiers died in the Korean War:* For the Korean War, age breakdowns are only available for the army. I assumed that the age breakdown for the other armed services was equal to the army's.

106 *To estimate war deaths for 2005, I assumed that the age breakdown:* Military fatality statistics for Operation Enduring

Freedom and Operation Iraqi Freedom break down deaths into five age categories: under 22, 22–24, 25–30, 31–35, and over 35. My estimates in Table 4.1 assume that 20 percent of all fatalities for those 31–35 are 35-year-olds, and 100 percent of 36+ fatalities fall in the 35–44 bracket.

CHAPTER 5

109 *Becker saw economics in the family:* See Gary Becker, *A Treatise on the Family* (Cambridge, MA: Harvard University Press 1993).

110 *The greatest perceived triumph of the economics of the family:* All total fertility rates are from "Total Fertility Rate (children per woman)," available at www.UNdata.org.

111 *A variant on the rising-women's-wages story claims:* See, for example, James Feyrer et al., "Will the Stork Return to Europe and Japan? Understanding Fertility Within Developed Nations," *Journal of Economic Perspectives* 22 (3) (June 2008), pp. 3–22.

111 *When the World Values Survey queried men and women around the world:* World Values Survey, Variable identifier D017, available at www.worldvaluessurvey.org.

111 *Condoms have been widely available since World War II:* Aine Collier, *The Humble Little Condom* (New York: Prometheus Books, 2007), pp. 236–238.

112 *"Children consumed more food than they caught":* Theodore Bergstrom, "Economics in a Family Way," *Journal of Economic Literature* 34 (4) (Spring 1996), p. 1913.

112 *Investing in your children is less lucrative than:* Ibid., p. 1914.

112 *One research team using the Survey of Consumer Finances:* William Gale and John Scholz, "Intergenerational Transfers and Accumulation of Wealth," *Journal of Economic Perspectives* 8 (4) (Fall 1994), p. 149.

112 *parents on average voluntarily gave a total of $25,000 more:* Ronald Lee, "Population Age Structure, Intergenerational Transfer, and Wealth: A New Approach, with Applications to the United States," *Journal of Human Resources* 29 (4) (1994), pp. 1051–1052.

112   *At the time, women earned 60 percent as much as men:* "Table
2. Employment Status of the Civilian Noninstitutional Population 16 Years and Over by Sex, 1970–2004 Annual Averages,"
Bureau of Labor Statistics, available at www.bls.gov/cps/
wlf-table2–2006.pdf; Francine Blau and Lawrence Kahn,
"The U.S. Gender Pay Gap in the 1990s: Slowing Conver-
gence," *Industrial and Labor Relations Review* 60 (1) (June
2006), pp. 45–66.

113   *Psychologists call this* hindsight bias: See Ulrich Hoffrage and
Rüdiger Pohl, "Research on Hindsight Bias: A Rich Past, a
Productive Present, and a Challenging Future," *Memory* 11
(4–5) (January 2003), pp. 329–335.

114   *When Social Security began:* "National Vital Statistics Reports: United States Life Tables, 2004," Centers for Disease
Control and Prevention (2008), Table 11.

114   *One careful study of elder care found:* David Cutler and Louise
Sheiner, "Policy Options for Long-Term Care," in David Wise,
ed., *Studies of the Economics of Aging* (Chicago: University of
Chicago Press, 1994).

115   *the decline of marriage and religion explains much:* In the
General Social Survey, I initially estimated respondents'
number of children as a function of YEAR, AGE, SEX, log of
real income (REALINC), and education (EDUC, with separate coefficients for men and women). The coefficient on
year was –.010. Controlling for marital status and church attendance reduced the coefficient on YEAR by more than
half to –.004.

116   *Look at thirty-something American moms who never married:*
General Social Survey 2008. This comparison assumes that
out-of-wedlock pregnancies are more likely to be unplanned,
which is indeed the case. About 70 percent of out-of-wedlock
pregnancies are unplanned, versus about 25 percent of in-
wedlock pregnancies. Lawrence Finer and Stanley Henshaw,
"Disparities in Rates of Unintended Pregnancies in the
United States, 1994 and 2001," *Perspectives on Sexual and
Reproductive Health* 28 (2) (June 2006), p. 93.

117   *makes you feel round and supple:* Rich Cohen, "A Woman in
Full," *Vanity Fair,* July 2008.

118 *Your feelings are important, but from a purely selfish point of view:* Of course, when you're predicting your future feelings, you should remember that there is some probability you will experience nothing at all because you'll no longer be alive.

CHAPTER 6

126 *He finally realizes:* Steven Seagle, *It's a Bird* (New York: Vertigo, 2005), pp. 116, 120.

127 *The main source of progress is* new ideas*:* For a good summary, see Paul Romer, "Economic Growth," in David Henderson, ed., *The Concise Encyclopedia of Economics* (Indianapolis, IN: Liberty Fund, 2008), pp. 128–131.

127 *"mainly an ongoing intellectual achievement, a sustained flow":* Robert Lucas, "Ideas and Growth," Cambridge, MA, National Bureau of Economic Research Working Paper, 2008.

128 *In the words of economist Julian Simon:* Simon, *The Ultimate Resource 2*, p. 407.

130 *The implicit dividing line, apparently:* The second most popular dividing line is probably between above-average and below-average intelligence. The famous eugenicist Karl Pearson maintained that "the sole condition under which . . . immigration should be allowed" is when the immigrants "form from the standpoint of intelligence a group markedly superior to our natives." Quoted in David Levy and Sandra Peart, "Statistical Prejudice: From Eugenics to Immigrants," *European Journal of Political Economy* 20 (1) (March 2004), p. 16.

132 *With almost 2 billion users worldwide:* "World Internet Users and Population Stats," available at www.InternetWorldStats.com.

132 *children have no legal obligation to repay their parents:* Even if they did, of course, many parents, if not most, would eagerly forgive the debt.

133 *In 1940, the United States had almost ten working-age adults:* "Social Security Area Population Projections: 1997," Social Security Administration, Figure 8, available at www.ssa.gov/OACT/NOTES/AS112/as112.html.

133 *Now it's about five workers per retiree:* "Table V.A2—Social Security Area Population as of July 1 and Dependency Ratios," Social Security Administration (2002), available at www.ssa .gov/OACT/TR/TR02/lr5A2–2.html.

133 *Japan, to take one of the worst cases: Population Projection for Japan: 2001–2050,* National Institute of Population and Social Security Research 2002, Table 4, available at: www.ipss.go.jp/pp-newest/e/ppfj02/ppfj02.pdf.

134 *"the addition of each person to the American population":* Paul Ehrlich, "Recent Developments in Environmental Science," 1998, available at dieoff.org/page157.htm.

134 *"Having children is selfish," she explained:* Natasha Courtenay-Smith and Morag Turner, "Meet the Women Who Won't Have Babies—Because They're Not Eco Friendly," *Daily Mail,* November 21, 2007.

134 *Yet adjusting for inflation, average commodity prices have fallen:* Paul Cashin and C. McDermott, "The Long-Run Behavior of Commodity Prices: Small Trends and Big Variability," IMF Staff Papers (2002), pp. 175–199, find that the inflation-adjusted price of the *Economist*'s index of industrial commodities fell by about 1 percent per year from 1862 to 1999. Stephan Pfaffenzeller et al., "A Short Note on Updating the Grilli and Yang Commodity Price Index," *World Bank Economic Review* 21 (1) (January 2007), pp. 151–163, report that, adjusting for inflation, the Grilli and Yang commodity price index (which includes metals, food, and nonfood agricultural products) fell by about .8 percent per year between 1900 and 2003.

135 *Most notably, air and water quality in the Western world improved:* See, for example, Lomborg, *The Skeptical Environmentalist,* pp. 163–177, 189–205.

135 *Around the globe, there's a standard two-stage pattern:* See, for example, Susmita Dasgupta et al., "Confronting the Environmental Kuznets Curve," *Journal of Economic Perspectives* 16 (1) (Winter 2002), pp. 147–168.

135 *most scientists say that our emissions of carbon dioxide cause global warming:* See D. Bray and H. von Storch, *The Perspectives of Climate Scientists on Global Climate Change* (Geesthacht, Germany: GKSS Research Centre, 2007).

CHAPTER 7

138   *The most comprehensive study ever done looks at the entire Danish population:* M. Murphy and L. Knudsen, "The Intergenerational Transmission of Fertility in Contemporary Denmark: The Effects of Number of Siblings (Full and Half), Birth Order, and Whether Male or Female," *Population Studies* 56 (3) (Fall 2002), pp. 235–248.

138   *The General Social Survey confirms the same pattern in the United States:* In the General Social Survey, the correlation between number of siblings and number of children is .20.

139   *Fertility runs in families because of nature, not nurture:* See Kohler et al., "Is Fertility Behavior in Our Genes?"; Rodgers et al., "Behavior Genetic Modeling of Human Fertility"; and Rodgers and Doughty, "Genetic and Environmental Influences on Fertility Expectations and Outcomes Using NLSY Kinship Data."

140   *Government preaching and nagging seem about as futile:* In practice, most government "awareness raising" tries to *reduce* birth rates rather than raise them. A comprehensive review of school-based pregnancy prevention experiments finds that many programs have no effect; for the rest, "the effects are relatively modest and may only last short-term." Sylvana Bennett and Nassim Asseffi, "School-Based Teenage Pregnancy Prevention Programs: A Systematic Review of Randomized Controlled Trials," *Journal of Adolescent Health* 36 (1) (January 2005), p. 78.

140   *The main researcher who studied Quebec's program concluded*: Kevin Milligan, "Subsidizing the Stork," *Review of Economics and Statistics* 87 (3) (August 2005), pp. 539–555.

140   *Another research team looked at the effect of paid parental leave in Austria:* Rafael Lalive and Josef Zweimüller, "How Does Parental Leave Affect Fertility and Return to Work? Evidence from Two Natural Experiments," *Quarterly Journal of Economics* 124 (3) (August 2009), pp. 1363–1402.

140   *Other researchers argue fairly convincingly:* See Anders Björklund, "Does a Family-Friendly Policy Raise Fertility Levels?" *Swedish Institute for European Policy Studies* 3 (April 2007).

142   *The late economist Bernie Saffran taped a rebuttal to his office door:* Saffran was probably paraphrasing George Bernard Shaw's *Man and Superman*: "Do not do unto others as you would that they should do unto you. Their tastes may not be the same." (Charleston, SC: Forgotten Books, 2010), p. 227.

144   *The Quebec experiment found of baby bonuses little or no effect:* Milligan, "Subsidizing the Stork," p. 552.

CHAPTER 8

148   *My colleague Russ Roberts named it:* Russ Roberts, "The Most Beautiful Toy Yet," Cafe Hayek, January 9, 2007, available at cafehayek.com/2007/01/the_most_beauti.html.

148   *Apple's crime: cutting the price by $200:* Katie Hafner and Brad Stone, "iPhone Owners Crying Foul over Price Cut," *New York Times*, September 7, 2007.

150   *65,000 babies—35,000 from their mother's husband's sperm: Artificial Insemination: Practice in the United States: Summary of a 1987 Survey* (Washington, DC: Office of Technology Assessment, 1988), p. 3.

150   *the number of babies born in the United States using IVF: Assisted Reproductive Technology Success Rates: National Summary and Fertility Clinic Report: 2006*, Figure 49, Centers for Disease Control and Prevention (Atlanta: 2008) available at www.cdc.gov/art/art2006/section5.htm. The CDC reports combined total results for all medical procedures "in which both eggs and sperm are handled" (p. 3). These include standard IVF, plus gamete intrafallopian transfer (GIFT) and zygote intrafallopian transfer (ZIFT).

150   *Doctors in Africa . . . already offer "no-frills" IVF:* Josie Glausiusz, "Cheap IVF Offers Hope to Childless Millions," *New Scientist*, August 26, 2009.

151   *Multiples have much higher infant mortality rates:* "National Vital Statistics Reports: Infant Mortality Statistics from the 2005 Period Linked Birth/Infant Death Data Set," Centers for Disease Control and Prevention (Atlanta: 2008), p. 5.

151   *"If Nature thought it was appropriate for homo sapiens to have litters":* Quoted in Liza Mundy, *Everything Conceivable: How*

Assisted Reproduction Is Changing Men, Women, and the World (New York: Knopf, 2007), p. 212.

151 *IVF is moving away from octomoms: Assisted Reproductive Technology Success Rates*, Figures 58, 64.

152 *Ninety-five percent of surrogates now get pregnant using IVF:* Elizabeth Scott, "Surrogacy and the Politics of Commodification," Columbia Public Law and Legal Theory Working Papers, pp. 39–40, available at lsr.nellco.org/cgi/viewcontent .cgi?article=1045&context=columbia_pllt.

152 *The booming economy of India has quickly become:* See, for example, Silvia Spring, "The Trade in Fertility," *Newsweek,* April 12, 2006.

153 *"Separated from her husband, she found that her monthly wages":* Amelia Gentleman, "India Nurtures Business of Surrogate Motherhood," *New York Times,* May 10, 2008.

153 *Japanese researchers managed to keep premature goat fetuses alive:* Jonathan Knight, "Artificial Wombs: An Out of Body Experience," *Nature* 419 (6903) (September 12, 2002), pp. 106–107.

153 *Hung-Ching Liu, director of Cornell University's Reproductive Endocrine Laboratory:* Gretchen Reynolds, "Artificial Wombs: Will We Grow Babies Outside Their Mothers' Bodies?" *Popular Science,* August 1, 2005.

154 *Sex ratio doesn't run in families:* Joseph Rodgers and Debby Doughty, "Does Having Boys or Girls Run in the Family?" *Chance* 14 (4) (Fall 2001), pp. 8–13.

156 *Only a handful of women can marry Nobel Prize winners:* David Plotz, *The Genius Factory: The Curious History of the Nobel Prize Sperm Bank* (New York: Random House, 2006). In practice, only a small fraction of the donors were actual Nobelists, and none of their donations ultimately produced a child.

156 *The Fairfax Cryobank will inseminate you for $355:* "Fees 2009: Donor Semen Services Fee Schedule," available at www.fairfaxcryobank.com.

156 *Elite Donors' wealthy clients typically pay ten times as much:* "Finding a Donor: How Much Does It Cost to Find an Egg Donor?" available at www.elitedonors.com.

157 *If you want a boy, sperm sortation boosts your odds:* Joseph Schulman and David Karabinus, "Scientific Aspects of Pre-conception Gender Selection," *Reproductive Biomedicine Online* 10 (1) (January 2005), pp. 111–115.

158 *A totalitarian government could use GE to root out individuality and dissent:* For more, see Bryan Caplan, "The Totalitarian Threat," in Nick Bostrom and Milan Ćirković, eds., *Global Catastrophic Risks* (Oxford: Oxford University Press, 2008), p. 515.

159 *Over 85 percent of Americans—and 100 percent of George W. Bush's Council on Bioethics:* Matthew Nisbet, "Public Opinion About Stem Cell Research and Human Cloning," *Public Opinion Quarterly* 68 (1) (March 2004), p. 151; The President's Council on Bioethics, *Human Cloning and Human Dignity: An Ethical Inquiry,* (Washington, DC: 2002), p. 202.

159 *Instead, they feel grateful for their special bond:* See Segal, *Entwined Lives*, pp. 97–115.

159 *"Identical twins . . . are born together":* Human Cloning and Human Dignity, pp. 103–104.

CHAPTER 9

167 *"Researchers have checked whether twins are more similar in intelligence or personality":* See Kenneth Kendler et al., "A Test of the Equal-Environment Assumption in Twin Studies of Psychiatric Illness," *Behavior Genetics* 24 (1) (January 1993), pp. 21–22; Peter Borkenau et al., "Similarity of Childhood Experiences and Personality Resemblance in Monozygotic and Dizygotic Twins: A Test of the Equal Environments Assumption," *Personality and Individual Differences* 33 (2) (July 2002), p. 262.

167 *"If similarity of treatment caused resemblance":* See Kendler et al., "A Test of the Equal-Environment Assumption in Twin Studies of Psychiatric Illness"; and Sandra Scarr and Louise Carter-Saltzman, "Twin Method: Defense of a Critical Assumption," *Behavior Genetics* 9 (6) (June 1979), pp. 527–542.

168 *"One study of families with both kinds of children":* Kyle Gibson, "Differential Parental Investment in Families with Both Adopted and Genetic Children," *Evolution and Human Behavior* 30 (3) (May 2009), pp. 184–189.

171   *"Average desired family size for men and women is virtually identical"*: World Values Survey 2005. Variable identifier D017, available at www.worldvaluessurvey.org.

171   *"Women are* more *likely than men to say that having kids is 'one of the most important things'"*: General Social Survey 2008. Variable identifier **IMPKIDS**.

INDEX

Abduction, child, 101–102

Accidents, as cause of children's deaths, 97, 98, 103

Activities, children's, 24–26, 168–169

Adoption, from Third World, 87, 178

Adoption studies
  on character, 58–62, 78–79
  direct *vs.* indirect effects, 43–44
  distinguishing nature from nurture and, 40
  effect of parents on children's future and, 4–5, 34–35, 76–80
  focus on middle-class, First World families, 83–84
  on happiness, 51–53
  on health, 46–49
  on intelligence, 49–51, 77–78
  nature and nurture effects and, 45
  nature-nurture effect size and, 73–74
  on religion, 79–80
  on success, 53–58, 78
  on values, 62–71

Age, mortality by, in 2005, 95

Agreeableness, nature *vs.* nurture and, 59–61

AI. *See* Artificial insemination (AI)

Altruism, having more children and, 7–8, 123

American Enterprise Institute, 16

American family, size of, 1

American War and Military Operations Casualties: Lists and Statistics, 106

Anger management, 33

Anna Karenina (Tolstoy), 69

Artificial insemination (AI), 150
  egg donation and, 156

Artificial wombs, 153–154

Ask the Children survey, 32–33, 172

Austria, paid parental leave in, 140

Baby boom, 112

Baby monitors, 21–22

Babysitters
  benefits of use, 30–31
  electronic, 25, 31

Battle Casualties and Medical Statistics: U.S. Army Experience in the Korea War, 106

Becker, Gary, 109–110, 111, 115, 116

Beethoven, Ludwig, 128